Machines like Us

Machines like Us

Toward AI with Common Sense

Ronald J. Brachman and Hector J. Levesque

The MIT Press
Cambridge, Massachusetts
London, England

The MIT Press would like to thank the anonymous peer reviewers who provided comments on drafts of this book. The generous work of academic experts is essential for establishing the authority and quality of our publications. We acknowledge with gratitude the contributions of these otherwise uncredited readers.

This book was set in ITC Stone Serif Std and ITC Stone Sans Std by New Best-set Typesetters Ltd. Printed and bound in the United States of America.

Library of Congress Cataloging-in-Publication Data is available.

Names: Brachman, Ronald J., 1949- author. | Levesque, Hector J., 1951-author.
Title: Machines like us : toward AI with common sense / Ronald J. Brachman and Hector J. Levesque.
Description: Cambridge, Massachusetts : The MIT Press, [2022] | Includes bibliographical references and index.
Identifiers: LCCN 2021031316 | ISBN 9780262046794 (hardcover)
Subjects: LCSH: Artificial intelligence. | Knowledge representation (Information theory)
Classification: LCC Q335 .B695 2022 | DDC 006.3—dc23
LC record available at https://lccn.loc.gov/2021031316

10 9 8 7 6 5 4 3 2 1

For Mom and Dad, for lifetimes of love.
—RJB

For my dear brothers John, Ray, and the late Peter and Paul.
—HJL

Contents

Preview

Imagine, if you will, a future where self-driving cars are much better than they are now. They reliably avoid obstacles, obey traffic lights and signs, and even respond to turn signals from other drivers. Autonomous carts are universally deployed at golf courses, movie lots, and residential communities, and self-driving vans fully service urban commuters in many cities. They have not caused an injury accident in years. In fact, these imagined cars are so safe and dependable that they don't even need human drivers as backup.

The technology has reached the first wave of consumers, and many of your neighbors now have self-driving cars in their driveways. You've joined them. Your new car is amazing, better than you at driving in adverse conditions like blizzards, changing lanes in heavy traffic, and navigating through intersections crowded with pedestrians, dogs, strollers, bicycles, and other vehicles. You just set the destination, and off it goes. Remarkably, many stores now provide curbside spots for cars like yours to have their trunks loaded up and sent on their way home—no human needed in the car at all.

Now picture this:

It's just before noon on Monday, and you send your car on a shopping run to Jones's Grocery Store. Today is the national Independence Day holiday, and Jones's is having a sale on its great steaks, which you're planning to barbecue this afternoon. You expect the trip to be quick because so many people are at the beach for the holiday and the store is not far away.

The car approaches the intersection of Bradford and Victoria. The traffic light is red so the car glides smoothly to a stop and waits for the light to turn green. Three minutes go by, and the light stays red. Five minutes go by, and the light is still red. The car's cameras detect some activity on the far side of the intersection, but no action is suggested. Your car's computers—excellent with obstacle avoidance and lane following—are not equipped to understand that drivers on the other side are getting out of their cars, talking to each other, and pointing. Your car's new external audio sensors, trained to detect honking and sirens, cannot make any sense of a somewhat distant musical sound coming from the right.

The car's navigation system has no rerouting suggestions; there is no traffic to speak of, and no known construction or accidents along the route. So the car sits there, waiting patiently for the light to change. Ten minutes go by, and then fifteen.

Meanwhile, at home, you begin to wonder why the car hasn't reported picking up the groceries. You know if it had a mechanical problem it would text you an alert. You check your app and see the car waiting at the intersection, and note that it hasn't moved in a quarter hour. Yet nothing is amiss. Your remote monitor shows that the car is just obeying the law, waiting for the light to turn green. Why isn't it doing something? You throw your hands up, bemoaning the fact that while your car drives like a pro, it occasionally makes these inexplicable blunders—like waiting forever at a traffic light while your guests are about to arrive.

Now imagine an alternate scenario. It's *you* driving this time. Same intersection, same stuck light, same five minutes gone by:

You ask yourself, What on earth is going on? Should I wait a bit longer just in case? Drive through the red light? Make a right turn to get around the intersection? Get to the store some other way? Forget about Jones's and go to another store? Give up on groceries altogether and head back home? (You can always order takeout.) You turn off the radio and ponder for a few seconds. The drivers on the other side of the intersection catch your eye. You look where they seem to be pointing. You see a bunch of flags in the distance and what looks like an open convertible with some people sitting atop the back seat. You hear some brassy-sounding music coming from that direction.

After a moment, you give up on Jones's, turn the car around, and head off to a different store.

Think about what was going through your head as you figured out what to do. It's not as if you remembered some specific rule that solved the problem for you. Certainly nothing you learned in driving school told you what action to take. There's really no single driving move that is the right thing to do in cases like this. Maybe you've experienced broken traffic lights before and followed other drivers right through the intersection (with great caution, of course). But in this particular case, you figured that the light was staying red because a parade was coming on the cross street. "Oh yeah," you remembered, "it's Independence Day!" You could have turned around and tried another route, but this was either going to take too much time or run into the parade at a different intersection. So you decided to go elsewhere. You could have gone to Smith's Grocery Store, which is closer to where you are, but the meat and produce there are nowhere as good. So you decided to head to Robert's instead.

You don't have to be some sort of driving expert, like a cabbie with thousands of hours on the road, to come up with driving behavior like this. Maybe it's not a learned routine you can just follow mindlessly while concentrating on something else like brushing your teeth or walking the dog. But it's not rocket science either. No pencil and paper required. You have to be able to take into account some things about your current situation, but beyond that, it's really just the ordinary common sense that any intelligent person would be expected to have.

An average adult will know many relevant, mundane things: you don't just wait forever at a traffic light; people talking and gesticulating likely indicates something interesting going on; flags and brassy band music likely presage a parade. And they'll put it all together quickly and make a fast, reasonable guess at what to do next: take the second-best choice if the first one no longer looks as promising. It's just common sense. And your supposedly intelligent car, while an excellent driver—maybe even an outstanding one—clearly doesn't have it.

This book is not a work of fiction about imaginary drives to imaginary stores. It starts with the art and science of artificial intelligence (AI) as it actually exists today, and how current AI systems can be amazingly good at some intellectually demanding tasks—in many cases, better than humans—but still be missing that uniquely human characteristic of common sense.

If the example above strikes you as improbable, numerous recent books illustrate many similar instances of blunders in the current world of AI. Simply put, AI systems are fragile. While they are quite adept at some things, they break down in unfamiliar circumstances in oddly unpredictable ways because they lack the broad capacity to deal with the open-ended world that humans get from common sense.

So what is this common sense that most people have, and what would it take for machines like self-driving cars to have it too? How could a nonhuman driver become more like one of us? This is what we set out to explore in this book.

As we will see, the answer is not a particularly easy one. There's no single magic ingredient, no silver bullet; just a number of issues to look into and resolve. Here we bring together a host of observations, technical ideas, and proposals from AI research that will help us address the challenge of common sense head-on.

This book is not intended for readers who mainly want to hear what the experts think will or will not come out of AI research in the next few years, how good self-driving cars are actually going to get, or whether autonomous AI systems will eventually rebel against humanity. There are other places to go for that. Instead, we hope to intrigue and satisfy the reader who wants to think about the nature of common sense as it relates to AI, what its main components are, and how it all works. It's for someone who is curious as to why AI has not yet produced fully functional autonomous robots, and wants to see if there is a route to a more capable AI. If you'd like your future self-driving car to truly manage on its own in the complex, unpredictable world we live in—and get you your groceries on time—this book is for you.

To such a reader we say welcome and let's get started.

1   The Road to Common Sense

We can only see a short distance ahead, but we can see plenty there that
needs to be done.

—Alan Turing, "Computing Machinery and Intelligence"

This is a book about common sense from the standpoint of artificial intelligence (AI). While only a small number of AI researchers actually work on
common sense directly, the topic has been around since the beginning of
the field. AI was given its name in the 1950s by US computer scientist John
McCarthy (1927–2011), and one of the first papers ever written about AI is
one he presented in 1958 called "Programs with Common Sense."

With a history like this, one might think that the common sense part of
AI would be well in hand by now, more than sixty years later. But in a 2019
book called *Rebooting AI*, Gary Marcus and Ernest Davis make this observation: "Unfortunately acquiring common sense is much harder than one
might think. And as we will see, the need for getting machines to acquire
common sense is also far more pervasive than one might have imagined."

The implication here is clear: AI systems could really use some sort of
common sense, but nobody has yet figured out how to provide them with
it. And it's not as if anyone thinks that common sense is some minor aspect
of intelligence; arguably, it's at the very core.

What we propose to do in this book is to take a hard look at this notion
of common sense to get a better sense of what it is, why it is important,
and what it might take to make it work in an AI system. But before setting
out on this long and winding road, let us have a look at where we will be
going.

A Guide to Commonsense Guides

A quick search on Amazon will reveal that there are over seven thousand books with "common sense" (or "common-sense" or "commonsense") in the title. About a tenth of them also include the word "guide." To get an idea of their range, here are a dozen of those guides:

The Common Sense Guide to Real Estate Investing

Nanny in a Book: The Common-Sense Guide to Childcare

Surviving the Ebola Virus: A Tropical Doctor's Commonsense Guide

A Commonsense Guide to Fasting

Freedom's Last Stand: A Common-Sense Guide to Understanding the Tyranny of Collectivist Ideology

Uncommon Fruits & Vegetables: A Commonsense Guide

Technical Writing A-Z: A Commonsense Guide to Engineering Reports and Theses

The Common Sense Guide to Handfeeding Baby Birds

Your First Gun: A Common Sense Guide to Selection and Usage for Novices and Dummies

Dude! What Were You Thinking? A Common Sense Guide to Dating & Relationships

Answers to Your Mule Questions: A Common Sense Guide to Understanding the Mule's Point of View

Gardening Nude: A Common Sense Guide to Improving Your Health and Lifestyle by Increasing Exposure to Nature, Cultivating a Green Mindset, and Building a Strong Community

Other than the "common sense" part, it is hard to see what these books could possibly have in common!

One thing to think about in the context of *this* book is what the term "common sense" in these guides is intended to convey. It is clearly not just an exhortation to use common sense; a commonsense guide to fasting should be a bit more than "use common sense when fasting." What the title *A Commonsense Guide to Fasting* suggests is perhaps something like this: "Here are some things to know about fasting, not to become an expert, but to guide your actions in a sensible way in ordinary situations." The same applies to investing in real estate, understanding mules, and presumably, gardening in the nude.

The premise here is that while it might be possible to become an *expert* on any of these topics, there are also some basic, commonsense things that even nonexperts will find useful. Here's the pitch at Amazon for the book on hand-feeding baby birds:

Breaking the myth that handfeeding baby birds requires years and years of training, this guide offers a common sense solution. Detailing a basic and workable knowledge of a baby bird's requirements for warmth, cleanliness, frequency of feeding, proper formulas, correct temperature and correct technique, this book will have you feeding baby birds like a pro in no time.

The goal seems reasonable enough. There is clearly a wide range of things that humans deal with every day not as experts, but in simple, ordinary terms. Indeed, how many of us truly understand how an LED TV displays a movie or Alexa tells us the weather? For most of us, a commonsense understanding of the technology is all we have. In some cases, we get our understanding through repeated experience (like how to eat a melting ice cream cone on a hot summer day); in some cases, we get advice from friends (such as what to wear—and not wear—for a party); and in other cases, our understanding may well come from something like a guide or manual (like how to set up a home printer).

What we intend to do in this book is to step back from individual topics like the Ebola virus and hand-feeding baby birds, and look at the underlying idea of common sense itself. We want an understanding of common sense that makes it clear how it leans on the knowledge gained from things such as prior experience, advice from friends, and commonsense guides. As computer scientists, we want to aim for an account of common sense that is specific and detailed enough that we could at least imagine building a computational machine that has it.

Artificial Intelligence

This takes us back to the topic of AI. In general terms, AI is the study of how intelligent behavior can be produced through computational means. At one extreme, we imagine sophisticated behaviors like playing chess, interpreting poetry, and classifying tumors; at the other extreme, we envision more commonplace activities like babysitting a toddler, preparing a meal, and driving a car.

What do these have to do with common sense? This will take some sorting out in the next two chapters, but the basic idea is that an AI system may be able to do remarkably well on certain specific tasks that demand intelligence in humans, but still be unable to behave in an intelligent way more broadly. What we will end up saying is that these AI systems display expertise, not common sense.

Consider the well-known AI system called AlphaGo developed by Deep-Mind Technologies. This system is unquestionably an expert when it comes to playing the game of Go and likely the top Go player in the world. But it does nothing else. It doesn't have even a rudimentary ability to deal with the rest of the world. We would never expect it to be able to order a pizza, recommend a movie, or diagnose a blood infection. The system can't really be criticized for this; it was never intended to do anything other than play Go.

To someone outside the field of AI, the fact that different AI systems perform different tasks might seem like a small detail. Can't you just take something like AlphaGo, marry it with Roomba and Siri, and end up with a system that plays Go, vacuums floors, and responds to voice commands? Throw in Google Translate, and will the system not respond to voice commands in any language? Keep on doing this long enough and will we not end up with a system with enough versatility to do a good job out there in the real world?

Things have not turned out this way. However impressive each of these AI systems is individually, they remain isolated from each other. They are like small islands of high achievement in a large sea of possible behaviors. There is still no clear sense within the AI community of how to get a system to behave in a reasonable way outside these localized areas of expertise. Even if we were to imagine an AI system armed with the hundreds of commonsense guides mentioned above, it would still be at a loss outside those specific topics.

To give a small example, the guide to uncommon fruits and vegetables listed above might well talk about pomegranates, but it almost certainly does not mention laundry baskets. Nor would we expect a guide for laundry baskets (or any direct experience with laundry baskets) to ever deal with pomegranates. So if we now imagine an AI system that has to decide whether a pomegranate would fit inside a laundry basket (for some reason), it will need something beyond what it has on each individual topic. It will be unable to make a sensible decision if it has no way of bringing these two separate topics together in a meaningful way.

This is of course not how things are in humans. We fully expect that a person who gets to be good at playing Go will still do well on a broad range of non-Go activities including, but not limited to (as the lawyers say), vacuuming floors and handling questions about pomegranates in laundry baskets. This ability to deal with what comes up in a way that is not tied to prowess in any particular domain is precisely what we expect of common sense.

We are not the first to observe that current AI systems and humans are different in this regard. It is one thing that virtually all AI scientists and technologists agree on. Where they do disagree, however—and sometimes quite loudly—is on what the implications are.

For (what might be called) AI boosters, the picture is somewhat like this:

We are in the early stages of AI, and the best of the systems built so far are already intelligent, but clearly not in the same way humans are. "Intelligent" is not a useful label in the end. The systems do better than humans in some ways, and worse in others. The goal is not to emulate humans to the letter, with all their limitations and failings, but rather to behave in a usefully intelligent way on a wide variety of tasks. There will always be a powerful synergy between AI systems and the humans they work with; each will make up for weaknesses in the other.

For (what might be called) AI skeptics, including many of the AI researchers themselves, the picture is quite different:

The AI systems built to date are nothing like intelligent. If real human-level intelligence is what you are after, the whole current AI approach is wrongheaded. Put aside proficiency in ultraspecialized areas like playing Go. You can't do better than humans in general terms if you can't do as well as a six-year-old child. And there is no evidence to date that an AI system will ever have the general intelligence of a six-year-old.

It is not our goal in this book to continue this debate; others have written about it. What we aim to do is to focus on just the common sense part: what common sense means, how it works, what it might take to build computational systems that have it, and why we should bother.

The Road Ahead

At the risk of spoiling all the suspense, here is where the book is going:

Chapter 2: Common Sense in Humans

We look at the idea of common sense as it exists in humans. We make the case that it is tied to knowing certain ordinary things. We argue that common sense is the ability to make effective use of this knowledge in deciding how to behave and plays a critical role in the spectrum of human cognitive capabilities.

Chapter 3: Expertise in AI Systems

We turn our attention to AI systems past and present. We make the case that no matter how these systems are built, they deliver expertise on certain tasks, not common sense. We argue that common sense is not a matter of additional expertise in yet another area. If we want AI systems that can deal with the wide range of unanticipated things that come up in real life, a different approach is called for.

Chapter 4: Knowledge and Its Representation

We consider the issue of knowledge and what it might mean to make use of it. We contend that an item of knowledge is somewhat like a number in that we can make use of it by representing it symbolically and working on the symbols. In the case of numbers, what the symbols should be and how to operate on them is well understood; it's what we call arithmetic. How this should play out for knowledge is much less clear and is the subject of the middle part of the book.

Chapter 5: A Commonsense Understanding of the World

We begin to consider commonsense knowledge by examining the high-level picture of the world it presupposes: there are things in the world with properties that change over time as a result of events that occur; among these things, there are physical objects with properties like size and location in space; and among these physical objects, there are animate agents with beliefs and goals who can cause events to occur.

Chapter 6: Commonsense Knowledge

We consider how specific items of commonsense knowledge might be formulated. We make the case that in addition to dealing with things and their properties, we need to deal with concepts—that is, ideas about the kinds of things there can be. We maintain that these concepts are understood in terms of typical, atypical, and borderline cases.

Chapter 7: Representation and Reasoning, Part I

We take the first step toward representing commonsense knowledge in symbolic form. We argue that we want to represent things and their properties separately from the concepts involved. We also talk about how a computational system would reason with these representations.

Chapter 8: Representation and Reasoning, Part II

We take a second step in the use of symbolic representations. We contend that we need to be able to represent propositions—sentences that can be either true or false—without believing them to be true. This will be essential for reasoning about what it would take to make a proposition true—the basis for planning. And again, we talk about how a computational system would operate on these representations.

Chapter 9: Common Sense in Action

We return to common sense at a high level and show how the pieces fit together. We consider a scenario where an agent, while engaging in a routine task, encounters something totally unexpected and needs to use common sense to figure out what to do next. We show how this application of common sense can be understood as computing a certain result from symbolic representations of the sort seen in earlier chapters.

Chapter 10: Steps toward Implementation

We look in more practical terms at what it would take to build an AI system with common sense. Besides considering commonsense reasoners, we spend some time thinking about where all the commonsense knowledge will come from, and looking at some interesting ways in which AI systems of the future will need to learn from experience and written texts.

Chapter 11: Building Trust

We begin to wrap up by considering whether society should even be thinking about building AI systems with common sense. We make the case that if we are ever going to build systems that make decisions for themselves, we will want them to have reasons for what they do that humans can understand, and then agree or disagree with. In particular, we will want them to have commonsense knowledge and goals, and for their decisions about what to do to be the result of applying this knowledge in pursuit of those goals.

The book also includes a bonus chapter for aficionados on the connection between logic and commonsense reasoning as well as chapter-by-chapter notes that add some color to the text and suggest further resources for the interested reader.

Setting Out

So this is our journey in a nutshell: from common sense, to commonsense knowledge, to commonsense knowledge representation and reasoning. It's a lot to take in. As the song says, the road is long with many a winding turn. This is a book about common sense, but not really much of a commonsense guide.

There are those who want to believe in a much simpler story for AI, where we would take some sort of learning system, hook it up to the internet (or maybe push a robot out the door), and have it learn to figure things out for itself. Why can't some version of common sense just emerge spontaneously from being embedded in the world over a period of time? All of this talk about computation over symbolic representations of knowledge might feel too mannered, too regimented, too cerebral for common sense.

While we understand the intuitive appeal of this simpler story, there is as yet no good specification of how it could possibly work. That said, we need to be clear that the more involved story we are about to tell here is only a hypothesis—one possible road to common sense. In practical terms, it could well turn out to be a dead end, or eventually be supplanted by more direct highways. But as we hope the reader will see, in intellectual terms, it is still a rewarding road to follow, with wonderful sites to visit along the way in philosophy, psychology, linguistics, logic, and computer science.

The road we are setting out on is one that we ourselves have explored for four decades in our own work. We have built AI systems, proved AI theorems, and led AI projects. We have been inspired by all the terrific people we have worked with and our involvement with the major international AI organizations. As your guides on this journey, we will do our best to make things informative, interesting, and fun. So buckle your seat belt and enjoy the trip!

2 Common Sense in Humans

Common sense is genius dressed in its working clothes.
—popularly attributed to Ralph Waldo Emerson

Before we can seriously contemplate endowing machines with common sense, we first need to get a good understanding of what it is. As a topic of serious study, there is not much scientific literature on it. Of course, we do have some sort of intuitive understanding of the idea. We use the term frequently in daily life, admonishing each other to "use a little common sense," for instance. So what do we mean by this?

In this chapter, we take a look at common sense in humans from several angles and create a working definition of our own—the first step on our journey toward AI with common sense.

Some Aspects of Common Sense

It is not hard to find interesting quotes about common sense, beyond the one by Emerson above. Here are some examples:

- Albert Einstein: "Common sense is the collection of prejudices acquired by age eighteen."
- Baron d'Holbach: "When we examine the opinions of men [sic], we find that nothing is more uncommon than common sense; or, in other words, they lack judgment to discover plain truths or to reject absurdities and palpable contradictions."
- Josh Billings: "Common sense is the knack of seeing things as they are, and doing things as they ought to be done."

- Bob Marley: "Me is a common sense man. That mean when me explain things, me explain it in a very simple way; that mean if I explain it to a baby, the baby will understand too, you know."

There are some revealing insights here, highlighting themes reinforced by many others: common sense is derived from experience; it's about easily apprehended facts and easily foreseen problems; it supports doing things that are reasonable and appropriate; and it favors simple explanations.

Let's explore these elements in a little more detail. First, there is general agreement that common sense is learned through personal experience rather than in school or by reading. Certainly some commonsense understanding is seeded through conversations with others or reading things like guides, but by and large, our understanding of how things work in the world is solidified by experiencing them ourselves.

The experiences that matter to common sense are generally those of relatively mundane, everyday life common to a large group of people. This group can be a culture, nationality, or maybe even all humans. We expect certain facts and tendencies to be known by virtually all the adults in the group. If someone draws a conclusion that fails to utilize such commonly known information, we think of them as not using common sense. Critiques about ignoring what "everyone knows" are familiar: "Why is he doing that? Everyone knows that you can't eat soup with a fork." There are many things that we learn growing up that we expect everyone else to know, and we expect them to use that knowledge to make the same kinds of decisions we believe we would make. (This is the "common" part of "common sense.")

Common sense involves noticing things that ought to be apparent to any normal person. If we are in a shared context, for example, we expect others to take that context into account. If a friend thinks that a husky-looking canine on a leash sitting on a neighbor's front doorstep is a wolf, we'd say they weren't using common sense. That would be flouting an easily observable context. Conversely, deciding that an animal in that situation was a dog, even if it looked somewhat wolflike, would be commonsensical.

Seeing these kinds of "plain truths" and "absurdities" is also essential in our internal mental world. A key part of common sense is being able to imagine (at least roughly) the consequences of actions. We use memories of lots of experiences along with an intuitive understanding of cause and effect to foresee what will lead to what. So when common sense suggests one action over another, it's based on an expectation of what will happen in each case. Thus common sense helps us envision whether a planned action, like trying to drive up a steep hill covered in ice, might fail. When choosing between multiple courses of action, common sense also gives us a rough idea of the costs and benefits of each, so that we can quickly compare the options. For instance, it will tell us how the social cost of asking a neighbor to borrow something might compare to the inconvenience and monetary cost of going somewhere to buy or rent it.

Underlying all of this is the fact that commonsense thinking is generally sound. Common sense relies on inference: the drawing of sound conclusions from premises. We envision how the results of one step of a plan will make the next step possible, such as getting into a taxi in order to get to the airport in order to board a flight in order to get to Rome. We understand intuitively how multiple facts can combine to yield useful new ones. We expect common sense to illuminate a reasonable conclusion based on logical justifications and evidence. We cannot make a commonsensical decision unless we can actually see how the pieces of our observations, envisioned outcomes, and other facts fit together. (This is the "sense" part of "common sense.")

Importantly, these kinds of commonsense inferences are quick and easy. They occur to us as intuitive rather than as consciously and exhaustively reasoned. We're reminded of some past experience related to our current situation, and adapt a remembered observation to fit a current need. Common sense is a shallow cognitive phenomenon, operating quickly compared to thoughtful, methodical analysis. It's not common sense if it takes a sizable amount of mental effort to figure it out. We can think of it as "reflexive thinking," with the "reflexive" being as significant as the "thinking."

Related to its contrast with complex reasoning, common sense displays a strong affinity for simple explanations. It follows Occam's razor: a convoluted account of some phenomenon when a clearly simpler one is available is not commonsensical. Author James Whitcomb Riley captured an important part of this when he famously said, "When I see a bird that walks like a duck and swims like a duck and quacks like a duck, I call that bird a duck." While there may be other possible explanations for a duck-like object, if it walks and swims and quacks like one, the commonsensical conclusion is that it's a duck.

Finally, as we noted with the commonsense guides in the previous chapter, common sense is often distinguished from expertise. Commonsense guides help us learn how to do things in quick, intuitive ways, explicitly targeting audiences that don't aspire to the specialized proficiency of experts. We will have much more to say about expertise later, but in a nutshell, we would not call on common sense to guide us in computing the trajectory of an extraplanetary space vehicle or even reconfiguring a home theater system with its six different remote controls (which can sometimes feel like rocket science). But we do rely on common sense to keep us from doing silly things like continuing to wait for water to boil on the stove after nothing has happened for an hour, or leaving a sharp knife on a low coffee table where a toddler could reach it.

A Definition of Common Sense

Having laid out the basics, we can now consider a more carefully crafted view of common sense. There are many opinions on what common sense is about, and it is easy to argue with almost any definition one might propose. But as we have seen, there are some key elements that distinguish it from other mental phenomena and on which there is much general agreement. Based on this (and our experience with knowledge and its use in AI systems), we propose a working definition that will guide our treatment in the rest of the book:

> *Common sense is the ability to make effective use of ordinary, everyday, experiential knowledge in achieving ordinary, everyday, practical goals.*

Many of the words we've used here are general and nontechnical, so a bit of elaboration is warranted. Given what we have said so far, the definition reflects these important points:

- "Effective" reminds us that it is not enough to merely know a lot of relevant things. Using common sense means being able to work through this knowledge successfully without being overwhelmed in order to find out how it bears on the goals at hand. The application of this knowledge should be fast and effortless.

- "Ordinary" and "everyday" imply that common sense deals with situations of the sort that humans regularly encounter in day-to-day life. Specialized education and expert analytic skills are not needed to develop and exhibit it. It is most frequently about mundane, familiar things.

- "Experiential" emphasizes that what counts as common sense is knowl-edge gained from repeated experience. It generally does not come from schooling or technical reading. Common wisdom can be passed from one person to another, but it is generally derived from personal experiences.
- "Practical" stresses that common sense is for making choices about what to do to be successful in the everyday world. We do not think of it as some kind of academic pursuit or foundation for philosophical argumentation.

The practicality aspect of common sense is one that is underscored by the psychology literature. Psychologist Robert Sternberg has spent years developing a theory of what he calls "successful intelligence," related to the ability to set and accomplish personally meaningful goals within one's cultural context. Sternberg's framework focuses heavily on adaptive behav-ior, understanding intelligence as primarily about the ability to adapt to the environment. He postulates four key types of abilities: analytical, creative, practical, and wisdom based. Regarding the third of these, he says this: "Practical intelligence is what most people call common sense." Sternberg and his collaborator, Richard Wagner, contend that practical intelligence is based largely on tacit knowledge—that is, "what one needs to know to suc-ceed in a particular environment that is not explicitly stated and often that is not even verbalized." Their theory emphasizes the role of personal experi-ence and suggests that this tacit knowledge is procedural—about knowing how to act in particular situations. As we have made clear, we agree with the former, but in our estimation, much of the tacit knowledge underlying commonsense inference is declarative (that is, factual).

Our definition of common sense is clearly related to what is usually called *rationality*, characterized by the psychologist Steven Pinker as "the ability to use knowledge to attain goals." Where the two concepts differ is that rationality is much broader; it does not constrain the kind or com-plexity of knowledge or reasoning that can be applied. Whereas common sense deals with mundane, experiential knowledge, rationality can deal with expert knowledge and require a more careful and thorough applica-tion than mere common sense. For example, a doctor may want to decide if a patient should undergo a certain cancer therapy. Given that the patient has just tested positive for this cancer, rational decision-making requires carefully weighing the reliability of the test against the unlikeliness of the cancer in the first place. A sensible thing to do, no doubt, but well beyond what we would expect of common sense.

Note that we need to distinguish commonsense *knowledge*—facts, patterns, principles, and generalizations—from commonsense *reasoning*—the ability to make use of that knowledge in certain ways. When we say that someone *has common sense* or *uses common sense*, we usually mean that they not only have the relevant knowledge but also can make appropriate use of it.

Regarding the word "knowledge" itself, we are following the practice common in AI of putting aside the difference between knowledge and belief, and using the terms more or less interchangeably. (The distinction is made more carefully in philosophy.) When we talk about commonsense *knowledge*, what we really mean, strictly speaking, is commonsense *belief*, allowing that some of these beliefs might be mistaken or held for the wrong reasons. Common sense does not limit itself to beliefs that are guaranteed to be correct or held with total conviction; there are too few of those. To its advantage, the term "knowledge" can be used in ways that have no equivalent with the term "belief": we can form useful sentences with "know" that we can't with "believe." For example, we can say, "Harry knows what card Ann is holding," but we can't say, "Harry believes what card Ann is holding." (To use "belief" correctly, we would need to say something awkward like, "There is a card such that Harry believes that Ann is holding that card.") Incidentally, while we certainly realize that there are *degrees* of belief, from the merest of suspicions to absolute certainty, we will not have much to say in this book about how numerical values for these degrees might be arrived at or managed, or how this would dovetail with the rest of common sense.

Bottom-up and Top-down Uses of Common Sense

Now that we have an understanding of the crucial aspects of common sense, it is useful to talk about when and how it is used. As noted, common sense is about practical responses to everyday situations. We can divide the ways in which it is invoked into two general categories, which we might call *bottom-up* and *top-down* types:

• The bottom-up (or event-driven) ones are where you observe, notice, or perceive something unusual and want to make some sense of it. It can be while you're engaged in some goal-directed activity or just sitting in a chair relaxing. The unusual thing can be something that happens unexpectedly or something expected that does not happen. You feel compelled to find a simple, intuitive explanation for what you have seen.

- The top-down (or goal-driven) ones are where you are considering what to do, and need to compare alternatives in your current situation or a future circumstance. This can involve the potential cost and benefit of engaging in one activity over another. For the cost, there are things like risk, the chance of failure, negative side effects, social considerations, and the like. The benefit aspect involves how successful an alternative is likely to be, or how preferable its result.

Let's start with the bottom-up scenario. Much of what we do each day is like running on a kind of autopilot. We regularly fall into routines that get us from one place to another and allow us to reflexively perform many of the activities of regular life. We walk, brush our teeth, play sports, and even commute to work for the most part without much conscious thought. Even if we are following a well thought-out plan, as we are starting to execute the plan's steps, we lapse into routinized behavior, like closing the door to our house, walking to our car, unlocking the car door, and adjusting our seat before setting out on a consciously planned car trip. These routinized steps have a certain set of expectations built in, based on repeated experience. When the expectations are met, we don't even notice. When we close the front door, we expect it to latch and lock; when we start the car, we expect the dashboard to light up, fan to start, and radio to go on. These things are done so automatically that we don't even remember them after we've done them. Our minds are free to think about other things, such as where we're planning to pick up food for dinner or an important presentation at work.

But sometimes things built into a routine's expectations fail to occur. If the door doesn't close well or the car doesn't start, we change mental gears; we are jolted from the routine and go into some sort of problem-solving mode. We say to ourselves, "Hold on a second. What's going on here?" (Note that the unexpected could be something that does *not* happen after a regularly experienced time interval, as when we've waited for twenty minutes and our coffee order still has not arrived.)

Common sense is the immediate resort when we are jarred by these interruptions. In some cases, we've experienced similar problems before, and previously learned routines help us make quick diagnoses and repairs:

if a door is not closing, we automatically look down to see if something is caught between the door and jamb, and push a toy out of the way; if the car lights do not come on, we try to remember if we left the headlights on last night, and check to see if the car's battery is dead. These are not as mindless as the activities we were engaged in before, but we don't use any kind of complex problem-solving either. As mentioned, one part of common sense is the innate urge to find simple, familiar explanations. If our first, commonsense-based approach to diagnosing a problem doesn't work, of course we may still resort to more detailed problem-solving, and imagine our way through rarer or more unusual causes: maybe someone attached a bungee cord to the front door as a joke; perhaps the new alarm system interlock shut down the car. But we don't go there first. Common sense jumps into play as the first responder when our regular behavior is met with something unexpected. It provides rapid, experience-based explanations and solutions for common problems.

Incidentally, we seem especially inclined to notice when others fail to use common sense. Familiar to many parents is the need to address these lapses: "You left Sally's house at 11:55 and you know it takes twenty minutes to drive home. Didn't it occur to you that you'd miss your midnight curfew?" Our commonsense recognition skills are well honed, and we are often inclined to ask others to "use some common sense."

Turning now to top-down scenarios, these are situations in which we are making plans in order to achieve goals. In making simple plans—without pen and paper or a computer to assist us—we use our experience-based power to mentally envision the key steps and their likely outcomes. Even without world-class skills in logic, we can all mentally project our activity into the future in a qualitative way. We do this all the time in everyday activity, thinking only a step or two ahead, like picturing a walk to the kitchen to open the refrigerator to look for something to drink, or many steps ahead, such as imagining a trip to the airport, a flight overseas, and how we will be met at the arrival lounge. Common sense is a powerful aid in such forward projection and our usual first resort when we decide we want to do something.

As noted, in this planning activity, previous experience allows us to take the obvious factors into account to quickly determine if a contemplated action might fail (if it's Sunday, the post office being closed will prevent us from picking up a package), whether there could be risks in a plan's step (if the upcoming stretch of highway has no gas stations, we could run out of fuel), or the relative risks and rewards of two alternative ways to achieve the same goal (if it's rush hour, the normally faster expressway may be jammed, but the surface streets have many traffic lights).

While we are all capable of forethought, however, some people are at least occasionally quite poor at weighing the assets and liabilities of contemplated plan steps. Subway stations need to post signs admonishing people not to jump onto the tracks to recover dropped cell phones. Comedian Jerry Seinfeld tells the story of a Halloween superhero costume whose manufacturer felt obligated to include a warning not to attempt to fly while wearing it. These kinds of notices are clear evidence that common sense doesn't always win the mental battle for our attention.

Note that bottom-up and top-down contexts can be intertwined. Unexpected events interrupt plans that are underway. If we spill coffee on ourselves during our travel to a meeting, we will spring into commonsense replanning mode to envision whether we have time to return home to change, and by what route. Sometimes while executing plans, we react to potential problems just before they happen. For example, just as we're placing a tray on a coffee table, we might think, "Hang on. I probably shouldn't leave these hors d'oeuvres here, or the dog will run over and start eating them." We didn't envision that as we were focused on getting food to our guests and leaned down to place the tray on the table. In this kind of case, our routine execution of a familiar plan can leave us on the brink of trouble, but then we catch ourselves—hopefully before something bad happens— and know that what we're about to do or have just done is problematic.

One area of life where we can easily see both the bottom-up and top-down operation of common sense is in the use of *language*. On the one hand, we listen to people and try to make sense of what they are saying, and on the other hand, we decide on things to say ourselves for our own purposes. Sometimes the language is so shallow that we connect words together, like verbs and their subjects, nouns and their modifiers, or pronouns and their referents, on what feels like the autopilot we mentioned above. But in instances where there is potential ambiguity, common sense comes into play.

To see this, read the following sentence:

The large ball crashed through the table because it was made of steel.

The "it" in the sentence is technically ambiguous: it could be the ball, or it could be the table. Yet we immediately and instinctively picture a heavy metal ball falling on a table and crashing through. We don't think of the "it" as referring to the table, and we don't even think about what the table might be made of. It's just common sense that heavy, metal things can break through items not made of metal. Interestingly, the reasoning is quite different if we change a single word in the sentence:

The large ball crashed through the table because it was made of cardboard.

Our knowledge of flimsy objects causes us to picture a cardboard table with almost any moderately heavy kind of ball breaking through. We just don't call to mind the other possibility that the "it" could be a ball made of cardboard. These kinds of inferences are made quickly and automatically, and are firmly based on a commonsense understanding of the world.

The crucial shared characteristic of all the above is that the reasoning does not take an expert in a specialized domain, like materials science or animal behavior or car mechanics, to figure things out or predict consequences. They represent everyday situations in which average people with normal experiences can predict or explain events with little cognitive effort, based heavily on observations they themselves have made in the past.

What Is Common Sense For?

Given the way it works, how does common sense provide value in the big picture of human cognition? Why exactly do we have it?

The human cognitive architecture is generally conceived of as having two end points: a reflexive action component that runs our routine autopilot activity, and a more methodical analytic component that supports in-depth deliberation and conscious problem-solving. The reflexive action autopilot lets us off-load from our conscious attention a huge portion of what we do every day. The analytic component allows us to bring our particularly human higher-level intelligence to bear on complex technical problems, future plans, thoughtful writing, and the general activity of building and maintaining civilization.

Common sense is the key to allowing this all to work effectively in a world where exogenous forces cause things to happen outside our control. By providing the first response to problems arising during routine activities, it avoids calling on the full power of our higher-level cognitive system for every little issue that comes up. The kind of shallow experience-driven thinking that common sense offers can handle a majority of the small hurdles we encounter every day, and thus it supplies a robust backstop for our autopilot. The scope of experience underlying common sense allows it to apply in a broad set of circumstances, and its basis in extensive observation of patterns in the world allows it to be successful most of the time.

Complex thinking and problem-solving is energy intensive and time-consuming. So common sense as an intermediary helps our brains to save precious energy and provides fast experience based shortcuts to conclusions that might otherwise take lengthy reasoning. In many situations, reaction time is critical, and common sense allows us to act quickly. In that respect, it can be literally a lifesaver. Thus common sense provides a linchpin capability situated between the reflexive and analytic ends of our cognitive spectrum. It makes the former more robust and preserves the latter for the more challenging work for which it is best suited.

This idea is backed up by some interesting work in psychology. Psychologist Kenneth Hammond and others in the field of judgment and decision-making claim that there is a *cognitive continuum* between endpoints that they call *intuition* and *analysis*. In their view, intermediate forms of cognition include combinations of both intuition and analysis, which aligns with our understanding of common sense as basically logical, but rapid, shallow, and memory driven. Hammond calls the position of common sense on the continuum "quasi-rationality." (That's nicely descriptive, but we'll stick with "common sense" for the rest of our journey.)

Even when our analytic capabilities are fully engaged, common sense continues to play a key role When planning a complex trip using the internet and a spreadsheet, we still rely on common sense to fill in gaps for many of the substeps. For example, we don't plan on where we will put our hand on the door to get into a taxi. Common sense allows us to skip that part, and envision the start and end of a ride to the airport. In other words, even the most thoughtful and analytic problem-solving relies on a foundation of common sense. This is in fact true for reasoning in general: common sense fills in the blanks between more esoteric steps with the mundane glue that allows us to derive complete chains of sound inferences.

Finally, we note that common sense plays its roles in a way that allows us to make efficient use of enormous amounts of experience. Perhaps we could have evolved to remember every single detail of every single experience we ever had, like a perfect video recorder. But if that were the case, finding a relevant prior experience to guide us in a new situation would be a burdensome search task. Instead, our memories are generally more stereotyped; we aggregate many similar things we experience into generic patterns that coalesce multiple experiences. Psychologists like Sir Frederic Bartlett have shown that we remember things in a schematized way and that memory use is reconstructive, rather than simply the equivalent of replaying a movie. We all know how our memories are flawed, and how we sometimes confuse one remembered experience with another that was similar. But while this kind of generalized memory can lead to problems (it famously makes people bad eyewitnesses, for example), for the purposes of common sense, it's a feature, not a bug. With this mechanism, we can learn aggregated lessons across multiple experiences and not have to remember them individually, and when we need to bring these experiences to bear, we can use a generic remembered version without having to sort out the differences between large numbers of similar memories.

As we will see later in the book, if only a limited number of things could ever happen to us, or if every event was under our control, we probably would not even need common sense. But given that we live in the real world with other agents and phenomena constantly adding to what happens to us, it is critical to have some mechanism to handle the range of things that our more robotic routines can't cope with automatically. Common sense might not be the last resort, but it is an excellent first resort. Its intuitive, generally sound practical basis gives us the flexibility to deal with unanticipated situations, and the robustness to cope quickly and effectively with an unpredictable world. In that respect, given that intelligence is generally regarded as learning and adapting successfully to the environment, *common sense is the core of intelligence.*

It's Important, but It's Not Everything

While common sense is a critical element of our everyday lives, clearly not all human thinking is commonsensical. And sometimes it just doesn't work, either because we fail to use it or its simple experience-matching approach is not up to the challenge. Much of our mental lives goes beyond what we might consider to be mere common sense, inhabiting different places on the cognitive continuum. To conclude this chapter, we want to briefly consider some departures from and limitations to common sense that will show up again later.

Expert knowledge: Most people learn some kind of specialty for their work or learn in school about subjects outside everyday experience. What we might call expert knowledge, gained through some combination of being taught explicitly and by hands-on experience, is an essential ingredient in the creation of new technology, solving of complex problems, and indeed progress of society. This kind of knowledge generally builds on a deeper understanding of how things work and why things are the way they are than we see with common sense, which tends to be more experiential, and less inclined to underlying causes and principles. The way expert knowledge is communicated and learned is different from that of common sense, and likely calls on additional memory as well as synthesis and inference mechanisms that are more deliberate and analytic than those we normally associate with common sense. (Expert knowledge does not so much supplant commonsense knowledge as enrich and deepen it. Even rocket scientists need to know that the people they work with will need air to breathe, for instance.)

Puzzle mode: Humans without extensive mathematical or problem-solving training are still able to solve nontrivial problems. We all learn to step back from problems that cannot be handled directly and try to work our way through to a solution, possibly using pencil and paper, or in consultation with others. This might be for recreational puzzles like sudokus and the logic puzzles seen in magazines, or decidedly less recreational activities such as filling out income tax forms or sorting a list of names into alphabetical order. It can also be for a broad range of more expert-level tasks like calculating the load on a bridge or solving a system of linear equations. Once we start thinking of a problem we are facing as something that can be dealt with by a specific *method* we know about (coming from algebra, logic, fluid dynamics, or wherever), we are outside the domain of common sense. If it takes pencil and paper to solve, or some complex procedure to puzzle through, then it is not really commonsensical. (Of course common sense does not go away when we are following a procedure. As we've mentioned, it is still needed to deal with each of the steps of any method we decide to pursue.)

Recognizing patterns: There are modes of thinking we engage in that have nothing to do with knowledge at all, commonsense or otherwise. Look at this pair of letter sequences: "wxyz" and "wyzx." Now look at this pair: "rbv" and "rvb." Here's another pair: "shout" and "south." And now this one: "gccewt" and "gcewtc." See the pattern? The mental process that took place to see the connection between the first and second elements of these pairs had nothing to do with any kind of knowledge or training. Nor is the process visual: typographic characters were used here, but you can repeat the exercise with sequences of sounds or taps on your body. Interestingly, the pattern is not really perceptual either. If the first element of a pair is the sequence of days Sunday, Monday, Tuesday, and so on to Saturday, what is the second element of that pair? The ability to recognize patterns like these in sequences or more complex structural arrangements is something we humans are good at, but is quite different from common sense. (Arguably, it feeds into common sense; we come to recognize analogies and part-by-part correspondences between commonsense categories such as hospitals and churches. More on this later.)

Primitive impulses: It is clear that humans take all sorts of actions that are steered more by emotions, urges, and compulsions than by anything like common sense or expressly articulated goals. What is less clear is how and when these impulses are actually beneficial to the human in question. Wariness of strangers, for example, is no doubt helpful to a point, but easily gives rise to a xenophobia that is counterproductive. The emotion of disgust can block people from putting unhealthy things into their mouths, but it too can degenerate into overly broad obsessions. At their worst, impulses like these push humans in directions that are diametrically opposed to common sense and considered to be psychological malfunctions. The example above of the cell phone on the subway tracks is one instance of some kind of primitive urge blocking out a commonsensical imperative to hesitate. (It is never really clear which side will actually win in a wrestling match between common sense and other conflicting impulses.)

Specious beliefs: Sociologist Duncan Watts has eloquently outlined his view of what is and is not common sense in his book *Everything Is Obvious** (**Once You Know the Answer*), and among the key features he posits is the relevance of common sense to "the immediate here and now of everyday life." He suggests that common sense breaks down outside that realm— that is, when "anticipating or managing the behavior of large numbers of people, in situations that are distant from us in time or space." While we are not sure of the "distance" aspect, Watts is no doubt accurate in his assessment and illustration of situations where commonsense beliefs can be mistaken. As a sociologist, he focuses on social phenomena like political conflicts, health care economics, and marketing campaigns, but he also discusses where commonsense intuitions about the physical world can lead us astray. Here is an example he cites: which bullet will hit the ground first, one fired horizontally from a gun, or one merely dropped from the same height? Even knowing from high school physics that they will strike the ground at the same time, it's hard to shake the feeling that firing a bullet will somehow keep it in the air longer. Some of our superficially plausible beliefs don't serve us well. (The subtitle of Watts's book is *How Common Sense Fails Us*, which is indicative of his focus on the inadequacy of common sense. While there are clearly situations where common sense fails us, we strongly believe that it is a critical component of human cognition and does succeed—largely unheralded—a great deal of the time.)

Cognitive biases: Psychologists Daniel Kahneman and Amos Tversky along with others have convincingly shown many places where common sense breaks down, especially in light of a variety of human cognitive biases ("systematic patterns of deviation from norm or rationality in judgment," as Wikipedia puts it). Fast, experientially driven, simplified thought patterns in humans leave us vulnerable to a host of mistakes: wishful thinking, confirmation bias, fallacies involving costs and benefits, overly optimistic mental shortcuts, and a host of other biases and illusions that can cause trouble.

Consider, for instance, what is called the *representative heuristic*. This is a mental shortcut that people take when thinking about categories of objects, where only typical or representative cases are considered. There is a famous Kahneman and Tversky experiment where subjects are told about Linda, a fictional student activist, deeply involved in issues of social justice, student demonstrations, and so on. Subjects are then asked to rate the likelihood of various career outcomes for Linda. One of the options is "feminist bank teller," and another is "bank teller." Subjects invariably end up rating the former more likely than the latter—a logical impossibility! The mistake, it appears, is to think of an unqualified category like "bank teller" only in terms of its typical properties. In other words, subjects seem to be comparing the "feminist bank teller" outcome to something more like a "stereotypical bank teller" outcome, and then having made this mistake, quite reasonably judge the former to be more likely for Linda than the latter.

In describing what is behind biases like these in humans, Kahneman posits a difference between a quick, reflexive kind of response to stimuli—executed by what he calls "System 1"—and a more thoughtful problem-solving-style response, invoked for activities that require attention—attributed to the equally neutrally named "System 2." The place for common sense in this framework is unclear. While commonsense inferences are also quick and intuitive, they don't align completely with System 1, which appears closer to what we were calling "reflexive action" or "intuition" above. Kahneman suggests that System 1 is capable of responding to "2+2=?" and driving on an empty road, but is it capable of resolving pronouns like the word "it" in the aforementioned sentence, "The large ball crashed through the table because it was made of steel"? System 2 handles activity that requires attention, but seems more aligned with the analytic component we discussed above. More analysis is needed to understand how Kahneman and his colleagues would account for common sense in their framework.

Whatever is at the root of the failures and limitations of common sense described by sociologists and psychologists, given the difference between commonsense and expert knowledge, and between commonsense and more puzzle-oriented thinking, it is quite apparent that common sense, while critical to life, is not the only kind of mental capacity we need. If your job is to run a nuclear power plant or fly a complex passenger aircraft, you cannot rely on common sense alone in your task.

When we eventually try to prescribe how a machine might gain and use common sense, we should be aware of these sorts of limitations and work to help machines recognize them too, either before they attempt to solve a problem, or in hindsight, when common sense seems to have fallen short. This will have important implications as we turn our attention to AI systems in the chapters to follow.

3 Expertise in AI Systems

A human being should be able to change a diaper, plan an invasion, butcher a hog, conn a ship, design a building, write a sonnet, balance accounts, build a wall, set a bone, comfort the dying, take orders, give orders, cooperate, act alone, solve equations, analyze a new problem, pitch manure, program a computer, cook a tasty meal, fight efficiently, die gallantly.

Specialization is for insects.

—Robert Heinlein, *Time Enough for Love*

This book is about what it takes to build machines that behave in an intelligent way. This is certainly not a new idea, and judging by recent headlines about AI, one might be excused for feeling that we must be pretty close to this goal by now, maybe in some well-funded research lab hidden somewhere, like we see in the movies.

But in our view, this is not the case. All the efforts to date have resulted in AI systems that are capable but highly specialized, and there appears to be some difficulty in getting off this track. To be clear about all of this, it is worth taking some time to understand where we are with AI today and how we got here. What we want to do in this chapter is highlight some of the field's major accomplishments over the last sixty years to illustrate the great strides that have been made, even as AI falls short of building a versatile, robust intelligence of the sort seen in humans. We will then step back and consider the lessons to be learned for the road ahead.

Building an AI

Devices and mechanisms that could be said to behave intelligently have been contemplated for centuries. But most would consider serious progress to have begun only with the advent of general-purpose electronic computers in the 1950s. A critical turning point was a conference at Dartmouth College in 1956 about a new field of study dubbed *artificial intelligence* by John McCarthy. As a field of study, AI took root in many university labs in the early 1960s, launched by computer and cognitive scientists from the Dartmouth conference like McCarthy, Marvin Minsky, Allen Newell, Herb Simon, and others. While there was no clear common understanding of what intelligence actually amounted to, the quest to program computers to behave in intelligent ways became one of the most exciting pursuits of the last sixty years. Recent growth has been even more dramatic; the amount of money that has been poured into AI and the number of people now familiar with the phrase "artificial intelligence" are stunning.

Much of the attention and investment in AI today is directed toward one way of building AI systems called *deep learning* (explained below). So much has been written about it that many people think of AI as synonymous with deep learning. And there is much to admire and be thrilled about with its success. In our opinion, however, the strengths and limitations of AI are best understood by taking a somewhat broader perspective. The field of AI has gone through a number of waves of thinking with quite different ideas about how to build AI systems. Each time, the wave was thought to be *the* game changer—the one that would supplant all the others. Deep learning is only the most recent.

In this chapter, we will look at five somewhat overlapping themes that have driven AI in useful and interesting directions. They started in different corners of the field, emphasizing different aspects of intelligent behavior, and each spans multiple decades. Each has resulted in notable successes, but each has also revealed key shortcomings in its approach to synthetic intelligence.

Before we begin, a caveat: we are not attempting to cover the entire history of the field here or even be comprehensive within the five areas we talk about. Others have written well about the history of AI, and we will not try to compete with them. Our focus is on the original grand vision of the field to create an autonomous AI system that can manage its way through the world we live in, accomplish its goals, and adapt on the fly to changing conditions. We will mention some of the better-known AI efforts, but always with an eye toward their implications for a robust, general AI endowed with common sense.

Theme 1: Game-Inspired Search

Since the earliest days of AI in the 1950s, getting a computer to play games of strategy such as chess (or checkers, Go, poker, and so on) has been a major preoccupation. There are three main reasons for this. First, success in this kind of domain is easy to evaluate: either the computer program can beat top human players at the game or it cannot. Second, games like chess and Go are considered to be major intellectual challenges. Not everyone can play well, and international champions are revered like sports heroes. The third reason is more practical: using ideas from mathematician Claude Shannon and computing pioneer Alan Turing, it appeared that game-playing computer programs could be built and deployed relatively easily.

The Shannon-Turing idea, roughly speaking, was this: to play a game like chess as well as an expert, it was not necessary to encode all the tricky chess knowledge that chess experts write about in books. Instead, it was sufficient to use the speed of a computer to search through the treelike space of possible moves, countermoves, countercountermoves, and so on, implicit in the rules of the game. At any point in the game, a computer program could determine the best move to make by looking ahead and considering how the game could be made to turn out after that move, even if the opponent played well. The tantalizing prospect was that of a chess program that would see far enough ahead to play a much better game than even its programmer.

The major stumbling block to this idea was the astronomical number of board positions that would need to be considered. Early computers in the 1950s were far from the powerhouses they are today, and so the first game-playing programs worked on much smaller games like checkers and 6x6 chess. A prominent checker-playing program by computer scientist Arthur Samuel was an early success in the 1950s, but it was only much later in the 1990s that a program by computer scientist Jonathan Schaeffer eventually became a world champion. In chess, it took until 1997 for the program Deep Blue from IBM to defeat Garry Kasparov, the world champion at the time. Deep Blue was built along the lines of the Shannon-Turing scheme, but with specialized hardware capable of looking at two hundred million chess positions per second.

Deep Blue was a major milestone in the history of AI. Here we had an AI program achieving success in a realm that everyone agreed required intelligence in humans. As such, chess had been a kind of holy grail for the field since its beginning. As far back as 1957, Nobel laureate Herb Simon had singled out chess and predicted that a machine would beat the world champion by 1967. The crucial ingredient of success here was not any deep knowledge or strategic competence, but rather techniques to manage and prune the enormous search space. Additional extensions and refinements were needed to develop world champions in games with elements of chance such as backgammon (as demonstrated by computer scientist Hans Berliner and colleagues in 1979) and incomplete information such as poker (as shown by computer scientist Tuomas Sandholm and colleagues in 2017). Interestingly, games like Go were still too big for any of these techniques and had to wait for more powerful ideas from machine learning, as described below.

Newell and Simon were probably the originators of the idea of effectively searching an enormous space of possibilities as a core element of intelligent behavior. Apart from games, a similar kind of search showed up in solving puzzles like the 15 puzzle (where a player tries to slide fifteen numbered tiles into numerical order on a four-by-four grid). This type of search even showed up in doing things like proving theorems in mathematics. In this case, the "moves" involve adding sentences to an ongoing proof according to certain logical rules, with the goal of arriving at the final theorem to be proved.

And yet while an important tool in the AI toolbox, this search-based view of AI has its clear limitations, even for games. To see this, consider the board game called Diplomacy, described as follows on Wikipedia:

Diplomacy is played by seven players, each controlling the armed forces of a major European power. Each player aims to move his or her few starting units and defeat those of others to win possession of a majority of strategic cities and provinces marked as "supply centers" on the map; these supply centers allow players who control them to produce more units. Following each round of player negotiations, each player can issue attack orders and take control of a neighboring province when the number of provinces adjacent to the attacking province that are given orders (written down and declared in advance) to support the attacking province exceeds the number of provinces adjacent to the province under attack that are given orders to support the province under attack.

What makes this game especially intriguing from an AI point of view is that between the board moves, which are synchronized for all players, time is allotted for players to negotiate with each other. Alliances are essential for players to bolster their military efforts and avoid having to constantly defend borders on all sides. Players who attempt to go it alone do not last long. But how these negotiations should proceed is left open by the rules. What the players choose to say to each other, privately or publicly, is totally up to them. In particular, what they may announce they will do in the next round and what their private written orders actually contain can be quite different. Of course, players who are found to be too untrustworthy may have a hard time finding allies—not only in the current game, but in subsequent ones!

Here we can see clearly how the idea of searching through a predetermined space of possible moves is only one part of the story. Moving an army on a map of Europe is indeed like moving a piece in chess or Go. But once negotiations are taken into account, the analogy breaks down. It is far from clear what "moves" players are selecting from during a negotiation phase. "Attacking Yorkshire from the North Sea" is one thing, but "making a deal with Russia that involves pretending to show support for France" is different.

What we have come to realize, in other words, is that the success of AI programs in games such as chess, Go, poker, and the like has depended on the fact that these programs operate in worlds that can be *circumscribed*, where moves can be enumerated and characterized in advance (perhaps probabilistically, when chance is involved). The moves in Diplomacy, similar to those in real life, are not like this.

Theme 2: Natural Language Understanding

One of the earliest ideas about how to ascertain whether machines could think came from Turing. Turing proposed yet another game, but of a somewhat different sort, wherein a computer and a human, hidden from a human judge, would each engage in a dialogue with the judge. The machine would be considered to be intelligent if the judge could not confidently distinguish between it and the human. (This is a bit of an oversimplification; the so-called *Turing test* has different variants.) This test had clear intuitive appeal: people generally believe that human-level competence in a conversation could not be achieved without being backed up by true intelligence. And as with other games, the test finessed having to take a position on what intelligence really comprised or how it actually worked in humans. The computer just had to win at this "imitation game."

Natural language (NL) also seemed quite amenable to computer programming. We learn grammar in school, and it feels like the regularities of verb conjugation and sentence structure should make an algorithmic approach to language understanding a natural for computer implementation. Work by linguist Noam Chomsky and others on structured formal grammars provided initial inspiration. The potential practical impact of machine NL understanding was clear too. Instead of having to use arcane artificial computer languages to ask questions and give commands to computers, why not use something more like English?

Work in NL processing started early in the history of AI—even before it was a field—as scientists in the 1950s tried to tackle automatic translation between languages. (We will have more to say about machine translation in the learning section below.) One of the most impressive early AI projects was a system at MIT called SHRDLU, developed by computer scientist Terry Winograd around 1970. SHRDLU was designed to work in a small world of simulated toy blocks on a table and allowed a user to issue commands in English to get the system to move the blocks around the table using a virtual robotic arm. A typical command might be something like this:

Find a block that is taller than the one you are holding and put it in the box.

From a research point of view, a big advantage of a system of this sort is that it was usually apparent whether the English command or question was being properly understood. The disadvantage was that the English in question was a slave to the kind of objects and properties (blocks with sizes, shapes, colors, and locations) anticipated in advance by its creators.

Systems like SHRDLU were general purpose in a way, in that the basic grammars and execution mechanisms did not have to be reprogrammed for new application domains. But a huge amount of human manual labor was required to increase their scope. And typically, the systems focused only on the input side of language, with only the crudest schemes for producing output. Even if they did a reasonable job of responding to restricted questions and commands, they could not hold their own in a natural conversation.

Work on text-centric NL processing has continued steadily since the 1970s, and has had some modest commercial forays—for example, with NL front ends to commercial databases. In the end, though, more significant impact came from systems built to process *spoken* language rather than typed text.

The processing of human speech has had its own focus for quite some time. Major advances were in part driven by consistent attention from the US Defense Advanced Research Projects Agency (DARPA) over a span of forty years. (DARPA supports a broad spectrum of research, including some basic long-term topics that go well beyond defense applications.) Early work, like that of text-based processing, tended to be driven by grammar- and structure-based approaches. But a significant evolution started in the late 1980s as statistical approaches augmented by large language corpora took over the field and even more dramatic advances came from machine learning.

Speech recognition is one of the great success stories in the history of AI. Systems like Siri, Google Home, Alexa, and Nuance's Dragon, whatever their other limitations, are able to deal with ordinary spoken language in ordinary noisy environments, and transcribe utterances with astounding accuracy. They do make mistakes in the conversion, of course, but much more significant is just how well they work overall. A speech technology this robust seemed a distant hope to experts even twenty years ago.

But alas, even after more than sixty years, getting machines to deal with language more broadly in a humanlike way remains an elusive goal. The problem is that language is generally used to talk *about* something, and it is this subject matter, as much as anything, that is the stumbling block. As stated by Winograd, "We assume that a computer cannot deal reasonably with language unless it can understand the subject it is discussing." While systems like Siri and Alexa are amazing tours de force, barely imaginable two decades ago but now in millions of pockets and homes, they frustrate us with their inability to answer questions whose subject matter wasn't anticipated by their creators—some of these questions so drop-dead easy that a six-year-old could answer them.

Lest it be thought that a lack of understanding only arises for complex sentences about esoteric subjects, a set of researchers (one of us, HJL, included) has offered up a more focused test of intelligence than Turing's imitation game—and one showing that perhaps the central challenge is not just the language per se or even dialogue but instead understanding the world itself.

Here's the idea, originally suggested by Winograd: simple two-sentence schemas show how NL utterances can only be processed successfully with some understanding of the world. A now-classic example is this:

The city councillors refused to grant the demonstrators a permit because they feared violence.

The city councillors refused to grant the demonstrators a permit because they advocated violence.

The challenge is to determine whether the pronoun "they" refers to the city councillors or demonstrators in each sentence. The only difference between the two sentences is a single verb, yet success at answering the question seems to require knowledge about what city councillors and demonstrators do. In fact, this is just another instance of the pattern seen in the previous chapter with the pronoun "it":

The large ball crashed through the table because it was made of steel.

The large ball crashed through the table because it was made of cardboard.

Examples like these, now called *Winograd schemas*, show that understanding even simple sentences can depend on substantial real-world knowledge of physics, social interactions, and frankly, almost anything else. (Much more on this later.)

Finally, a section highlighting NL systems would not be complete without a mention of the Watson system from IBM. In 2011, after an enormous programming and knowledge acquisition effort, Watson played in a three-game head-to-head contest on the TV show *Jeopardy!* against two of its most prominent human champions. On national television, Watson overwhelmed its human opponents. The fact that it could do this in real time without any idea in advance of the domains of the clues was remarkable. Watson used a variety of NL processing methods and was trained on a massive amount of world knowledge from many sources, including a huge archive of categories, clues, and correct answers from all prior *Jeopardy!* games.

Watson became the toast of the popular media, with former champion and defeated contestant Ken Jennings acknowledging in his final answer, "I for one welcome our new computer overlords." IBM subsequently moved to commercialize its core system and apply it to many domains, including health care and medicine, albeit with mixed and somewhat disappointing results. But Watson already had issues with a few of its answers on *Jeopardy!* such as answering "What is Toronto?" to a question in the US cities category. While Watson showed unprecedented versatility and did so in full view of the public on broadcast TV, its gaffes also revealed the still-unmet challenge of dealing with NL: understanding the world and using common sense to talk about it.

Theme 3: Rule-Based Problem-Solving

Sharing some of the same challenges that underlie work in NL understanding, an important thread in AI research revolved around tasks requiring humanlike problem-solving. One of the earliest focal points of this theme was at MIT, where in the 1960s Minsky guided researchers on a variety of human cognitive challenges, such as solving algebra and deduction word problems (computer scientists Daniel Bobrow and Bertram Raphael), making geometric analogies (mathematician Thomas Evans), and finding associations between concepts (cognitive scientist Ross Quillian; work done at Carnegie Mellon).

Inspiration from human thinking was very much front and center in early AI work at Carnegie Mellon. A more psychologically based point of view had taken root there, and AI programs were being written premised on observing human subjects asked to think aloud while solving problems. Newell and Simon postulated that problem-solving could be understood in terms of operations over a somewhat stable long-term memory made up of IF/THEN rules (see below for an example) and a more volatile short-term memory for intermediate results. The problem-solving process itself was quite generic: repeatedly find rules that were judged applicable given what was in the current short-term memory, and use them to determine how to change that memory for the next round in the cycle. All the specifics of the problem being solved were encoded in the rules themselves.

The idea of using rules in this way had a remarkable impact on the field as a whole, and led to an explosion of excitement about AI and, for the first time, generated a number of systems with clear impact in the commercial world. The cluster of efforts in the 1970s based on this idea

IF
1. The time frame of the patient's headache is acute,
2. The onset of the patient's headache is abrupt, and
3. The headache severity (on a scale from 0 to 4) is greater than 3

THEN
1. There is suggestive evidence (.6) that the patient's meningitis is bacterial,
2. There is weakly suggestive evidence (.4) that the patient's meningitis is viral, and
3. There is suggestive evidence (.6) that the patient has blood within the subarachnoid space.

Figure 3.1
A gloss of an IF/THEN rule for MYCIN

generally became known as *expert systems* since they focused on emulating the problem-solving of human experts using rules obtained from them in interviews.

Much of the seminal work in this direction came out of Stanford, where the first expert systems were created. The MYCIN system from computer scientist Ted Shortliffe demonstrated the power of rule-based systems in medical diagnosis and therapy such as prescribing disease-specific drugs. By the late 1970s, MYCIN was able to show competency in infectious disease therapy recommendations on a par with human doctors—a remarkable accomplishment. A gloss of a typical MYCIN rule appears in figure 3.1.

Among the earliest important industrial expert systems were Prospector and XCON. Prospector, from computer scientists Richard Duda and Peter Hart and colleagues at SRI International, was a system for predicting mineral deposits that emulated the specific expertise held by a limited number of geologists. Prospector was quite successful in its assigned task, including predicting a previously unknown molybdenum deposit in Washington State. XCON, from computer scientist John McDermott at Carnegie Mellon, was used to configure computers at the Digital Equipment Corporation. It entered use in 1980, and by 1986 was estimated to have processed eighty thousand orders and saved its parent company $25 million. This was the most complex expert system at the time, with about twenty-five hundred rules.

Once commercial viability was demonstrated by these early trailblazing efforts, the field of expert systems exploded. Investment in AI companies grew dramatically, and thousands of such specialized systems were deployed across a large number of industries. This was the first great wave of international recognition of AI as a commercially significant field.

The success of expert systems and the fact that all the expertise was encoded in a collection of rules gave rise to an AI bumper sticker slogan, "knowledge is power." (The original use of the phrase is often attributed to Sir Francis Bacon, but is traceable back to the tenth century.) When it came to expert-level problem-solving, clever algorithms were not the issue; knowledge—and lots of it—was the key. But left unsaid was that "knowledge" here really meant "expert knowledge in the form of IF/THEN rules." This implied two significant weaknesses in the paradigm. First, there is what became known as the knowledge acquisition bottleneck: the manual collection of an adequate supply of rules from human experts was an enormous burden. And second, while the systems indeed allowed the emulation of specific problem-solving in specialized areas, they were strongly limited to those narrow types of expertise. When asked questions beyond their strict competence, they failed miserably. Computer scientist Melanie Mitchell puts it this way:

Expert systems ... were increasingly revealing themselves to be *brittle*, that is, error-prone and often unable to generalize or adapt when presented with new situations. In analyzing the limitations of these systems, researchers were discovering how much the human experts writing the rules actually rely on subconscious knowledge—what you might call common sense—in order to act intelligently.

We will have more to say on this in the next chapter.

Theme 4: Autonomous Integrated Systems

As AI technology was succeeding well in specialized areas, the trend was clear: to make AI software work at an industrial-grade level and provide performance that would satisfy real, paying customers, the work had to be deep, but it could be narrow. With a bit of care, the brittleness mentioned above did not get in the way of successful applications.

But AI ambitions from the beginning were always broader than that. People envisioned autonomous robots that would be able to decide for themselves what to do and then carry out actions based on the resulting plans. And letting a robot loose on its own meant that it had to be prepared to handle unforeseen situations.

The Shakey project at SRI International was an AI effort in the late 1960s to build a robot that could roll around an indoor space, and make and execute fairly complex plans to move from one room to another as well as move objects around. (The robot was called Shakey because it shook when it stopped.) It was one of the earliest efforts to put a (somewhat) autonomous mobile system into the (somewhat) unpredictable world and have it perceive its surroundings, plan its actions, observe the effects of those actions, and adapt its plans and next actions. It could, for example, determine that in order to push a box off an elevated platform, it should roll up a ramp and move something else out of the way to get to the box.

After Shakey, robots gradually moved out of the lab and into the outside world. In 1998, computer scientist Sebastian Thrun and colleagues developed an interactive mobile robot called Minerva that worked without human intervention to guide visitors through the Smithsonian's National Museum of American History over a period of two weeks. Museums are often filled with people, making safe navigation quite complex, and Minerva was specifically designed for safe navigation in this unpredictable and dynamic environment. (There are wonderful videos of children blocking its way, trying to distract it or climb on for a ride.)

Perhaps the environments most clearly in need of autonomous AI systems that can adapt are those like deep space where humans are far enough away to make teleoperation or real-time communication impossible. Because of this, the National Aeronautics and Space Administration along with its Jet Propulsion Laboratory have always been a source of leading-edge thinking about autonomous systems. The Sojourner rover deployed on the surface of Mars in 1997 was one of their first autonomous robotic systems. In the 1999 *Deep Space 1* mission, an AI software system was allowed to run the onboard computer system for two days, more than sixty million miles from Earth. This AI system was presented with several simulated spacecraft failures (a faulty electronics unit, sensor providing false information, and stuck attitude control thruster) and reportedly handled each well.

While work continued on individual robotic systems, an interesting development moved research toward *teams* of robots. Based in part on a suggestion by computer scientist Alan Mackworth in 1992, Japanese and US researchers posited a grand challenge for AI: to beat the human World

Cup championship soccer team with a team of autonomous robots by the year 2050. As with other real-world-embedded robots, the openness of the soccer world, including playing against an adversary, challenged core AI algorithms and demanded real-time perception coordinated with real-time decision-making. The RoboCup soccer challenge was born. Since that time, teams from all over the world have been creating and dramatically improving robot soccer teams in simulation as well as with wheeled or legged robots of various sizes.

We are currently seeing one important area where autonomous integrated systems are slowly emerging into routine use: self-driving cars. A major push in this area began with a grand challenge from DARPA for a vehicle to drive by itself over a demanding 132-mile course through the desert between California and Nevada. The first competition was held in 2004, and the best vehicle only got 7 miles into the course, at which point it got hung up on a berm after making a switchback turn. But in the second competition in 2005, five of the twenty-three finalist vehicles completed the course, with the car called Stanley from Thrun and his team from Stanford coming in first. This success led directly to work on self-driving cars first at Google and eventually at a number of car manufacturers. Of course, the commercial vehicles that have come out of this work to date are still far from autonomous. They are good at automatic lane following and reactive speed control, and even parallel parking, but simply cannot yet react appropriately to never-before-seen items on the road and the boundless creativity of humans to do unanticipated, unfathomable things while driving.

Not all AI interest in integrated autonomous systems has been focused on robots or other mobile systems. Research in the field has continued around software systems that can combine perception, learning, and reasoning. For example, the DARPA "Personalized Assistant That Learns" project (conceived and initiated by one of us, RJB), which led directly to Siri—and then Google Home and Alexa—was intended to create an integrated but disembodied system to emulate a human office assistant. And prior to that work, many years' worth of research on integrated knowledgeable systems led to a series of cognitive architectures suggesting ways in which a complete AI system could be constructed from elements inspired by human cognition and perception. One of the more ambitious and long-lived efforts along these lines is the Soar architecture, originating in the work of Newell and Simon. It attempted to characterize the full range of capabilities of an intelligent agent, including an ability to examine its own problem-solving, and posited multiple forms of memory (episodic, semantic, and procedural) in a single integrated framework.

The area of integrated autonomous systems is perhaps the one thread of the field that has ended up focusing on what the founders generally thought of as AI. But even then, the systems ended up being fairly limited, or just used statistics or metrics to try to avoid limitations in their abilities to get things done. None has really resorted in a serious way to the kind of common sense that humans find so critical to getting through their everyday lives.

Theme 5: Data-Driven Learning

In the earliest days of AI, researchers like Minsky, mathematician Seymour Papert, and others felt that a reasonable inspiration for an AI would be a natural organic brain. Borrowing from neuroscience work like that of Nobel Laureates David Hubel and Torsten Wiesel, and earlier work by neurophysiologist Warren McCullough and logician Walter Pitts on what they called "artificial neural networks," these scientists implemented and studied models of human neurons, and devised computational devices based on their triggering mechanisms and connectivity.

Minsky and Papert showed some significant limitations on the computational power of simple forms of these networks in 1969, prompting general enthusiasm in the area to wane. But work by a dedicated core of scientists continued on more complex multilayer neural networks. An important development came in the mid-1980s in the form of a learning algorithm for neural networks called backpropagation. Backpropagation is a way of making small adjustments to the weights between neurons after an incorrect classification, from the output layer all the way back through the inner, so-called hidden layers of a network. This allows the network to improve its performance over time without overreacting to any single training example. Also in the 1980s, computer scientist Yann LeCun proposed a network model well suited to image processing called convolutional neural nets (or CNNs). These start with an input layer that covers the input image in overlapping grids, and where subsequent layers are convolutions—matrix multiplications—of earlier layers. LeCun's group at AT&T Bell Laboratories created networks that allowed machines to read and classify handwritten zip codes on envelopes—technology that eventually found its way into common use in the US Postal Service in the 1990s as arguably the first real-world application of AI neural nets.

Despite the digit-recognition success, early CNNs did not scale well, and interest ebbed again in the mid-1990s. But the idea of an AI system trained on a large data set of labeled examples remained enticing. Eventually in 2012, with developments from computer scientist Geoff Hinton and students (especially Ilya Sutskever and Alex Krizhevsky), massive amounts of image training data could be processed effectively by multilayer networks. A system based on this work called AlexNet trounced its competition in a public third running of a contest called the ImageNet Large Scale Visual Recognition Challenge. (ImageNet was a multimillion image repository created at Princeton and Stanford.) Networks with more than one layer of hidden units eventually began to be called *deep networks*, and the training on these networks became known as *deep learning*.

The ImageNet CNN success solidified the view that deep learning was significantly applicable to perceptual tasks like object recognition in images. Companies like Twitter, Facebook, Microsoft, and Google jumped energetically on the deep-learning bandwagon, using CNNs to allow users to find similar images, classify emotions in photographs, label people and tag objects in images, and generally improve a wide variety of image-related services.

Since then, the deep learning wave has swept the field and been used in effective ways on each of the four themes discussed above. Machine learning has been a key element in self-driving car technology, for instance. Around the same time that image processing was being revolutionized by deep learning, speech recognition was also conquered in a surprisingly fast and unexpected way. According to Jeff Dean at Google, the application of deep neural networks provided the "biggest single improvement in 20 years of speech research." This is a pivotal reason why Siri, Alexa, and related products have been so successful.

Other applications followed suit. Product advice services of various sorts, from Amazon to Netflix to YouTube, use deep learning to improve the performance of their recommendation engines. Large-scale advertising platforms, like Yahoo, Google, Facebook, and others, trained their ad servers using machine learning on the data collected over user sessions, allowing uncannily relevant advertisement recommendations to be made.

(It is worth noting that the achievement of the most stunning gains came initially from companies like Google, IBM, and Microsoft, which had access to enormous amounts of data.) In 2017, astronomers discovered an eight-planet solar system more than twenty-five hundred light-years away by applying a neural network trained on a huge data set collected through the Kepler telescope over four years. The Nest home thermostat uses machine learning to regulate temperature by learning from manual changes by users over the first few weeks after installation, and then inferring people's schedules and temperature preferences. By 2015, the battle cry had changed from "knowledge is power" to "data is king."

One of the more impressive achievements of modern machine learning is Google Translate. Machine translation between human languages had been an aspiration for AI since almost its beginning, and Google Translate, using a data-driven, statistical-model-based approach, was a promising new entrant when it was introduced in 2006. But a breakthrough by Google in the application of deep learning in 2016 changed the game completely. Using a novel representation of words and word sequences from computer scientist Yoshua Bengio and others, a special network was trained on a staggering number (estimated to be more than thirty million) of human-translated pairs of sentences. Many of these came from government sources in multiple languages, like the records of the Canadian Parliament. The switch to Google's neural machine translation radically improved the quality and scope of its abilities. As anyone can confirm online, Google Translate is an extraordinary achievement that currently supports more than a hundred languages, and one that keeps improving over time. On the other hand, like many such translation systems, it doesn't do well on paragraph-length texts and can get easily mixed up with different senses of the same words. (Many authors, including Marcus, Davis, and Mitchell, have cataloged failures in Google Translate and other deep learning systems.)

Another recent product of deep learning technology in the area of NL is a system called Generative Pre-trained Transformer (GPT) from the OpenAI research lab. What GPT does, roughly speaking, is to guess at a completion of any input it is given—typically some fragment of text. A user might type in

I grew up in Athens. I speak fluent …

and GPT responds with

... Greek. I've been writing Greek since elementary school.

How does it manage to do this? It uses a gigantic network (175 billion parameters in the latest version) trained on staggering amounts of text—hundreds of *billions* of words. The entire Wikipedia—all 6 million articles—is said to be less than 1 percent of its training set. The *New York Times* called it "the most powerful 'language model' ever created." The results can indeed be impressive and have facilitated a wave of new applications, including question-based search engines, code generation engines, and even chatbots that allow you to "talk" to historical figures.

And how well does it work? The latest version (as of the time of this writing) is called GPT-3, but an earlier version, GPT-2, is available online for free use and testing. What emerges is this: sometimes the answers it produces are perfect; sometimes the answers are quirky and not what you might have expected, but still relevant and thought-provoking; and sometimes the answers are just plain gibberish. Here's one example:

I want some birthday cake. I should ...

... go to a more dangerous place and get arrested.

For informal use, GPT is great fun. But when the answers *matter*, it is tough to take what it produces seriously. It's not just that it makes occasional mistakes; it's that with no hesitation at all, it flubs in a way no human ever would. And there's no rhyme or reason as to what will set it off. (We will see this issue again with AlexNet in chapter 11.) While the output GPT produces is invariably fluent and mostly on topic, it does not reflect any real understanding of the world. Like Google Translate, it has no idea what it's talking about.

Finally, no account of the recent success of machine learning technology can fail to mention the stunning success of Google's DeepMind group in game playing. Following a sparkling display of competence in arcade video games at a conference in 2013, DeepMind was acquired by Google in 2014 and set its sights substantially higher: learning to play the ancient Chinese game of Go, taken to be much more complex than chess. After improving its ability by playing against itself millions of times (borrowing a technique originated by Samuel with his checkers-playing program years before), the AlphaGo program from DeepMind shocked the world in 2016 by defeating one of the world's premier Go players, Lee Sedol. Apparently some two hundred million people watched at least part of the match—an astounding audience, bigger than the worldwide audience for the most-watched Super Bowl. AlphaGo then went on to defeat the world's top player, Ke Jie, in 2017.

Given its dramatic rise to public recognition and commercial prominence, deep learning has had an astonishing impact on the field of AI. Impressive and in some cases superhuman performance has been achieved on a wide variety of tasks. In the public eye, AI means deep learning. But the reliance on training data alone also entails a major deficiency: if the training sets don't match the expected context of use, the systems have nothing else to fall back on. In other words, having data as the primary fuel for massive learning is both a blessing—eliminating the manual knowledge acquisition challenge of expert systems—and a curse, in that success is totally dependent on that data used for training. As researcher François Chollet puts it, "Although we are able to engineer systems that perform extremely well on specific tasks, they have still stark limitations, being brittle, data-hungry, unable to make sense of situations that deviate slightly from their training data or the assumptions of their creators, and unable to repurpose themselves to deal with novel tasks without significant involvement from human researchers."

Data may have become king, but it rules over only its own limited domain with no sovereignty beyond its sharply delineated borders.

The Lesson from AI Systems

What can we learn about the strengths and limitations of AI systems from the examples presented above? On the surface, they seem to have little in common—different applications in different domains realized in quite different ways. One common thread we saw is that success often depends on *brute force* enabled by immense computational resources. For Deep Blue, it was brute-force search; for Google Translate, it was brute-force data.

But if we reflect further on the examples, we can see that they do share the following two properties:

1. The AI system exhibits a high level of performance in some area of expertise. It might be in recognizing photos of cats, diagnosing blood infections, or playing arcade video games. In many cases, the performance exceeds what humans are capable of.

2. The AI system performs extremely poorly outside its area of expertise. Assuming it can be presented with input it has not been explicitly designed to handle, it fails to achieve even a minimal level of competence. The system exemplifies a kind of brittleness in its ability to cope.

Because of these two properties, it is difficult to relate the behavior of these systems directly to what we know of humans. In attempting to characterize their overall performance, proponents sometimes say that their systems exhibit "intelligence," but not as the term is normally applied to people.

There is in fact a term applied to humans that does match the two properties fairly closely. An "idiot savant" is a person with a severe mental or learning disability that is nonetheless superbly gifted in performing certain specialized mental feats. A well-known illustration is the character played by Dustin Hoffman in the movie *Rain Man*. Property (1) above is the "savant" part, while (2) is the "idiot" part.

When we say that a system performs poorly outside its area of expertise, what is missing is not high-level expertise in a second or third area. It's not that we expect a blood diagnosis application to play grandmaster-level chess or a language translation system to prove theorems in mathematics. It's more that we expect some sort of general-purpose ability that even nonexpert humans have: common sense. What makes AI systems so hard to characterize in human terms is that they somehow manage to acquire an impressive level of specialized expertise without having first acquired even rudimentary common sense. This is the great irony of AI: it's been virtually the exact opposite of people. Almost all humans exhibit common sense, and only rarely possess deep expertise in challenging areas like medical diagnosis, mineral prospecting, or Go, yet AI systems have most commonly achieved excellence in such limited special domains, and none of them have common sense.

But what would an AI system with expertise even need common sense for? The answer is that common sense would allow it to deal in a reasonable way with things beyond its immediate area of expertise so as to at least avoid obvious blunders the way a nonexpert human would, as we discussed in chapter 2. If all a system ever encounters are chessboards, and all it ever has to worry about is winning the game, common sense really adds nothing to the mix. Where common sense will have a role to play is when we venture beyond the chessboard and think of a chess game as an activity that takes place in the real world.

Open and Closed Systems

To get a sense of what a game like chess in the real world might mean, consider what parents have to deal with when playing competitive games with their children, especially when they want their children to come away with a positive experience of the game.

A "chess parent" of course has to be able to play chess reasonably well. Only the youngest of children enjoy winning too easily. But playing well is far from the whole story. A parent has to clearly distinguish between winning a game and trouncing the opponent. No child will want to be humiliated in one-sided contests. So a chess parent will either have to lose some games, or come close enough to keep the child interested and motivated. Still, the parent must never be seen to be deliberately throwing the game either. Nobody likes being condescended to. So there is a complex line between winning and losing that a chess parent needs to follow. (Similar considerations apply to a "chess pro" in a chess club or "tennis pro" in a tennis club.)

In existing AI chess programs, the current chessboard (or maybe a list of the moves that led to it) is really all that is taken into account in deciding how to move. For a chess parent or chess pro, though, there is more to consider in deciding how to move, and in particular, when to try harder and when to ease up somewhat. How well is the child playing *today*? Is the game intended as light recreation or a more strenuous workout? Is the child feeling frustrated by the game or are they anxious to take on more demanding challenges? A chess move in this context is more like a sparring move in boxing, and ought to be responsive to the current needs and abilities of the opponent. Each move communicates something like this: "This move is maybe not the best one I could make on this chessboard, but it is a good one, and let's see your response to it." Moves that are seen by the opponent as overly strong or overly weak defeat the purpose.

Of course, a chess parent does more than make legal chess moves. The tricky part is characterizing the factors beyond the chessboard that might be relevant in deciding what to do next. Consider, for example, what might compel a chess parent to stop or postpone a game in progress. Some of these will be ordinary things—the dog has knocked over the chess-board, the game has gone on for too long, it's getting close to mealtime, or the child is getting cranky—but some of them will be much rarer—the child is injured by a chess piece, the house catches on fire, a long-lost cousin from a distant country arrives for a visit, or a tornado sweeps through the neighborhood. So some of the factors will be chess related, some will involve being an attentive parent, and some will be just common sense.

In talking about present and future AI systems, it is useful to consider how the behavior of the system reflects the environment it is working in. Let us call a system *closed* if we can enumerate in advance all the parameters in the environment that the system will be able to use in deciding how to behave. So for example, current chess systems are closed: their behavior is solely in response to the current chessboard. They live in an imaginary world where chessboards and pieces are all that exists. A more elaborate chess system that also takes into account the skill level of its opponent (with the ability to play better or worse according to that level) would still be closed. In this case, once the chessboard and level are specified, nothing else matters.

What makes a system *open* is that we cannot predict in advance what features of the world might need to be considered in deciding how to behave. So while current chess systems are closed, a chess parent needs to be open. We cannot expect to make a list in advance of all the things a chess parent might need to take into account in deciding when to interrupt a game. Would the list mention tornadoes? Long-lost cousins?

Of course, nobody is contemplating building AI systems to serve as chess parents. This was just to illustrate a point. But the issues raised here arise in more realistic systems that are being developed now—many of which will have profound impacts on human lives such as self-driving cars. (We will return to them and open systems in chapter 11.)

In sum, then, we can see that current AI systems—whether deep learning trained, expert systems, or game players—are similar in the following way: within the closed environment determined by the parameters they have been designed to deal with, they can perform well, and sometimes amazingly well; outside those limits, they perform poorly. They have nothing like the common sense that people have to deal with the many unpredictable things that happen outside the box in real life, like tornadoes and long-lost cousins. And we can't even steer them when we see them going astray.

Beyond Expertise

Before we roll up our sleeves to get into the details of common sense and how we imagine it could work in an AI system, it is worth briefly considering whether we could take an easier path and avoid all the complications. Why, it might be asked, would we not continue to build AI systems as we currently do, but with ever-larger domains of expertise, until those systems are broad enough to be experts on virtually everything they will get to see? Common sense could then emerge spontaneously, without us having to do anything special about it.

This idea of *emergent phenomena* may sound a bit like magic, but it is evident in areas where macroscopic effects result from a large number of microscopic events. An example in economics is how appropriate prices are arrived at automatically by the to-and-fro of self-interested buyers and sellers in a free market—in theory anyway. In biology, the concept is most often applied to the large-scale structures that result from the individual actions of tiny animals such as termite mounds.

Think, for instance, of an AI system based on deep learning. The idea would be to provide the system with enough data (over a long period of time, of course) so that its training would eventually be sufficient to cover anything the system might need to deal with. The most common types of things would be seen frequently in the training, yet if the data is truly massive enough, much rarer things (maybe even tornadoes or unexpected visits from long-lost relatives) would eventually be seen as well. With more and more data to lean on, the system would start making fewer and fewer blunders. There certainly would still be some extremely rare things that the system would not get trained on, and might then not do too well on, although if they really are that rare, why should we worry about them? The resulting system might not be absolutely perfect, but as we saw already, neither are humans. Isn't the perfect the enemy of the good?

It is important to understand why this argument is wrong. There are really two issues to consider: the scope of the events that occur in the real world, and what is sometimes called the long tail of their distribution.

First, the scope. Perhaps we can rest our hope on the fact that while a huge number, there are only a manageable number of objects in the universe that a system would need to deal with. But that won't save us. When we think of events in the world, we understand them as involving collections of objects, but collections arranged in a certain way. It's not enough to say that there was a biting event involving a dog and person; we need to know if the dog bit the person or the person bit the dog. We've all seen alarm clocks, life jackets, grocery carts, and bear cubs, yet it is safe to say that nobody has ever witnessed a bear cub wearing a life jacket pushing a grocery cart loaded with alarm clocks. The objects might all be familiar, but it's the arrangement of the objects that makes up the event, and the arrangement can be new and quite unfamiliar.

Even a small number of objects can be arranged in an astronomical number of ways. We can see this most clearly with words. Again, it's not the individual words that matter; it's their arrangement in phrases and sentences—the difference between "dog bites person" and "person bites dog"—that is overwhelming. Consider, for example, four-word English sentences. Even if there were only one thousand words to use at each point, there would still be a *trillion* different four-word sentences. With eight-word sentences, it's a trillion trillion. This explains why new pieces of text we read—including short ones—continue to be so fresh and original. We can even see the phenomenon with pairs of words. Consider "fearful symmetry" in the poem "The Tyger" by William Blake. The two words themselves are unremarkable; it's their combination in that poem that is so striking and memorable.

More dauntingly, even if we were to read the first sentence of every novel ever written, we would still only get a slight hint at the range of possibilities. The first sentence of the very next novel might be totally different and unexpected. It might say this:

Yesterday, when all my troubles were somewhat farther away, seven notes of Mahler's seventh symphony—the famous horn call that arrived from another star in 1986—drifted into my room from a wireless down the hall and Geneva Farewell was instantly restored to me.

Who could have predicted this? Could we have used an analysis of the first sentences of all the other novels to come to anticipate something like this one? The words are certainly familiar, but the arrangement is unique and quite unlike any that preceded it.

Now consider the distribution of events. Here is the idea in simplified form: imagine a lottery with a hundred million tickets. The chance of picking any given ticket will be miniscule—that is, one in a hundred million. Now suppose that every minute of every day a lottery ticket is chosen at random (and then replaced). Because the lottery is so big, the chance of seeing a particular ticket even after a century is still less than fifty-fifty. Nonetheless, *some* ticket is drawn every minute, meaning that in this world, an extremely rare event happens every minute.

The real world is somewhat like this lottery. There are so many different exceptional things that can happen at any time that extremely rare ones happen all the time. Of course it would be tough to confirm this claim mathematically—we would need a count of how many things can happen—but we can see this so-called long-tail phenomenon quite clearly in an actual real-world example involving words once again.

The British National Corpus is a gigantic database of English text drawn from a variety of sources. It has about 100 million words in total. Most of the words are common and occur often. The word "the" is the most common, occurring 6 million times. The word "time" is the most common noun, occurring 183,000 times. Yet there are some rare words that show up only once in the entire corpus. The British adjective "niffy," meaning "stinky," is one such case. So the chance of selecting one of these words at random from the corpus is one in a hundred million, just like a lottery ticket above. There are so many of these single-occurrence words in the corpus, however, that they make up roughly 0.5 percent of the total overall. An easy calculation shows that if we were to draw 140 words at random from this massive corpus—fewer words than in this paragraph—the odds of picking one of those rare single-occurrence ones would be better than fifty-fifty. Extremely rare words are quite common!

What conclusion can we draw from these considerations? The world is made up of a sequence of events drawn from a pool of astronomical size. While most of these events are familiar and expected, many of them—like those that make it into newspapers every day—are extremely unlikely. An AI system that has acquired a form of expertise that takes into account all but the most extremely unlikely events will still miss out on events that occur all the time. In other words, if we want AI systems to be able to deal in a reasonable way with things that happen in the real world quite commonly, we need something beyond an expertise that derives from sampling what has already occurred. Given the overwhelmingly large numbers, predicting the future based simply on seeing and internalizing what has taken place in the past won't cut it, no matter how brutish the brute force. We need common sense.

In concluding this chapter, we do not mean to suggest that AI has completely avoided the topic of common sense. Although the overall emphasis in AI has clearly been on developing systems with specialized expertise of various kinds, we will see in the next chapter that the single-largest project ever undertaken in AI was in fact aimed squarely at common sense.

4   Knowledge and Its Representation

It's not an idea until you write it down.

—Ivan Sutherland, reported in *History of Computer Graphics*, by Dan Ryan

It is far from obvious how common sense is supposed to work to allow humans to deal effectively with the new and unanticipated situations they experience. Recall that we defined common sense as the ability to make use of everyday knowledge for this purpose. But what does this really mean? Just how does one "make use" of something abstract like an idea? Is this just a figure of speech, like getting ahold of yourself or flying off the handle? Is it something that only people can do, or do we think machines might be able to do it someday too? To answer these questions, we need to look at the notion of knowledge more carefully.

Expressing Knowledge

When we first think about knowledge, what it is we acquire when we learn something, we have the tendency to imagine it as some sort of general impression about the world. What do you know about your hometown, for instance? It seems more like a big, permeating feeling than a collection of small, individual thoughts. More like a stew, say, than a bunch of individual ingredients.

Part of the problem is that so much of what we know is hard to put into words, to actually write down, as per Sutherland. This is most obvious when we talk about what is called *procedural* knowledge such as how to control a yo-yo or knead dough. But a lot of what we know about specific things, people, or places feels similar. We might be asked, "What was it like to be at Woodstock in 1969?" or "What is the sound of a *Saturn V* rocket?" and we might throw up our hands and answer, "You had to be there!" Being at a loss for words happens so often that we may be tempted to think that the most important things we know cannot be expressed in words.

But this is too simplistic. In the main, what we really mean when we say that words cannot express something is that it would not be easy. While we might not be accustomed to putting certain things into words, with a bit of mental effort, we can do it, and more frequently than we might first suppose. And when we do, we come to realize that much of what we know is not really some sort of undifferentiated stew. It can be *articulated*—described piece by piece.

We can see this most clearly when we need to use what we know to actually do something. Consider, for example, answering questions like the following:

Could a crocodile run a steeplechase?

Would a pomegranate fit inside a laundry basket?

Should you wash a birthday cake before eating it?

Can you drive from Sudbury, Ontario, to Wilmington, Delaware?

What these four questions have in common is that there is nothing you have ever experienced and nothing you have ever been told that gives you the answer directly. In other words, there is more to answering each question than just using your memory and *recalling* what the answer is. The words are old and familiar, but the questions are new.

Take the first one, for instance. This is almost certainly the first time you have ever considered this whole crocodile and steeplechase issue (unless you have read some of our previous work since we have used the example before). The fact that you have a hunch about how to answer the question at all is because you already have some crocodile knowledge (independent of steeplechases) and some steeplechase knowledge (independent of crocodiles). If you were missing one or the other—for example, if you had no idea what a steeplechase was—you would be stuck. Then, although you were most likely not aware of doing so, you had to bring those two pieces of knowledge together to answer the question.

This is precisely the sort of commonsense reasoning we have been talking about. What you have is a new, unanticipated event—in this case, an arrangement of words different from any other you have ever seen—and you were able to deal with it in a commonsense way.

So what is required to do this? At a minimum, you have to be able to bring to bear pieces of knowledge you have and somehow put them together to get the response you want. Knowledge about crocodiles is somehow combined for the first time with knowledge about running steeplechases to produce the new idea that crocodiles cannot run steeplechases.

But what exactly took place in your head? What does it mean to combine two pieces of knowledge, one about crocodiles and the other about steeplechases, and somehow produce a new third item about crocodiles being unable to run steeplechases? This is the key theoretical question that needs to be resolved to make sense of common sense. It is not something we can find an answer to in other areas of science like physics, biology, neuroscience, or even psychology. The answer—or at least the answer we will be considering in this book—actually comes from an unlikely source: the German philosopher Gottfried Leibniz, who lived and worked more than three hundred years ago (1646–1716).

Symbolic Representations

In a nutshell, the Leibniz proposal for answering this theoretical question is that we should think of using knowledge the same way we think of using numbers.

So consider numbers for a moment. Although they are purely abstract ideas, we still work with them and put them to use in a variety of ways. For example, given two numbers, we are able to produce a third number that is their sum. The way we actually do this is by using symbolic representations: we represent each number as a sequence of decimal digits, we operate on these two sequences to produce a third sequence of digits (with carry digits and so on, the way we were taught in elementary school), and the number we are after is the one represented by that third sequence. In the end, we do not have to resolve the thorny question of how to make use of abstract ideas like numbers; we only have to resolve how to represent them symbolically, and how to properly manipulate those symbolic representations. This of course is what we call arithmetic.

Leibniz's proposal is that we should think of using knowledge in a similar way: we represent the two thoughts in some symbolic form; we do some sort of arithmetic over these symbolic structures to produce a third symbolic structure; and the final thought we are after will be the one represented by this new symbolic structure. Here it is in a translation of Leibniz's own seventeenth-century words:

> It is obvious that if we could find characters or signs suited for expressing all our thoughts as clearly and as exactly as arithmetic expresses numbers or geometry expresses lines, we could do in all matters insofar as they are subject to reasoning all that we can do in arithmetic and geometry. For all investigations which depend on reasoning would be carried out by transposing these characters and by a species of calculus.

Again we will not have to resolve the thorny question of how to make use of abstract items of knowledge; we only have to resolve how to represent them symbolically (what he calls "find[ing] characters or signs suited for expressing" them), and how to properly manipulate these symbolic representations (in what he calls a "species of calculus").

So the Leibniz proposal has two strong requirements:

1. We have to be able to take any bit of knowledge we are interested in dealing with, and represent it symbolically (to get the analogue of a sequence of digits, in other words).

2. We have to figure out how to properly operate on those symbolic representations to produce a representation of the new idea we are looking for (to do the analogue of arithmetic).

Let us begin with the first requirement. Among other things, it implies that more than merely having knowledge, we have to be able to *express* it: write it down in symbolic form. If all the knowledge we care about is so deep and holistic that it cannot be broken into parts and expressed, the Leibniz proposal will not work.

A good starting point in coming up with a suitable symbolic representation is to try to express knowledge in a language like English. We want to be able to say in English what it is we know about crocodiles (that might be relevant) and what it is we know about steeplechases (that might be relevant). It may well be true that there are all kinds of things we know that we can never articulate. But if we can articulate them at all, there is a good chance we will be able to do so in sentence-like form. In other words, if we cannot express something we know as sentences, it is unlikely we will be able to represent it at all. (There are symbolic representations that are not sentence-like, and we will discuss them below.)

Representing numbers symbolically is much less of a problem. We are so used to doing this that we seldom even distinguish between numbers and their representations—that is, between numbers and numerals. Where the distinction does arise is when we want to think of representing numbers in different ways for different purposes. The one number, fourteen, might be represented by numerals like 14 in the decimal system, or 1110 in binary, or XIV in the Roman system. The important part about the symbolic representation is that it breaks the number into small pieces using an arrangement of characters from a fixed alphabet. This alphabet does not have to be made up of digits; in Roman numerals, the letters I, V, X, L, C, D, and M are used.

Of course, there are other symbolic representations of numbers that are less useful for arithmetic. For example, the number fourteen can also be represented by strings of letters and spaces such as "fourteen," "catorce," "the sum of eight and six," and even this:

the predecessor of the product of the two smallest odd primes.

There is nothing wrong with any of these representations of fourteen; they are just less useful for the sorts of arithmetic operations we care about.

This ties into the second requirement above. What sorts of operations on symbolic representations of knowledge are we expecting to need? In the case of numbers, the basic operations were clear: arithmetic. Leibniz was the first to work on the precise relationships between numbers and numerals in terms of bases. Each piece of a numeral tells us how many powers of the base to include. For instance, 14 in the decimal (base ten) representation system means (starting from the right and moving leftward) including four of 10^0 and one of 10^1; 1110 in the binary (base two) system means including zero of 2^0, one of 2^1, one of 2^2, and one of 2^3. The reason Leibniz's analysis was so significant is that it made crystal clear how the operations we cared about (sums, products, quotients, least common multiples, prime factors, and so on) could be carried out purely symbolically. The magic of computation is that we can operate on two sequences of digits in a certain way and end up with a third sequence of digits that is then guaranteed to represent the sum of the numbers represented by the first two sequences. Operations on symbolic structures capture key relationships among the purely abstract ideas they represent. This is what makes it possible for machines to do meaningful computation. Machines can do arithmetic exactly *because* the symbols that they manipulate correspond to the numerical abstractions we care about, and the symbolic manipulations correspond to operations like addition and multiplication. (Some might be reluctant to say that machines can actually "do" arithmetic, but they surely do some sort of symbolic processing that lines up exactly with arithmetic.) What is much less apparent, however, is how all of this can be done in the case of knowledge. It will not be enough to find any old symbolic representation of knowledge; we need one where we will be able to perform a "species of calculus," the analogue of arithmetic that Leibniz had in mind, where we bring together one symbolic structure representing crocodile knowledge with another representing steeplechase knowledge, perform some computation over those representations, and end up with a new symbolic structure representing the desired conclusion.

At the time Leibniz was thinking about these ideas, there were really no good systems of symbolic representations to use for this. The work on logic dating back to Aristotle showed how certain combinations called syllogisms could be made to work. You started with "All men are mortal" and "Socrates is a man," and ended up with "Socrates is mortal." But Aristotle was interested in the structure of sound argumentation, not in commonsense knowledge. And the kind of reasoning being considered was highly restricted. It was only much later, in the twentieth century (starting perhaps with Gottlob Frege a little earlier, in 1879), that proposals for what is now called symbolic logic started to show clear promise in this regard. Finally we had systems of symbolic representations that had both a certain level of generality and the precision of arithmetic. Logicians at the time, however, were worried about the foundations of mathematics and interested primarily in representing mathematical truth, like the fact that the equality relation is transitive, but not commonsense truth, like the fact that crocodiles have short, stubby legs. Commonsense knowledge had to wait until the mid-twentieth century.

Incidentally, as noted above, there are symbolic representations that are not sentence-like, such as digital pictures or diagrams. The problem with them is precisely that there are no plausible stories about how they would be combined to produce representations of new ideas. Think of the crocodile and steeplechase. Even if we tried to represent the required crocodile knowledge using a picture of some sort (maybe one showing those short, stubby legs) and the steeplechase knowledge using another picture (or movie) of horses jumping high enough to clear the hurdles, nobody has any idea at all about what kind of operation on those two representations would produce the desired one showing crocodiles unable to run steeple-chases. But this raises an even more fundamental problem: there are simple ideas for which there appear to be no clear pictorial representations. Think of negations, for instance. What picture should represent the idea of John not walking? If the picture shows him just standing there, why would this not be mistaken as a representation for the different idea of John not lying down? Or of George Washington not being there? Or even of John wearing pants—assuming that is what he is wearing in the picture? Although pictures may be worth thousands of words, by themselves they seem to be ill suited for representing certain ideas easily expressible in words.

The Knowledge Representation Hypothesis

The move to represent commonsense knowledge in symbolic form and then draw conclusions from it in a computational way really began with McCarthy, one of the founders of the field of AI. In 1958, he wrote a com-pletely unprecedented paper titled "Programs with Common Sense," where he proposed the development of a computer program that would process symbolic representations of commonsense knowledge as a way of making decisions about what actions to take. The representation scheme he sug-gested for this purpose was a dialect of the recently developed symbolic logic called the *first-order predicate calculus*, and the processing he had in mind involved calculating the logical consequences of this represented knowledge—a computation that had been studied for two decades since Turing first made it clear what it meant to compute something. Here is what McCarthy says:

> One will be able to assume that [the proposed system] will have available to it a fairly wide class of immediate logical consequences of anything it is told and its previous knowledge. This property is expected to have much in common with what makes us describe certain humans as having common sense.

This was the first proposal for building what is now called a *knowledge-based* computer system—that is, a system built along the following lines:

- Much of what the system needs to know will be stored in its memory as symbolic expressions of some sort, making up what we will call its *knowledge base*.

- The system will process the knowledge base using the rules of some sort of logic to derive new symbolic representations that go beyond what was explicitly represented.

- Some of the conclusions derived will concern what the system should do next, and the system will then decide how to act based on those conclusions.

This should sound familiar. The structure of the expert systems we mentioned before was exactly this, with the knowledge bases being populated by symbolically represented rules extracted from conversations with human experts.

McCarthy's main point was that if we were really interested in computer systems with human-level intelligence—that is, systems that are able to do more than perform a set of tasks circumscribed in advance—the systems would need to be knowledge based in just this sense.

There is a lot to quibble with in the McCarthy proposal, not the least of which was its dependence on the language of the predicate calculus. This is a language well suited to representing mathematical truth (for which it was invented, after all), but in the end, not so well suited for common-sense truth.

To give one example, in mathematics, we often want to say something of the form "All *P*'s have property *Q*," as in "All even numbers greater than two are the sum of two primes," or "All planar graphs on nine vertices have a nonplanar complement." The predicate calculus has special notation for just this sort of quantification. But in commonsense knowledge, we most often do not want such absolute, categorical statements; instead, we think in terms of normal and exceptional cases. It is part of our commonsense knowledge that birds fly, for instance (as opposed to fish, which swim; snakes, which slither; and dogs, which walk and run), but we certainly do not believe that each and every bird flies. In fact, we are hard-pressed to state anything we believe unequivocally in the form "All birds have property *Q*." (We will have much more to say about this matter later.) As McCarthy and others soon discovered, the logic of the predicate calculus would need to be radically revised to deal with things like the typical, atypical, and borderline cases of commonsense categories.

But all quibbles aside, how do we really know that McCarthy was right and that the best route to common sense is one based on the processing of symbolic representations of commonsense knowledge? How do we even know that symbolic representation is the right way to look at knowledge at all? The answer is, we don't. It's a hypothesis only, something called the *knowledge representation (KR) hypothesis* by philosopher Brian Cantwell Smith. Here it is in his own words:

> Any mechanically embodied intelligent process will be comprised of structural ingredients that a) we as external observers naturally take to represent a propositional account of the knowledge that the overall process exhibits, and b) independent of such external semantic attribution, play a formal but causal and essential role in engendering the behavior that manifests that knowledge.

In other words, the hypothesis behind McCarthy's manifesto is that the memory of an intelligent system will need to contain symbolic structures with two important properties: first, that we (from the outside) will be able to understand them as representing propositions making up part of the knowledge of the system, and second, that the system will act the intelligent way it does because of the presence of these structures in its memory.

Note that the KR hypothesis says nothing about *how* those symbolic structures are supposed to engender this intelligent behavior. (This is something we will be spending a lot of time on in this book.) It also says nothing about the kind of knowledge involved. McCarthy obviously had commonsense knowledge in mind, but subsequent work on expert systems starting in the 1970s applied the idea to expert-level knowledge only. Not too surprisingly, the resulting systems failed to demonstrate anything like common sense, as we saw before; they were brittle and broke down in unexpected ways when straying out of their narrow lanes. There was too much work involved in representing complex medical knowledge about varieties of blood infections, say, to leave any time for more mundane knowledge, whose utility was much less apparent. And the creators of the systems never anticipated the critical role of mundane obvious general facts and rules in supporting even expert inferences; interviews with experts focused on specialized problem-specific rules rather than the boring, generic facts that all humans know and use but rarely articulate. (In all fairness, we would be hard-pressed to say why it would be important for a blood infection diagnostician to know about the jumping limitations of short, stubby legs, say. Individual items of commonsense knowledge do not come with a promise of usefulness or practicality.)

But it's not as if AI researchers failed to notice the limitations of these expert systems. By the 1980s, it was quite apparent that those systems were at best idiots savants: highly capable on certain specialized tasks maybe, but totally lacking in the robustness and versatility of common sense. While the field was marching in a more expertise-focused direction, a small number of researchers wanted to follow McCarthy's lead more directly and concentrate on commonsense knowledge.

There were two different approaches, broadly speaking. On the one hand, there were researchers who saw their job as expressing as clearly as possible what a commonsense agent would need to know about this or that aspect of its world in order to be able to behave in a commonsense way. The attention was on articulating sentences in some sort of artificial language, with an eye toward the commonsense conclusions that could be drawn from them according to the rules of logic. In some cases, a language like that of the predicate calculus would suffice; in other instances, a more expressive logic had to be worked out. In addition to McCarthy himself, a number of thought leaders like Patrick Hayes, Jerry Hobbs, Ernest Davis, Raymond Reiter, and Joseph Halpern vigorously pursued this agenda in their quest to capture commonsense views of physics, time, space, minds, beliefs, plans, and society.

On the other hand, there were researchers who seriously questioned the role of logic in the McCarthy proposal. As Minsky later put it, "'Logical' reasoning is not flexible enough to serve as a basis for thinking." These researchers, who included Roger Schank and students of his like Janet Kolodner and others, saw their job not as articulating sentences but rather as building complex symbolic structures that could serve as the memory of a commonsense agent. These structures, with names like "frames," "scripts," and "schemata," were still intended as representations of knowledge (and thus were guided by the KR hypothesis), but with an emphasis more on the memories of past experiences than on general truths about the world. The focus was less on deriving conclusions from other facts, and more on recognizing patterns and drawing analogies between current circumstances and these remembered experiences as a way of solving new problems.

The Cyc Project

Both of the approaches highlighted above offer useful insights on the nature of common sense and, as we will see later in the book, ingredients that we believe to be critical in the realization of common sense in machines. But the work lacks in the breadth needed for a serious comparison with human common sense. It tends to center on isolated examples and limited areas of knowledge.

The challenge of the *scope* of commonsense knowledge was one that a Stanford University researcher named Douglas Lenat decided to tackle. In the mid-1980s, starting at the Microelectronics and Computing Technology Corporation in Austin, Texas, Lenat and his colleagues began a multiyear project called Cyc (as in "en*cyc*lopedia") to develop a commonsense knowledge base—a symbolic structure totally in keeping with the KR hypothesis of what an AI system would need to know to exhibit some form of common sense and escape the brittleness flaw of expert systems. Lenat's hypothesis was that expert reasoning needed to be undergirded by typically unstated commonsense facts, and he set out to create a comprehensive repository of such under-the-radar facts. (This is what we described earlier as declarative tacit knowledge.) It was a massive undertaking, probably the largest and most ambitious project ever tackled in AI—and certainly the longest-running one. The Cyc knowledge base is currently claimed to contain "more than 10,000 predicates, millions of collections and concepts, and more than 25 million assertions"—an amazing accomplishment.

So did Cyc actually succeed in what it set out to do? Unfortunately, there is not a clear answer. The bulk of the work has remained proprietary and impossible to evaluate critically. As others have observed, hardly anything has been said about the work publicly for the last decade, and there has been virtually no peer-reviewed publication about Cyc in quite some time. (A similar lack of transparency has made the IBM Watson system hard to assess.) This is unfortunate. It is understandable to want to protect intellectual property in work like this, but it prevents the scientific community from understanding what was achieved and assessing claims.

Lenat did publish two interesting opinion pieces in *Forbes* in 2019 that reaffirmed the Cyc philosophy and offered some examples of the kind of conclusions it could draw in the context of understanding plot points from the play *Romeo and Juliet*. The anecdotal examples—explained through English description, a few Cyc formulas, and two screenshots—are compelling in many respects. It has also been reported that there have been successful commercial applications of the Cyc knowledge base. But despite all of this, suffice it to say that AI systems with general common sense have not emerged spontaneously into the public light as a result of this work.

Why not? Isn't common sense supposed to derive from commonsense knowledge? One lesson to learn from this is that while knowledge may be *necessary* for common sense, it is not *sufficient*. Most critically, it is not enough for an AI system to have access to all of this knowledge, represented internally in some symbolic form; it needs to be able to bring the knowledge to bear in an effective way on what it is trying to do.

One thing to notice about Cyc is that a huge percentage of the enormous effort that went into it—estimated to be around a thousand person-years of work—was about building a gigantic knowledge base, not about how that knowledge should be processed and deployed. In the terminology from before, the Cyc project was foremost about commonsense *knowledge*, not commonsense *reasoning*. This is not just a Cyc issue. We see it in related projects like Never-Ending Language Learning (NELL) from computer scientist Tom Mitchell and colleagues at Carnegie Mellon University. In this case, instead of handcrafting a large knowledge base, the NELL system constructs the knowledge base automatically by scanning for information on web pages. Since NELL's inception in 2010, a collection of almost three million assertions has been obtained in this way. But as with Cyc, there is virtually no study of how those assertions can be brought together and processed, and to what end.

Over the years, there has been considerable attention in AI to automated reasoning, but mainly for solving expert-level problems like those found in advanced mathematics and logic. For researchers interested in plain common sense, however, the main emphasis to date has been on the knowledge itself, or what McCarthy called the *epistemological adequacy* of the system.

To be fair, reasoning was not ignored in Cyc. Because of the number and complexity of its knowledge structures, Cyc's creators needed to grapple with ways to make inference fast enough for use in applications. The Cyc team considered the complement of McCarthy's epistemological adequacy—*heuristic adequacy*—related to "how to search spaces of possibilities and how to match patterns." To support computation, Cyc engineers started to represent the same information redundantly in different ways, each with its own idiosyncratic structures and reasoning procedures. According to Lenat, "By 1989, we had identified and implemented about 20 such special-case reasoners, each with its own data structures and algorithms. Today [2019] there are over 1100 of these 'heuristic level reasoning modules.'"

An architecture with a large number of special computing modules might make perfect sense as a way of managing a pool of reasoning methods used by experts (for example, specialized analytic techniques for solving problems in electric circuit analysis, fluid dynamics, or the integral calculus). But why should we think it will be any good for common sense? The Cyc reasoning modules are claimed to work together cooperatively like some sort of "community of agents." But do they?

While Lenat and colleagues have written extensively about the kinds of knowledge in the Cyc knowledge base, and what conclusions can be drawn from this knowledge when it is used properly, they have had little to say about what Cyc actually does for itself with all of this knowledge in an *automatic* way, especially when different pieces of knowledge need to be brought together for the first time. Much of the discussion around reasoning in Cyc emphasizes engineering issues—appropriate in support of a working software system, but with no real bearing on common sense more broadly. In fact, the reasoning approach in Cyc is not really inspired by the benefits that common sense might offer in support of appropriate reactions to unanticipated circumstances or in avoiding blunders in planning and action.

It might seem like a strength of Cyc that it allows flexibility in how its massive knowledge base can be put to use by these reasoning modules in different applications. But what it really means is that AI system builders using Cyc have to figure it all out for themselves. Cyc simply fails to spell out how ordinary, everyday knowledge (about crocodiles and steeplechases, say) gets to be exercised without human intervention in service of ordinary, everyday goals, other than to say that many methods can be involved. With eleven hundred reasoning modules ranging over twenty-five million assertions, the ingredients might all be there, and in abundance, but the final recipe is still missing. Too many questions are left unanswered.

For example, assuming an AI system has all the knowledge it needs represented in symbolic form, how exactly will those pieces of knowledge come together in an automated way to allow totally new conclusions to be drawn? What is the process that will go looking for facts about crocodiles and steeplechases, and then bring them together to draw the desired conclusion? How does this process get started, and when does it stop? What role will symbolic logic play in this regard (or symbolic probability theory, for that matter)? And where classical logic and probability are not used, just what species of calculus (in Leibniz's terminology) is being proposed as the alternative? As a range of new conclusions are being considered and developed, how is this process going to be kept in check to work quickly enough in real circumstances? In other words, how will the overall behavior of an AI system be *enhanced* by having massive amounts of knowledge available and not be stymied by the sheer number of items that might turn out to be relevant? Lenat has mentioned "metaknowledge" and "microtheories" as ways of controlling how the knowledge will be processed, but how will the processing of these things be constrained?

Without clear and definite answers to questions like these, it is hard to see how Cyc or any other reasoning system will work in practice. Seeing example after example of commonsense conclusions that can be drawn by stringing together items from the Cyc knowledge base does not address the concern. We have no way to know what kind of stringing Cyc will be able to do for itself as a matter of course without getting lost or overwhelmed.

Putting the Hypothesis to the Test

Given all these concerns about knowledge-based systems like Cyc, we might well ask, What alternative to the KR hypothesis is there for common sense in AI systems? The answer: so far, none, really. As explained earlier, despite the impressive achievements of AI systems based on deep learning—systems that are clearly not based on symbolic representations— there are good reasons to believe that those ideas alone will not be up to the job. A recent attempt from the deep learning community—a project called COMET—actually resorts to a conventional knowledge base to train a language model. And even then, the focus remains on commonsense knowledge and not on what we have called commonsense reasoning.

But what makes us think that systems based on the KR hypothesis will turn out to be any better? For many current AI researchers, all of this talk of knowledge and symbols seems tired and outdated. It's that "good old-fashioned AI" (GOFAI) that philosopher John Haugeland talked about a while back. They might say, "Symbolic AI? Really? We tried that in the seventies and it didn't work!" This is too simplistic, though. After all, for quite some time, AI people might well have said, "Neural nets? Really? We tried them in the sixties, and Minsky and Papert showed they didn't work!" As we saw in the previous chapter, the real story about these AI efforts is more subtle and involved.

In the next part of the book, we want to do more than argue *on principle* about what will or will not work. We want to take on the KR hypothesis in a more constructive way by laying out what we see as all the necessary ingredients: the kinds of commonsense knowledge that would be needed, the symbolic structures that might be used to represent them, and also the sorts of computational operations that can then process these representations in a practical and effective manner. This will be done in chapters 5–8. (While prior work may be valuable to keep in mind, we will be doing this from first principles.) In chapter 9, we will then show how those pieces can come together to support an agent needing to use common sense to deal with an unanticipated situation.

This will not settle the question, obviously; the KR hypothesis will remain a hypothesis. But we do hope our analysis will at least give it some credence as a way of making sense of common sense.

5   A Commonsense Understanding of the World

You can't have everything. Where would you put it?

—Steven Wright, quoted in "Headwaters for a River of Stand-Up,"
by Jason Zinoman

The picture we are developing of common sense is one of a certain ability, namely the ability to make effective use of a large store of mundane background knowledge in deciding what to do in ordinary situations. But what underlies this ability? What kind of knowledge are we talking about? How is it going to be used? And when is this use effective?

In the next four chapters, we want to propose some answers to these questions. The reason this will take four chapters is that we want to do more than suggest how some sort of *illusion* of common sense might be achieved. This is not about shortcuts and clever tricks, who they might fool, over what percentage of test cases, or for how long. We want to outline how we think common sense in machines can actually work.

Note that our intent is to provide an outline only. The story will be presented slowly and in a certain amount of detail—perhaps in too much detail for some readers—but in nowhere near enough detail for an engineer tasked with building a computational system along these lines. Our belief, however, is that while many issues remain to be resolved, they are fundamentally of the same sort as the issues that we will discuss in detail.

The starting point for this part of our journey will be commonsense knowledge—that is, beliefs about ordinary situations and things expressible in everyday language. Note that when we talk about what people know about their world, we are not looking for an account that scientists or other experts would necessarily find agreeable. For one thing, we do not want to limit ourselves to the sorts of topics that have been given precise analyses by scientists. We do not expect numerical precision to play a big role in commonsense thinking at all—what do people know with any kind of precision about cheese sandwiches or changing diapers, say? Nor do we want to couch our story in terms that only experts would use, like *quanta* for physicists, or *qualia* for philosophers.

When we talk about what people commonly know, who do we have in mind? How old are these people? What culture do they belong to? The answer is that we have adults in mind (mostly), and we want to give a story that applies to a wide range of backgrounds and cultures (mostly). Different people will know different things, of course. Canadians typically know a lot about black ice (certain ice on paved roads), but not so much about *haka* (a certain ceremonial dance), while the reverse might be true for New Zealanders. Our account of commonsense knowledge will be agnostic as to what topics it should cover. What should hold for every culture is that there will be ordinary, everyday knowledge that the adults in that culture expect each other to know.

What constitutes common sense will depend on the knowledge it leans on. We might want to say that it is just common sense to avoid going to the airport when there is a riot going on there. Yet it is not a failure of common sense to go to the airport if you don't know about the riot, or if you know about it but you think a riot is just people having a good time together.

We will dive into commonsense knowledge itself in the next chapter. But first we need to set the stage. In this chapter we look into what we might think of as the presuppositions of this knowledge—that is, the kind of understanding that has to be in place *before* you can even start to make sense of knowledge about the world. As with the knowledge itself, there need not be a single way to do this. We will suggest one way, but it will certainly be possible to carve up the world in different ways (as psychologists interested in cognitive development have done).

Things and Their Properties

To start thinking about knowledge, and specifically mundane knowledge expressible in ordinary language, here is a thought experiment to consider. Suppose you have lived your life without ever having heard of the game of soccer (or what is called "football" in much of the world). Imagine you ask somebody to explain it to you. Here is how they might begin:

Soccer is a sport somewhat like hockey except that …

Of course this is not much help if you do not already know what hockey is. You might prefer an explanation that does not make reference to other sports:

Soccer is a game played with a ball by two teams on an outdoor field …

(This is a somewhat dry formulation, not something you would expect to hear in an actual conversation, but ignore that for now.) To make sense of this, you would still need to have some understanding of the following: what a game is, what a ball is, what it means to play with a ball, what a team is, what it means to have two of them competing in a game, what an outdoor field is, and what it means to play on one. If, for example, you have no idea what a ball for soccer might be like, you could ask, and get something like this:

A soccer ball is a hollow spherical thing about the size of …

To make sense of this, you would again need to have some sort of understanding of what a sphere is, what it means for something to be hollow, and so on, any of which might call for even further clarification.

Where would this all end? It seems like it might never end; you can always ask follow-up questions like "Ah yes, but what do you mean by … ?" On closer examination, however, the talk does have to end somewhere; you will get to a point where you can still ask for explanations, but the words you get in response are not going to tell you anything new.

For instance, you may be told that a soccer ball is a certain thing of a certain size, but suppose you interrupt right there and ask what a thing is, and what it means for it to have a size? Someone might try to offer an explanation:

A thing is anything at all, and things can have certain properties …

But this is really just another way of saying this:

There are these things called "things," and they can have certain properties called "properties."

In other words, the explanation is no explanation at all! If you do not already understand what a thing is, it does not really help to be told that it could be anything. If you do not already understand that things can have properties, it does not help to be told that this is a property of things. When you are told that a soccer ball has a certain size, a soccer team has a goalkeeper, or a soccer field has nets at each end, you have to *already* understand that these are all things, and that they can have properties. This is a presupposition of whatever else you might need to be told about soccer—or anything else in your world.

A Theory of Everything

Let us say a little more about things and their properties.

There are things, and they have properties.

There are different kinds of things depending on the properties they have. Some things like numbers, beliefs, and stories are not physical. Some things like owls, refrigerators, and lakes are physical, and so have properties like size and location.

Some of the properties that things have are just qualities like being alive or being held every Tuesday. Other properties concern relationships between the thing and other things, such as being born in a city or being the sum of two numbers. Some properties hold to a greater or lesser extent, such as being heavy or being fond of something.

Time points are nonphysical things that are ordered linearly, and so have the property of being before or after other time points. When we talk about what things exist or what properties they have, this is always relative to a time point. A thing may not exist at one time, may come to exist at a later time, and then may cease to exist at an even later time. Similarly, a thing may have a property at one time and fail to have it at another.

Event occurrences are nonphysical things whose existence is responsible for change. What things exist and what properties they have are considered to stay the same over time unless an event takes place at some point to change them. Some events happen as the result of agents. Others occur as the result of earlier events. Some events occur spontaneously.

Some events happen only at a single time point and result in an immediate change. Other events, called processes, take place across a number of time points and produce a gradual change over time. More than one event may be occurring at the same time. There is a process called the passage of time that is always taking place and gradually changing all physical things.

What can we say about this little "theory of everything"? Maybe the most obvious thing is that the worldview it presents is one we believe in! The language might look strange and there are some obscure parts. We might not express ourselves in this way. And there are some fine points that we might even disagree with. Maybe we don't think of there being events that occur spontaneously. Or maybe we prefer to say that certain things just change by themselves like the growth of hair, say, without attributing this to some ongoing process. But by and large, the picture it paints is one that feels quite familiar. We would expect everyone we meet to just know these things, to have learned them through experience at a young age, even if never articulated explicitly as above.

The second point worth noting is that the worldview it presents is again one presupposed by commonsense knowledge. For example, if we did not already understand that things could change over time, it is hard to imagine what we would have to know so as to later be informed about this possibility.

One important part of this worldview is what is sometimes called the *commonsense law of inertia*: things will stay the same unless they are changed by events. This is like Sir Isaac Newton's first law in physics except that it is not just for the constant motion of physical objects. Whenever we paint a bench yellow and expect it to have that color the next day, or tune a piano and expect it to sound right the next day, we are applying this law.

To apply the law to something we care about, we have to believe that nothing will occur to change it. What makes the law so potent is what might be called the locality of change: as we accumulate commonsense knowledge about the world, we come to realize that each event changes only a narrow range of things, and each property of a thing is changed only by a narrow range of events (the wing action of distant butterflies notwithstanding). So although events of a variety of sorts are taking place all the time, there is an overall *steadiness* to the world. We do recognize, however, that there are certain cataclysmic events such as the astronomical or seismic ones that can have broad effects on the things we care about, even if their impact on the universe as a whole remains quite localized.

The law of inertia and the locality of change are what make living in the world as manageable as it is. Among many things, they allow us to learn from experience: the second time we encounter something, we can expect it to be largely as it was the first time. This also means we can work on what we care about piece by piece. In many cases, we can finish one task and move on to the next, expecting the first to remain finished. So we can park the car in the parking lot, do our grocery shopping, and expect to find the car where we left it. We also recognize full well that we cannot park the car, go to Fiji for three years, and expect to find it in the same place on our return. There is a steadiness to the world, but not a glacial steadiness.

Incidentally, this steadiness is also what makes the so-called displacement property of human languages—the ability to talk about things that are not nearby—so valuable. It might be entertaining to hear about the dangerous things currently out of sight that someone encountered recently, for example. But what can make a report like this so consequential is the expectation that these dangers are still there, even if we can't immediately see them.

The little theory, though, is incomplete. It mentions physical things without saying enough about them, and similarly for agents. We turn to these next.

Naive Physics

Among the many things we have knowledge about, almost all of our attention is on physical things. What can we say about them in general? Here is one attempt:

The physical world is made of matter located in space.

Points in space are nonphysical things that are ordered linearly in three separate dimensions. A collection of points that are contiguous in space is called a region. The border of a region are those points in the region that are contiguous with points outside the region. Each region has a certain volume, which is a measure of the amount of space it contains.

Bits of matter are things that have a spatial presence—that is, for each bit of matter, there is a point in space called its location that it alone occupies. There are many distinct kinds of matter such as air, granite, and ginger ale, with different characteristic densities. Bits of matter also have nonspatial properties called energy properties, such as their motion, heat, light, sound, and electric charge.

A physical object is a thing made of contiguous bits of matter. The total amount of matter involved (taking density into account) is called the mass of the object. The smallest region that encloses all the matter is called the shape of the object, and the total volume is called the size of the object. Sometimes the border where one object stops and another object begins is unclear.

Among the properties of a physical object, its location in space is perhaps foremost. This is because a physical object must be located nearby to be acted on or made use of in some way—for example, to play a guitar, eat an apple, or pick up a comb. One object can be kept in close proximity to another by putting it inside or attaching it securely to the other.

The bits of matter that make up an object can change over time. Some objects like clouds and rivers change constantly, while others like rocks and plastic bags change more slowly. The shape of an object can also change over time. An object can be in a solid, liquid, or gaseous state, according to how readily it changes its shape. Some solid objects like buildings tend to keep their shape; liquid objects like puddles take on a shape according to the solid objects around them; gaseous objects like puffs of air change their shapes spontaneously over time. Objects can also be made of component parts in different states: a glass of milk as an object has a solid outer shell surrounding a certain quantity of liquid.

This second treatise is only a first step toward a naive physics. (By "naive" here, we do not mean mistaken; we mean something like unsophisticated or prescientific.) Unlike real physics, it does not dig into any of the micro-level details. A carrot is made up of small bits of carrot matter, and that's that. There is reference to quantitative properties like mass and energy, but not even the stub of a theory about them. (We will return to quantities in a separate section below.)

Naive physics is concerned primarily with physical objects that are not too big and not too small—what we might call *medial macro-objects*, like beetles, dishwashers, and drugstores. This is a special case of the things we know about, but one that means a lot to us since this is the kind of thing we perceive through our senses and act on directly.

One problem with the idea of physical objects is that of their spatial boundaries. This is most evident for nonsolid things, but the problem is there for solid ones too. Is this one particular bit of pavement part of the main highway or the exit ramp? The commonsense answer is this: nobody cares. We recognize the issue, but shrug it off and say that the precise boundaries of physical objects like these almost never matter. This is also true for the boundaries of some events—say, the exact moment that was the end of the French Revolution. Similar considerations apply to classifications of objects based on properties that hold to a degree. Just how wide does a creek have to be before we consider it to be a river? When is something not a rock because it is too small? And similarly, when does a snack become a meal? When does an acquaintance become a friend?

Another difficulty with thinking about physical objects as discrete things is how their existence unfolds over time. A house can be destroyed in a fire; a cell can divide and be replaced by two new ones; a puddle can evaporate; and a door can be created by installing a piece of wood in a jamb. But despite complexities like these, we still do tend to think of the objects of the physical world as steady enough to work with on a human timescale, not as the sort of volatile stew suggested by quantum mechanics. There is no contradiction here. Macroproperties can be quite stable even when the underlying microproperties fluctuate wildly.

Implicit in the above account is what we might call the *commonsense law of collocation*: if an object is contained in or attached to another, then changing the location of the latter also changes the location of the former. This can be thought of as an explicit exception to the commonsense law of inertia. Normally, the location of something like a passport would not be affected by events involving other objects, like playing a guitar, eating an apple, or picking up a comb. But if the passport is in a suitcase that is in the trunk of a car, then driving the car to Montreal changes the location of the passport where it might later be needed. One challenging truth about the world is that not only can you not have everything, as Steven Wright reminds us, but you also cannot even have everything you need nearby, and appropriate measures have to be taken.

Naive Psychology

The final major topic in the theory of everything above is that of agents. Among all the physical objects, we spend perhaps most of our time trying to make sense of what agents are up to and why. Of special concern, of course, are those that are like us.

Agents are physical things that can actively make certain events take place. The events in this case are called actions, and the agent is said to perform the action. Intentional agents are ones that perform actions in accordance with a mental state, made up of propositions.

Propositions are nonphysical things that have the property of being either true or false. Atomic propositions are those whose truth depends on whether something has a certain property or a certain thing exists. Complex propositions are those whose truth depends on the truth of a collection of other propositions, such as whether every person in a certain room was born in Philadelphia.

At any point, there will be certain propositions that an intentional agent believes to be true (quite apart from whether those propositions really are true) and others that it desires to make true; the latter we refer to as the agent's goals. Although an intentional agent may perform an action unwittingly, the signature case is when the agent performs the action with the goal of doing so at that point, and the belief that doing so will bring about a change that it desires.

An intentional agent is behaving intelligently to the extent that it is making the best possible use of its beliefs to achieve its goals and get what it desires. In practice, however, there is no guarantee that an agent will choose the right action to perform, even by its own standards. Among other things, an agent may fail to appreciate all the consequences of its own beliefs and desires.

Agents will often have goals that they believe can be realized by the actions of other agents. Of course, those other agents will be acting on their own beliefs and desires. Yet one strong link between two agents is that of a mutual belief: two agents mutually believe a proposition when they both believe it and both believe that they mutually believe it. An agent will sometimes choose to do an action when it believes that it is mutually believed with another agent that the other agent wants it done by the first agent (and may even be willing to reciprocate later). To get to such a state, agents will perform communicative actions like informing and requesting, whose purpose is to change the beliefs of another agent about what they mutually believe.

So while agents are considered to be the things that make events occur (including toasters, say), the emphasis is on intentional agents: those that choose actions in accordance with beliefs, general desires, and specific goals. A much simpler story about these agents is that they choose what to do according to the way the world is. For example, we might have said that agents take their umbrellas when the forecast is for rain. This simpler account aligns quite well with experience. So it is a subtle but crucial insight about the world that this story is wrong, that it is the *beliefs* of the agents that matter; the agents would not take their umbrellas when the forecast was for rain if they mistakenly believed the forecast was for sun. Famously, young children do not get this insight until about the age of four, when they first construct a *theory of mind*, allowing that other agents could have and be acting on false beliefs.

Perhaps the key fact about intentional agents is what might be called the *commonsense tendency of agents*: agents will choose actions they believe will advance their goals, and avoid actions they believe will hinder them. This is a tendency, though, and not a strict law. For one thing, agents will sometimes make choices willy-nilly without taking even important goals into account. A person who cares deeply about the value of money can still end up spending injudiciously—a choice that may be inexplicable except as some sort of primitive impulse, or perhaps as an exercise in sheer free will ("I am doing it because I can!"). For another, agents will sometimes fall prey to faulty modes of reasoning that may lead them astray. So it is hard to develop any confidence about what agents will actually do in particular situations, and virtually impossible to have certainty about their behavior. It is an oversimplified view of intentional agents to expect them to act like some sort of ideal logical/rational machines, always making the best use of what they know to get what they want. It turns out that even as a rough approximation, this view of how people behave is not that helpful (as already discussed).

The final paragraph above is the stub of a theory of communicative actions (or *speech acts*, as they are called). Once one agent recognizes another as an intentional agent, it opens up a whole new dimension in how to achieve certain goals. An agent can either walk over and open a window, or in the right circumstances, stay put and just say the words, "It's stuffy in here, isn't it?" and the overall effect on the window can be the same. Similarly, groups of agents can achieve things together that individuals cannot. For a complete picture, it would be important to take into account broader social conventions as well as interactions between groups, or what we might call naive sociology.

Quantities and Limits

While commonsense thinking might not resort to the sort of precise numerical reckoning seen in science and mathematics, it certainly deals with quantities, such as things being heavier or lighter, brighter or darker, or older or younger. It is commonsensical that an adult elephant will not fit into a car. How then to characterize quantities like size? Here is one way:

Natural numbers are abstract things that are linearly ordered. A number is larger/ smaller than another if it occurs later/earlier in the ordering. There is a smallest number called zero. The successor of a number is the next largest number in the ordering. Every number other than zero has a predecessor, which is the next smallest number in the ordering.

Things can have numerical properties. Some of those numerical properties are for identification only—that is, different things will be associated with different numbers (like phone lines and citizen taxpayers). But there are abstract things called quantities (or amounts) that have special numerical properties that categorize them as big or small. Examples of quantities are things like areas, weights, voltages, costs, and durations. The numerical properties here measure the size of the quantities in certain standardized units. Given a specific length, for instance, we can ask for its measure in meters, football fields, or light-years, getting different (but related) numbers in each case.

Quantities are typically introduced as properties of other things: the area of a rug, weight of a person, voltage of a battery, cost of a bicycle, or duration of a meal. Two things might be associated with the same quantity, like two people having the same age. Quantities can also be for more than one thing, like the distance between two cities.

When something changes, it can come to be associated with a different quantity as a property. A person can gain or lose weight, for example. We say that a quantity is incremented for something when that thing is changed so that it is associated with a new quantity whose measure (in some fixed units) is a bigger number than the old. Similarly, a quantity is decremented when the new measure involved is a smaller number. One key feature about a change in quantity like this is that if a quantity is repeatedly decremented, it will eventually end up with a measure of zero.

A basic case of this is a (finite) collection of things, where the quantity in question is a count of the number of items in the collection. In this case, removing something from the collection decrements the count so that repeatedly doing so will eventually result in a collection with a count of zero—the empty collection.

This treatise on quantities begins with a description of the natural numbers, without much by way of standard arithmetic terminology (except for the name "zero"). The main motivation for this ordering is to be able to talk about one quantity being more or less than another, and compare differences.

An important feature noted near the end is what might be called the *commonsense law of limits*: a quantity that is repeatedly reduced will eventually be reduced to zero. Like the law of inertia discussed above, this is a powerful principle that allows us to think about a wide range of problems that might otherwise be overwhelming.

Suppose, for example, that we want to get a pile of bricks onto the back of a truck. With this law, common sense tells us that we can do this by repeatedly picking a brick up from the pile and putting it on the truck. The brick we choose to move each time is not important. Specifically, to be confident of the outcome, we do not have to first come up with a plan that determines which brick to pick up when. (We do have to be confident that it will always be possible to transfer some brick.) Similar considerations apply whenever we have a collection of things to deal with in a uniform way, like reading all the mail or peeling all the potatoes.

This law of limits also allows us to easily draw certain conclusions without having to resort to mathematics, assuming we can identify the quantities involved. For example, we can see that a king on a chessboard can get to any other square on the board once we realize that it can always move to reduce the distance to that square. That conclusion is no harder to get to for a thousand-by-thousand board. (Incidentally, a knight can get to any square on an eight-by-eight chessboard too, but in that case, the quantity being reduced by each move is far from obvious.)

The treatise on quantities only talks about natural numbers. We are assuming that quantities are measured in units small enough to avoid fractions, but this is not crucial. Some care with fractions is needed, though. For instance, we want to be able to conclude that when two objects are moving closer and closer together, they will eventually come into contact. But if distances are measured in fractional units, and we allow arbitrarily small changes in distance, a much more complex analysis is needed.

In talking about subjects like the size of the Statue of Liberty, we end up talking about three distinct things: the statue (the physical object), its height (an abstract quantity related to that statue), and the number ninety-three (a measure of that quantity in meters). For many purposes, however, we can bypass the quantity and talk about two things: the statue and its height in meters—the number ninety-three. (We will see this simplified form in later chapters.)

Counterfactuals and the Ways of the World

In talking about the way things are and how they change as the result of events, we are allowing that things can be different from the way they currently are. Similarly, in talking about the beliefs and goals of agents, we are at least contemplating the possibility of things being different from how they have ever been or will ever be.

There is a perhaps unfortunate tendency to talk about these matters in terms of other "worlds." For instance, we might say that someone is imagining another world where some desirable condition holds. This is unfortunate in that it suggests that there is something broader than the world, something made up of many such worlds. (Physicists—and comic book writers—sometimes talk about a "multiverse.") We happen to live on one such world, say, but could imagine observing another one using some sort of magic telescope or even traveling to another world, somewhat like visiting a distant planet. We might go exploring, investigating what is the same and different there, perhaps tracking down our counterpart in that world, and so on.

But this type of story, if it can be made coherent at all, is not really how we think about the way things were in the past. Things might have been different, but we do not think of the past as some other world where, for example, our counterpart lives; we're the ones who lived there. It is part of a commonsense understanding that the person I was yesterday is not someone distinct from me, a doppelgänger; it's just me. Similarly, assuming I don't die, it will be me again tomorrow, not something that resembles me.

Rather than talking about other worlds, the commonsense understanding is more like the following, which applies equally well to the past and future as well as the more extreme possibilities imagined by agents:

> There is one and only one world, but there are many different ways that world can be, which we call states of the world. A state is completely determined by the things that exist and the properties they have. So at any given point in time, the world is in one state, called the current state, and events can change the world from one state to another.
>
> Any state of the world distinct from the current one is called a counterfactual. The beliefs and desires of agents deal with counterfactuals in that the propositions they believe to be true, or want to be true, may only be true in states other than the current one.
>
> Of special interest is a state that is almost like another: the things in it are almost the same, and their properties are almost the same. In thinking about the world and the actions at their disposal, agents consider counterfactuals where things are almost the same as they imagine the world to be, except for what they imagine to be changed by the action.

Although we talk about the current state of the world, the state of the world five minutes ago, and the state of the world five minutes from now, what these states actually are will be unknowable to agents. Quite apart from false beliefs, there will be always be matters that agents fail to know for a variety of reasons. To any agent, it will always seem like there are many different ways the world could be, could have been, or could turn out to be. Part of the difficulty here is practical; agents can only observe, measure, and verify so much, and these apply to the current state only. But there are conceptual problems as well. The lack of precise boundaries on what constitutes a physical object or event, say, can result in legitimate disagreements about the true state of the world. This is quite apart from the various subjective opinions agents have, such as whether or not a movie was boring, where there are really no objective facts about the world under consideration.

In thinking about counterfactuals, we can end up talking about things that we do not believe currently exist. For example, in talking about the future, we might discuss the house that George is having built. This is not a problem as long as we are clear about what state of the world we have in mind. We might insist, for instance, that the house has five bedrooms, even though, strictly speaking, there is no house to be talking about. Similar considerations apply in talking about topics like the London street address of Sherlock Holmes or the color of Santa Claus's boots.

Causality and Other Advanced Topics

The premise of this chapter is that there are certain topics that are part of a commonsense understanding that might be difficult to acquire through language. (We used language here to go through them, but only to remind the reader about them, not to introduce them from scratch.) In some cases, we mentioned topics but only hinted at the details. For physical objects, we talked about mass and energy, but left out forces such as gravity. For agents, we talked about beliefs and goals, but left out emotions, such as what agents find exciting, are afraid of, or are shamed by, and how these might contribute to the choices they make. The omissions were simply to keep the discussion of reasonable length and should not be taken to imply that the unmentioned items are not important.

There are many additional topics we might have discussed, and which ultimately are likely to be needed as foundations of the commonsense knowledge of an intelligent machine. At this stage, it is hard to tell which of them might best be understood in terms of other topics. For agents, we will want to understand the idea of morality, such as how agents view some choices as good or evil according to certain precepts. In the Bible, this particular topic ends up being the primal subject of what is called the Tree of Knowledge. (Of course, understanding what some agents take as being good or evil, and why, is different from actually taking some things to be good or evil. Both are required.) There are issues of control, freedom, and responsibility that would be worth capturing—assumptions about agents' freedom to act or coercion by others that can be useful in everyday circumstances. People understand appearances of physical objects, how they can change over time, and how they relate to underlying properties of those objects as well as to external coverings. And there is also the notion of causality—a subject worth looking at here in more detail.

Much of what we believe about the world across a wide variety of subject areas is expressed in terms of causality. We want to know what causes what because we want to know who or what is responsible when things happen, or what action can bring about something we want to happen. We might believe that Jane was late for the meeting because she slept through her alarm, Jimmy was not allowed on the waterslide because he was too short, or Trump was elected because of Russian meddling. On a more generic level, we might believe that smoking causes cancer or carbon emissions cause global warming.

These are not simple facts about the world but rather complex ones involving counterfactuals. It's not just that there are two events, where one happens before the other: Jane sleeps in and then Jane is late. This is the fallacy that lawyers call *post hoc ergo propter hoc*. Causality means that if you imagine a state of the world where the first event does not take place (or where some property does not hold), then all other things being equal, the second event no longer takes place. So what we might know is this: had Jane not slept in, she would have arrived on time; had Jimmy been taller, he would have been allowed on that waterslide; or had the Russians not meddled, Trump would not have won.

Nevertheless, the counterfactual story by itself is not quite right; it is neither necessary nor sufficient. Consider this: we might happen to know that the bus Jane takes was stuck in traffic on the day she slept in, but we still want to say that she was late because she slept in, even though she would have arrived late anyway. Or consider this: if Tommy pushes Timmy down the stairs, we want to say that Timmy fell because Tommy pushed him (since he would not have fallen otherwise), but we do not want to say that Timmy fell because he was on the stairs (even though he certainly would not have fallen had he not been there). If an event involves more than one person, they need not all be causes. This is important since it means that the parties involved need not be equally to blame.

These are subtle features of causality that are hard to be precise about. As we have already alluded to, however, there are two fundamental aspects of causality that will be central to our project, and that we will be dealing with repeatedly in this book:

1. Events can cause the world to change; a rain shower can make the grass wet, a birthday party can leave a mess in the living room, a purchase can change the ownership of a car, or a drive to Montreal can change the location of a passport.

2. Under the right circumstances, agents can cause certain events to take place; an agent can pick up a brick, eat an apple, sing a song, or drive to Montreal.

But in the end, how best to make sense of causality in the more full-bodied way that respects our commonsense usage of the term is something that even the experts have yet to come to an agreement on.

As a final thought, we might wonder if instead of having missed some important topics, we have included too many of them. This chapter was about the presuppositions of commonsense knowledge, or what needs to be in place before you can make sense of what you find out about the world. But are we presupposing too much? Aren't the kind of topics presented here really the whole game? Sorting out a commonsense worldview may feel more like the ultimate goal of intelligence rather than its starting point. Or as Brian Cantwell Smith puts it, "Ontology is an achievement of intelligence, not a presupposition." Our only defense is to say that this is a question of perspective. We are indeed presupposing a lot, but as we will see in the next chapter, this is all just preparation for a much larger game that remains to be played.

6 Commonsense Knowledge

The time has come, the walrus said, to talk of many things:
of shoes—and ships—and sealing-wax—of cabbages—and kings.
—Lewis Carroll, "The Walrus and the Carpenter"

Now that we've seen how common sense carves up the world, it is time to talk about commonsense knowledge itself. So what is this knowledge about in general? The answer is easy: it's about the everyday things around us— taxi drivers, elevator doors, Ferris wheels, front-yard lawns, car loans, mystery novels, apple pies, court verdicts, and yes, even cabbages and kings. As suggested in the previous chapter, it's also about events like city council meetings, game shows, traffic jams, restaurant meals, forest fires, trips abroad, and all the things that happen every day that can cause the properties of other things to change over time.

Recall that we defined common sense as an ability to make effective use of ordinary, everyday, experiential knowledge in deciding what to do. In this chapter, we consider some of the issues involved in *articulating* this knowledge—knowledge of commonplace things, their properties, and how they change.

Just to be clear about our approach and end goal, ultimately we want to consider what it would take to get computers to have and make use of commonsense knowledge. To do that, we'll have to find ways to represent the knowledge in a manner that a computational device could manipulate and operate on. As discussed before, that will be in some sort of computer-processable, symbolic form. But rather than jump right into that, we need to first spend some time getting a better sense of the sorts of things we will want to represent. And as we will see, there are some interesting nuances and complexities in this. So we will use the ability to state things in a natural language like English as a temporary surrogate for representing them in a form that a computer could operate on, which we will get to in the next chapter.

The Overall Organization

Most of what we know about the world seems to be about specific, individual things—the things we've encountered, the people we've interacted with, and the experiences we've had. As we saw, we can think of these as making up a state of the world. In addition, we allow for states of the world that do not exist right now, but that could exist or we expect to exist in the future. People are good at recalling previous states of the world, and imagining, at least in a limited way, what the outcomes of actions and events might be, and also at making plans for imagined futures. When we think of those scenarios, they generally look more or less like the actual situations we are in; they have individual people, places, and so on, the same way our current world does.

So what do we know about all these individual things? It is pretty clear that humans organize what they know, such as related to their families and jobs, geography and time, and even with respect to ideas. It will be useful to think of certain kinds of things in the world as being conceptually close and/or structured similarly to one another. We tend to think of things as clustered in types or categories.

So in talking about common sense, we need to go beyond the individual things themselves and consider what we will be calling a *conceptual structure*. It's not just that we know about things like hospitals and birthday parties; it's that we think of them *as* hospitals and birthday parties. So separate from the individuals themselves, there are these generic ideas called *concepts* (like the concept of a hospital) that serve to organize how we think about the individuals.

Imagine looking at some people on a field outdoors. One person might see a game of baseball, with one person playing the role of pitcher and another the catcher. Another person might see the same scene as just a collection of people throwing and catching a ball, hitting it with a stick, running, and so on. The two people might agree completely on what things are on the field, the properties they have, and the observable events taking place. Where they disagree (or maybe just fail to communicate) is that one of them has a conceptual structure involving the game of baseball, and the other does not.

So a conceptual structure concerns the kinds of things we imagine there to be and the kinds of properties we imagine them to have. Before we can know that John was born in Boston, say, we need to see John as the kind of thing that can have the property of being born somewhere. In other words, we need to have the concept of a person and the idea that a person is the kind of thing that will have a birthplace. Similarly, we can have the concept of a baseball team and the idea that each person will play a position on the team, such as shortstop; we can have the concept of a hospital along with the idea that it will have operating rooms and patients; we can have the concept of birthday party along with the idea that there will be guests and a birthday cake; and so on. A conceptual structure like this gives us huge leverage for thinking about the world by allowing generalizations and analogies to be made between individual things, and allowing us to understand things much more richly than as disconnected, individual items.

In its most elemental form, a conceptual structure like this can be expressed in English sentences using the verbs "to have" and "to be":

A hospital is a building, and has patients who are people and operating rooms that have bright lights.

The "to be" portion induces a generalization hierarchy, or *taxonomy*. Hospitals are buildings. Buildings are physical enclosures. Houses are buildings. Vacation houses and lake houses are houses. The "to have" portion also induces a hierarchy. Cities have hospitals. Hospitals have patients. Patients have injuries or illnesses. Injuries have treatments. Thinking in terms of these hierarchies—for example, thinking of certain concepts as being more general or more specialized than others—is a powerful way of dealing with large numbers of them manageably. Dictionaries and encyclopedia entries are often built around the idea of starting with a general category, and then specifying how a term at hand is different and more specific than that category.

As we will see later, there are other important relationships between concepts that are more causal or temporal in nature. In other cases, the relationships between concepts involve location and structure, like how a hand relates to an arm. The main point, however, is that these ideas are all generic and not about any particular individual in the world. This generic knowledge is critical to cognition for many reasons and certainly is a significant part of common sense.

So in the end, when we talk about expressing commonsense knowledge, we are interested in more than individual things and their properties; we are also interested in the concepts that help us make sense of these things. Common sense will need to make use of a conceptual structure. For example, faced with something new and unanticipated, we ask ourselves, What *kind* of thing is this, and on that basis, what else might I know (or guess) about it, and what does that suggest I do next? This double-barreled organization of knowledge—beliefs about individual things in the world, framed within a conceptual structure—is the fundamental basis for commonsense knowledge.

What's in a Concept?

A conceptual structure is made of a collection of concepts interrelated in various ways. But what can we say about each one? Just what is our concept of a hospital, for instance? When we think of a hospital, what idea do we have in mind? And does it even make sense to try to express this in words?

Here are two observations to begin. First of all, we want more than a definition of the word in question. Here is what *Merriam-Webster*'s dictionary says:

A hospital is an institution where the sick or injured are given medical care.

Another dictionary, geared to children, says this:

A hospital is a place where people who are ill are looked after.

While these definitions are fine as far as they go, they clearly fall short of what we'd expect to reflect a commonsense understanding of hospitals. They don't tell us many things we'd need to know when thinking about, getting around, or making decisions about what to do in a hospital. In characterizing our idea of a hospital, there is a lot more to talk about. There is the building itself: emergency entrances, operating rooms, intensive care units, patient wards, and nurses' stations. Then there are the people there: patients and their visitors, doctors, nurses, orderlies, gift shop clerks, and other personnel. There are the medical services that take place there: examinations, surgery, the administration of medicine, and the application of bandages. We might talk about hospital departments: intensive care, maternity, coronary, oncology, and billing. We might speak of the furniture: patient beds, medicine carts, gurneys, and operating tables. We might also want to talk about other services: pharmacies, cafeterias, gift shops, and long-term parking. A dictionary entry would not be expected to cover any of these. An encyclopedia might, except for the fact that encyclopedias tend to focus on things that are not encountered as routinely as hospitals.

Second, when we talk about expressing our concept of a hospital, we mean expressing what we might call a hospital's *basic* properties, not the many conclusions that can be drawn from them. For example, here is something that common sense tells us about hospitals:

A hospital is bigger than an ice cream truck.

While this is commonsensical, the idea of an ice cream truck is not really part of our idea of a hospital. There are indeed an enormous number of things we imagine a hospital to be bigger than, but we expect them to be *derivable* from something more basic about the sizes involved. To take a more extreme illustration, consider sentences of this form:

A hospital is a building with fewer than N floors.

It is certainly commonsensical that a hospital building has fewer than, say, 279 floors. Indeed, there are an infinite number of sentences like this that we know to be true. But again, we expect them to be derivable from more basic properties about the number of floors in a hospital. (Hospitals are not skyscrapers; the tallest one so far is in Hong Kong and only has 38 floors.)

In sum, what we are after in our concept of a hospital is something more than a dictionary definition, but less than all the facts we might know about hospitals. Overall, there are two main things to focus on: first, how the concept of a hospital fits within the rest of our conceptual structure— that is, how it specializes or generalizes other concepts we know about (like that of a building or medical institution) in terms of the properties it has; and second, how things other than hospitals (like patients, waiting rooms, and gurneys) have a role to play. As noted above, this can often be expressed using just the English verbs "to be" and "to have." In many cases, however, events will be involved, and it will be more natural to use other English verbs for them. For example, instead of saying something awkward like,

> *A hospital is a building that has medical service events that have a location in that building and recipients who are patients.*

we prefer to say,

> *A hospital is a building where patients receive medical services.*

where quite apart from hospitals, we are now imagining medical services as events that have locations and recipients (and other properties, such as providers—that is, the medical personnel).

Annotating Generalities

In trying to put into words our concept of a hospital, here is what inevitably happens: we start saying something about hospitals in general, and just before finishing, we realize that what we were going to say is not quite right. It is almost impossible to complete a sentence like "Every hospital has ..." or "All hospitals are ..." because there is so much variation. No sooner do you begin to say something than you want to correct yourself and qualify it in one way or another. We feel a need to elaborate, discuss special cases, and inevitably, hedge almost everything.

How then to get started? One possibility is this: we take everything we say with a grain of salt. We make blunt, unqualified statements about hospitals in general, using expressions such as "A hospital is ..." or "A hospital has ... ," with the understanding that these are preliminary and subject to annotations to come later. The simple statement might be all there is for the knowledge of a child. But as we come to learn more, the concept will evolve; we will want to annotate the statement, adding refinements and subtleties, and revising the original unqualified claim. The more we learn, the more we annotate.

One way to visualize this annotation in text is in terms of footnotes, as suggested in figure 6.1. Each line written in annotations like these is itself subject to further annotation. Overall, a linear string of words like an English sentence can feel ill-suited for the job.

In a 1974 piece, Minsky suggested that what we know about things like hospitals should be represented not by a linear string of words at all but

A hospital is a building[1,2] where patients[3] receive medical services[4,5] ...

---

[1] A hospital can be made of brick and mortar, but some are just tents. Sometimes a hospital is just an area outdoors, with perhaps a roof and wall coverings to keep out the rain and dust.

[2] We might want to distinguish between a hospital as a physical enclosure and a hospital as an organized collection of medical services. Instead of saying that a hospital is a building, we might prefer to say that a hospital is housed in a building. That way, we could say that a hospital moved to a new location, even if the building itself was torn down.

[3] Patients are people who are sick or injured and are under the care of medical personnel. Many other people are in a hospital, too: physicians, nurses, orderlies, visitors, support staff, administrators. Sometimes people needing urgent medical care show up unexpectedly at the emergency entrance of a hospital, but are not yet patients. There are also animal hospitals where the patients are household pets, and the medical personnel are veterinarians and their helpers.

[4] There are a variety of medical services in a hospital, such as surgery, intensive care, long-term treatments, and lab tests. Some medical services like eye exams and routine physiotherapy are typically not found in hospitals. Hospitals also provide nonmedical services for patients and others, like gift shops and cafeterias.

[5] The difference between a hospital and a medical arts building where a number of physicians maintain a practice is mostly one of scale. A hospital is typically large enough that it can afford expensive medical equipment by sharing facilities across many physicians and patients.

Figure 6.1
A description of a hospital annotated with footnotes

instead by a complex structure of entities and relationships he called a *frame*. Minsky has some useful thoughts on these kinds of conceptual structures, and we include here some of what he said (from his paper "A Framework for Representing Knowledge"). Note that he is talking about symbolic representations (networks of nodes and relations) here; ignore that aspect for now, and just get a sense of his view about this kind of conceptual framework:

When one encounters a new situation (or makes a substantial change in one's view of the present problem) one selects from memory a structure called a Frame. This is a remembered framework to be adapted to fit reality by changing details as necessary.

A frame is a data-structure for representing a stereotyped situation, like being in a certain kind of living room, or going to a child's birthday party. Attached to each frame are several kinds of information. Some of this information is about how to use the frame. Some is about what one can expect to happen next. Some is about what to do if these expectations are not confirmed.

We can think of a frame as a network of nodes and relations. The "top levels" of a frame are fixed, and represent things that are always true about the supposed situation. The lower levels have many terminals, "slots" that must be filled by specific instances or data. Each terminal can specify conditions its assignments must meet. (The assignments themselves are usually smaller "sub-frames.") Simple conditions are specified by markers that might require a terminal assignment to be a person, an object of sufficient value, or a pointer to a sub-frame of a certain type. More complex conditions can specify relations among the things assigned to several terminals.

Collections of related frames are linked together into frame-systems. The effects of important actions are mirrored by transformations between the frames of a system. These are used to make certain kinds of calculations economical, to represent changes of emphasis and attention, and to account for the effectiveness of "imagery."

For visual scene analysis, the different frames of a system describe the scene from different viewpoints, and the transformations between one frame and another represent the effects of moving from place to place. For non-visual kinds of frames, the differences between the frames of a system can represent actions, cause-effect relations, or changes in conceptual viewpoint. Different frames of a system share the same terminals; this is the critical point that makes it possible to coordinate information gathered from different viewpoints.

Much of the phenomenological power of the theory hinges on the inclusion of expectations and other kinds of presumptions. A frame's terminals are normally already filled with "default" assignments. Thus, a frame may contain a great many details whose supposition is not specifically warranted by the situation. These have many uses in representing general information, most likely cases, techniques for bypassing "logic," and ways to make useful generalizations.

The default assignments are attached loosely to their terminals, so that they can be easily displaced by new items that fit better the current situation. They thus can serve also as "variables" or as special cases for "reasoning by example," or as "textbook cases," and often make the use of logical quantifiers unnecessary.

The frame-systems are linked, in turn, by an information retrieval network. When a proposed frame cannot be made to fit reality—when we cannot find terminal assignments that suitably match its terminal marker conditions—this network provides a replacement frame. These inter-frame structures make possible other ways to represent knowledge about facts, analogies, and other information useful in understanding.

Once a frame is proposed to represent a situation, a matching process tries to assign values to each frame's terminals, consistent with the markers at each place. The matching process is partly controlled by information associated with the frame (which includes information about how to deal with surprises) and partly by knowledge about the system's current goals. There are important uses for the information, obtained when a matching process fails.

We can of course unpack the content of a frame system into a sequence of English sentences, but it will be important to remember that those sentences do not live in isolation. They will be commented on by other sentences, suggesting related ideas, elaborating, clarifying, hedging, and sometimes even contradicting them by bringing up variations as well as exceptional cases.

Consider this, for example:

A hospital has six floors ...

This is a reasonable default for the size of a hospital building (that is, hospitals do tend to be shorter than skyscrapers yet taller than bungalows), but we know that there is considerable latitude in how many floors we might expect to see. Hospitals with other than six floors are common.

This idea of latitude is key. Consider this:

A bird is an animal about the size of a human hand.

While we may accept this rough statement about the size of birds, or as a statement about some sort of prototypical bird, here we allow for great latitude. A full-size royal albatross is nowhere near the size of a hand, nor is a young bee hummingbird. But we recognize that these are extreme cases. It is part of commonsense knowledge that insects are smaller than birds, which are smaller than dogs, even though we well know there are exceptions. We cannot afford to be overly strict or categorical in how we make use of what we believe.

The idea of latitude also connects to those vague properties that hold only to a degree. It might make sense to think of a green X as no more than an X whose color is green, but we cannot think of a tall X in this way. What the adjective "tall" means depends on the X in question and is something more like "having height that is in the high range for things that are X." A tall hospital might have twenty floors, but a tall high school would be expected to have fewer, while a tall downtown hotel would probably have considerably more. This suggests that a concept might include not only a default value but default high and low values too, and maybe default very high and very low values. (Going further, we can even imagine a full distribution of default values, from the most common one to various less likely ones.)

One interesting way to think about typical quantities like the height of a hospital or duration of a haircut is in terms of *orders of magnitude*. A small number N might mean a value taken to be between 10^N and $10^{(N+1)}$ in some suitable units. For example, we might have a default order of magnitude cost (in US dollars) of a hardcover book as 1, an air conditioner as 2, an engagement ring as 3, a car as 4, and a house as 5 (with luxury versions of these items perhaps one number higher, and low-end budget versions one number less). These small numbers do the job of qualitative orderings for which we tend to use adverbs in English like "extremely," "very," "somewhat," "barely," and so on. They allow us to easily conclude that a night in a hotel is more expensive than a hamburger without having to know the exact quantities involved.

So when we think of what we know about something and try to write a sentence to express it, we should be thinking along the lines of Minsky's frame systems. The sentences will tell us what to expect under normal, typical circumstances, what to look for, and what questions to ask. But the sentences need to be richly annotated and cannot be taken in isolation. Of special interest is that a frame system may be used for "differential diagnosis," proposing alternatives to the current best guess as to the kind of thing under consideration.

Similarly, we should not be too hasty about dismissing a sentence that we think is wrong. Consider a statement like this:

A dog is a brown mammal.

The issue here is not so much whether we take the statement to be true or false in reality (but more on this in the next section); it is how strongly we are prepared to hang onto what it says. We should not be surprised at all by a black dog, for instance, but we should be much more surprised by a green one. (Further annotation: dogs are considerably less constrained when depicted in cartoons, such as Huckleberry Hound, the blue dog that can talk and sing (one horrendous song, anyway), and Clifford, the red dog that is the size of a garage.) On the other hand, there is much less latitude when it comes to a dog being a mammal. We recognize that there are robot dogs and toy dogs that are not alive, but we do feel that those that are alive should be mammals. It would be quite unusual to imagine a dog that had a dry, scaly skin and laid eggs. We might want to say that that was something other than a dog.

The Minsky idea of a frame captures some important high-level ideas about commonsense knowledge of stereotyped situations. It is worth noting that this idea also covers knowledge about sequences of events. Other early work by AI scientists like Schank focused on stereotypical sequences of actions based on everyday experiences, which were often referred to as "scripts." A classic example captures the typical sequence of events related to eating at a restaurant, with "scenes" related to entering, ordering, eating, paying, and exiting. The same kind of annotation, situation-matching, and expectation-driven recognition apparatus described above can be applied to these sequences of events. Note that commonsensical notions of time and causality would be essential ingredients to support such a mechanism.

Getting a Concept Right

It is not too surprising that we should have a hard time writing anything categorical of the form "Every hospital has ..." Philosophers of language have long made the case that we cannot expect to find satisfactory characterizations in language for many of the kinds of things that are part of our world. For example, how do we characterize something like our commonsense notion of a game, philosopher Ludwig Wittgenstein asked, given the extreme range of variations?

A big part of the problem has to do with boundary conditions. The conceptual boundaries of what constitutes a hospital (like the boundaries of what constitutes a creek, from the previous chapter) need not be clear-cut. We might prefer to use a term like "medical arts building" for institutions that are more limited in scope (only some doctors' offices and a few medical services) and something like "health care facility" for institutions that are less limited in scope (institutions that include things like hospices and long-term psychiatric wards), but we do not expect exact boundaries in this classification.

Once we accept that in formulating commonsense concepts, however, we need not pin down the facts that are true of all and only things of that kind, the task is eased considerably. To repeat, we can start with a blunt and unqualified version of the idea, perhaps one that is suitable as a first explanation to a child. This version might make an adult cringe in the same way an adult might cringe at reading how the concept of democracy is presented in a fourth grade school text. It ignores so many issues, special cases, variations, and subtleties. To compensate for this, we allow for the possibility of annotations to refine the description as necessary.

To see this in action, consider the concept of a children's birthday party, prior to annotation of any sort, as in the following:

A children's birthday party is an event put on by the parents of a child in their home to celebrate the anniversary of the birth of that child. The party takes place on a weekend close to the date of the birth of the child, and is attended by about six other children, usually friends or relatives, who have been previously invited. Each attending guest is expected to bring a wrapped gift to give to the birthday child.

The following events take place in sequence:

1. *The party begins with party games for the children, organized by the parents, such as pin the tail on the donkey.*

2. *The children are then seated at a table for a light snack.*

3. *At the end of the snack, the lights are dimmed and a cake decorated with small, lit candles on the top is brought out; the number of candles matches the age of the birthday child in years.*

4. *The guests sing the song "Happy Birthday!" while the cake is placed on the table in front of the birthday child.*

5. *At the end of the song, the birthday child is told to make a wish, and the child blows out all the candles, after which the guests clap.*

6. *The cake is then cut into pieces by the parents and distributed for everyone to eat as the snack dessert.*

7. *After this, the birthday child is presented with the gifts brought by the birthday guests.*

8. *Everyone watches as the birthday child unwraps each gift in turn, thanking the guest who brought it.*

9. *Once all the gifts have been unwrapped, the children may play for a while, and the party then comes to a close.*

The script, of course, is quite familiar: the designated birthday child, guests, gifts, cake, candles, and a number of scenes, including most crucially, the singing of the birthday song and blowing out of the candles. But the description does not make any attempt to be true of *all* children's birthday parties; things are stated too bluntly. It says the event takes place at the home of the parents of the child, without mentioning the possibility of using a nearby restaurant or craft shop, as many parties do. It says that the event takes place on a weekend, without allowing for weekdays when there is no school. It does not even distinguish between a party for a two-year-old and one for a ten-year-old. Similarly, each of the subevents of the party are specified categorically, in a certain fixed order, with little or no room for variation. All of these would need to be dealt with in annotations.

So with the aim of being able to express commonsense knowledge at all, we are advocating for a simple description of children's birthday parties that we admit is not true of all of them. In fact, if the description is detailed enough, we may know that it is not true of the *majority* of them. But this then raises a troubling question: If we are seemingly unconcerned with notions of accuracy or truth, will any description do? Is there no way to get one wrong?

There's an old joke/riddle that goes like this:

Q*: What's big and gray, has a trunk, and lives in a tree?*

A*: An elephant. I lied about the tree.*

The reductio ad absurdum version of this riddle is this:

Q*: What's big and gray, has a trunk, and lives in a tree?*

A*: The number seven. I lied about everything.*

What this raises is the prospect that we could characterize commonsense concepts in arbitrarily fanciful terms, with the idea that annotations could be superimposed to cancel any missteps. We might, for example, have proposed a concept of an elephant that goes,

An elephant is a big, arboreal creature. …

with annotations to hedge the "arboreal" part. Is this not a problem?

It is. The description goes to the trouble of including the word "arboreal," where we know (that is, our commonsense knowledge tells us) that it would have been much better to use something different like "terrestrial." The concept of a big, arboreal creature is fine, but as a characterization of what we think of as an elephant, it's just wrong.

More generally, we say that a description of a concept (like that of an elephant, hospital, or birthday party) is wrong if we know a change to it at the same level of detail that would be more accurate. This might be easiest to visualize in terms of editing: a description is wrong if you can put a red line though some part of it and replace it by something at that same level of detail that you know would be better. Conversely, the description is not wrong if for any part you find objectionable or cringeworthy (including within any of the annotations you are considering), you would be forced to write a more detailed correction somewhere in the margin (that is, you would be forced to write an annotation). So going back to the birthday party, it's fine to say that it takes place at the home of the parents since a more accurate account would need additional detail and discussion.

Incidentally, the idea of describing events like stereotypical birthday parties helps to explain how to handle some general experiential knowledge that is tough to find a place for otherwise. Consider, for instance, the fact that people (tend to) eat cake at birthday parties. This doesn't seem to be part of what we mean either by a person or cake. But it does fit well within our concept of a birthday party and in particular the people playing a certain role in that event, as described above. Similar things could be said about people cheering at hockey games, washing dishes after a meal, and wearing warm clothing in the winter months.

Prototypes and Exemplars

While much of the above is built on ideas like stereotyped situations, let us take a moment to examine this a little more closely. Throughout this chapter and the previous one, we have emphasized simplified, commonsensical views of the world rather than strict dictionary definitions, carefully crafted encyclopedia entries, or expert knowledge. We even used the term "naive physics" to contrast with the perspectives held by trained physicists. The worldview of the average person includes simplistic ideas like "unsupported objects fall" instead of notions like distorted space-time or gravitational waves.

This is because commonsense knowledge is derived from experiences by everyday people of everyday situations. We develop our theories of the world in childhood by observation (with occasional instruction from parents and teachers), and so our central views of how the world works, why people do things, and how events cause change tend to be intuitive and shallow. Even before we can understand language (and certainly well before we can read books), we experience objects and people interacting in the world around us. We develop a localized view. So the ideas that a birthday party is thrown at the house of the parents of the birthday child or a dog is an animal that is brown are arrived at quite naturally, and can easily become strongly lodged before we ever experience exceptions to them. We eventually learn about things different than those we've experienced, and come to understand more complex and hidden rules about the universe through reading and schooling. But the core of our mundane knowledge comes from personal experience.

While our knowledge of the world is initially driven by our specific, individual experiences, we also have a natural drive toward generalization. We notice that the second, third, and fifth dogs we encounter seem to share some obvious characteristics with the ones we've seen before: tails, black noses, four legs, and so on. Of course there will be differences, like color, shape of the snout, or whether we hear them bark. Yet it's an inevitable tendency after seeing a few of them to come to believe that there is an underlying commonality in all of them. This urge to generalize has great value since it allows us to know what to expect when we see other things that we believe to be instances of the same class: the first dogs we encountered wagged their tails and licked our faces so it's natural to assume that the next ones will do the same.

There are different methods one can imagine for retaining our knowledge of first experiences and their generalizations. When it comes to humans, some work in cognitive science tends to favor what are called *prototypes* or ideal representations for categories, built on a person's first experience with something. If a child's first experience with a dog happens to be a collie, the child's prototype for dogs takes on the most salient features of that collie. This representation then gets abstracted as well as refined as more dogs are encountered and new features are noticed. What we've covered here directly acknowledges the fact that commonsense knowledge seems to be built on concepts driven by a few personal experiences and then generalized; it allows generalizations to be expressed and default values to be retained. Our mechanism also allows for the inevitable exceptions and nuances that need to be added incrementally via annotations.

There is an alternate view of how to retain everyday knowledge and apply it to new situations via *exemplars* of a given class rather than abstracted prototypes. In that case, new items would be compared to knowledge of specific individuals we'd encountered (like the dog Tramp in the movies, that specific dog we first saw in our yard, our current pet Fido, and so on) as opposed to a made-up representative that exemplifies the category. Some psychologists have found that people may use both prototypes for the central characterization of categories and also exemplars surrounding the prototypes.

While we have no strong stance on matters like these, anyone building an artificial commonsense cognition will probably need to arrive at one view or the other. The important thing is that the kind of conceptual apparatus we have been talking about should be adequate to handle any of these approaches. (But see the last section of this chapter below for a more radical take on the issue.)

Change: Events, Actions, and Their Effects

Birthday parties, like other events, change the world: candles are lit and blown out, a cake is eaten, and the ownership of each gift is transferred from the guest to the birthday child. Understanding the changes caused by a birthday party involves looking at the various subevents that take place. But some events have an additional aspect. Alongside having subevents, we think of them as actions that agents perform deliberately as a way of working toward goals they care about.

Consider opening a door, for example. There may be many things we know about doors (including their material, installation, handles, hinges, and locks), but from a commonsense point of view, the main thing about them is their location along with the fact that they can be opened and closed. Why do we care? As already noted, we care about getting close to certain objects to be able to act on them, and to do so often involves going into a room where the objects are located, and this in turn may require going through a door. And if the door is not open? There are specific actions that agents can do to cause the state of a door to change. We can express this door knowledge as in the following:

A door has a state that is open, closed + locked, or closed + unlocked.

An agent can close a nearby door provided its state is open, and the effect is to change its state to closed + unlocked.

An agent can open a nearby door provided its state is closed + unlocked, and the effect is to change its state to open.

An agent can lock a nearby door provided its state is closed + unlocked and the agent is holding a key for the door, and the effect is to change its state to closed + locked.

An agent can unlock a nearby door provided its state is closed + locked and the agent is holding a key for the door, and the effect is to change its state to closed + unlocked.

This describes four actions that agents can perform using a before-and-after story for each one: what has to be true before an agent is able to successfully perform the action (by sheer force of will), and what changes are caused by the agent successfully performing the action. The former are called the *prerequisites* of the action; the latter, its *effects*. In this case, what specifically actually happens during the action is left unspecified. For most purposes, door events might be thought of as having no subevents at all. For example, the actual use of a key is something that would be described only in a supplementary annotation.

The pattern here is familiar. Just as door states are affected by opening, closing, and locking events, marital status is affected by weddings, divorces, and deaths. Likewise, the ownership of an object is affected by events like sales, donations, and repossessions. The location of an inanimate object is affected by transportation events, complicated by the commonsense law of collocation. Certain actions performed by agents have the effect of initiating or terminating other longer-term events. So pulling the plug in a bathtub filled with water immediately starts a water-draining event. The amount of water in the tub is a quantity that is then affected over time by this draining event. Similarly, length of hair is a quantity that slowly increases over time unless it is suddenly affected by a haircutting event.

Before-and-after stories like those above are geared specifically to deciding what actions to perform, and in particular, the *means-ends analysis* (that is, the analysis of how to achieve goals and by what means) necessary for commonsense behavior. It is part of common sense that if you want to get a book from a certain room, you may need to start by going in a completely opposite direction, as preposterous as this might seem at first. Why? Because you may know that the door to the room is locked, and you first need to get the key to unlock it, which will then allow you to open the door, enter the room, and get the book.

While attempting to string actions together to achieve a goal is certainly part of common sense, another part is knowing when certain actions would not be suitable, either because the effort is not warranted or is likely to fail, or because the actions might have undesirable side effects. For example, if you don't know where the key to the door is, it is still possible to get into the room in other ways: taking the door off the hinges, getting a locksmith to remove the lock, cutting a hole in the wall, exploding a small bomb near the door, and so on. While there might be far-fetched cases where each of these actions would be a reasonable choice, part of common sense involves knowing the typical effort (or inconvenience, cost, or risk) associated with performing an action, and using that knowledge to rule out courses of action that are inappropriate for the goals in question.

Of course, one way of getting a shared key when its location is not known is to ask somebody who does know. Using other agents as a means to achieve an end is a familiar strategy used by people and other social animals. This requires recognizing that other agents are not only involved in events but can also cause them to take place. As noted before, if an agent can be made to share a goal you have, this may be sufficient to have the agent do what it takes to achieve that goal. So communicating what you want can be a powerful way of getting things done, including finding out where a key is and possibly even achieving higher-level goals like actually getting the book from the locked room.

But it is also important to keep in mind the effort it might take to get other agents involved—and the side effects there as well. If you need to know what time it is, it makes perfect sense to ask someone, even a complete stranger. If you need a car for the weekend, however, trying to convince a complete stranger to lend you their vehicle is a fool's errand. (If that stranger happens to have a car rental business, then that's a different story.) It is part of common sense that an agent will take on certain goals quite readily, sometimes just by being asked, but will not take on others without specific reasons that might be difficult to contend with.

In the end, there are certain events that take place as the result of the efforts of agents, although under such specific circumstances that they might best be thought of not as actions but rather more as naturally occurring events like thunderstorms or traffic jams. For example, we might not think of a birthday party as an action that is performed by an agent for every effect it achieves. Even though we may be quite confident that the guests at a birthday party will be given cake to eat, it would never occur to us to try to get cake by finding a birthday party to get invited to. In contrast, a complex event like buying cake at a bakery will be understood as something that can be done just for this effect, even though many of the changes caused by its subevents (like doors opened, service numbers picked, display cases opened, and cash registers used) will be considered to be side effects only.

Factual Information about Individuals

As noted at the start of this chapter, much of what we know about the world is about specific individual things. It is true that we carry around a large number of concepts to describe these things. But the number of individual things we know at least one distinctive thing about is much larger. To take a trivial example, we know that the number 7,503, and 7,503 alone, has 7,502 as its direct predecessor.

Most of our commonsense knowledge of individuals reads like a fact sheet: John, the person who lives next door, was born in Boston, works as a barber, and has a mother called Sue; the Saturday night poker game took place in John's basement, had five players, and lasted until three in the morning. But as noted in the first section, there is a strong connection between knowledge about individuals and conceptual structures: to believe that a thing has a certain property, it must be thought of as the kind of thing that can have such a property. The conceptual structure, in other words, determines the *scope* of the fact sheet—the range of what can be known about the individual things in the world.

One thorny issue in expressing knowledge about individuals in English involves the use of noun phrases designating things in the world. Who or what do we mean by "John," "John's basement," or "Boston"? How should we understand sentences containing the phrase "John's basement" when John does not have a basement? Or has two of them?

The philosopher Bertrand Russell had a useful suggestion regarding the use of noun phrases like this in English, including names. Whenever we write something like,

John was born in Boston.

we should interpret it as saying something more like,

There is a person whose name is "John," and that person was born in a city whose name is "Boston."

What we should do, to put it another way, is clarify just what things are claimed to exist and what properties they are claimed to have. So when we say,

A game took place in John's basement.

we should interpret this as,

There is a basement that is the only one owned by a person called "John," and a game took place there.

In other words, the suggestion is to replace all noun phrases describing individuals (except maybe for strings of characters within quotation marks and numerals) by claims of the existence of things of various kinds with various properties, and where, in some cases (such as for noun phrases that use the definite article "the"), there may also be claims of uniqueness.

When it comes to knowledge about individual things, the issue of basic and derived knowledge noted above again comes into play. Suppose, for example, that we know the following:

1. *Mary is in John's basement with a flashlight.*

We might expect to then know each of these:

2. *There is a person in John's basement with a flashlight.*
3. *Someone other than Joe is in John's basement with a flashlight.*
4. *Either Alice or Mary is in John's basement with a flashlight.*

Each of these would be easily derivable from (1). The difference is that (1) identifies the individual in question as Mary, while (2), (3), and (4) leave that identity open.

The interesting possibility, however, is having something like (2) as basic knowledge, without knowing anything like (1). For example, we might spot somebody in the basement through a small, dirty window without being able to identify who it is. Similarly for (3), we might see enough to know that the person in the basement cannot possibly be Joe (who is much taller, say), but no more. For (4), we might be able to tell that it is either Alice or Mary (because they look alike, say), without being able to narrow it further.

In talking about knowledge, philosophers sometimes distinguish between *knowing that* and *knowing who*. We can know that somebody is in the basement with a flashlight without knowing who it is. We can know that a playing card has been drawn from a deck without knowing what that card is. This is an instance of what is sometimes called *incomplete* knowledge: we know that there is a sentence of the form

X *is in John's basement with a flashlight.*

that is true, but we cannot yet say what sentence it is. For (2), the X could be any person; for (3), it must be someone other than Joe; for (4), it must be Alice or Mary. We also get a similar sort of incomplete knowledge using a universal quantifier like "all":

All the paint cans in John's basement are covered in dust.

In this case, we are saying that a group of individuals have a certain property without identifying who or what those individuals are. (We will have more to say about what it means to identify an individual below.)

Why do we care about knowledge that is incomplete in this way? Primarily because when we learn about the world, whether through language or experience, we frequently acquire information in a piecemeal fashion and sometimes will need to make do with just the information we have. We may spot somebody in John's basement and need to decide what to do before we have identified the person in question as Mary.

This type of incomplete knowledge leads to serious complications when it comes to reasoning, for both machines and people. In a nutshell, we are forced to move away from a direct representation of things and their properties toward a representation of *information* about things and their properties. Putting these pieces of information together to draw conclusions can be like using clues to solve some sort of puzzle.

To see this more concretely, consider the example about three couples going to the prom presented in figure 6.2. In this case, all the relevant people and their properties are identified. If this is what we are told, then we see immediately that Gina is going to the prom with Bob. Common sense also tells us that she will not be going with Bill.

But now consider the variant presented in figure 6.3 (in the form of what is sometimes called a *logic puzzle*). This time we do *not* automatically see who is going to the prom with Gina. (For the record, it has to be Bob again. See the next paragraph below.) Identifying Gina's date using the three given

Three boy-girl couples are attending the prom. The boys that are going are Bob, Bill, and Brad, and the girls are Gabby, Gail, and Gina. Also:
- *Bob is going to the prom with Gina;*
- *Gail is going to the prom with Bill;*
- *Gabby is going to the prom with Brad.*

Who is going with Gina?

Figure 6.2
A first example concerning three couples going to the prom

Three boy-girl couples are attending the prom. The boys that are going are Bob, Bill, and Brad, and the girls are Gabby, Gail, and Gina. Also:
- *Bob is going to the prom with someone other than Gail;*
- *Gail is going to the prom with someone other than Brad;*
- *Gabby is going to the prom with Brad or Bill.*

Who is going with Gina?

Figure 6.3
A second example concerning three couples going to the prom

clues is obviously still a form of thinking, but thinking of a specialized sort: it requires a certain amount of effort, it may require pencil and paper, and not everyone is good at doing it. The conclusion that Gina is not going with Bill, while still true, is beyond the reach of mere common sense. One of the more subtle challenges in explaining the workings of common sense is accounting for the difference between these two cases. (This is something we will take up in detail in the bonus chapter at the end of this book.)

Regarding the prom puzzle, here's the reasoning. We see by the first clue that Gail is not going with Bob and by the second that she is not going with Brad either. So Gail must be going with Bill. By the third clue, Gabby is going with Brad or Bill, but since Gail is going with Bill, Gabby must be going with Brad. This leaves Gina and Bob as the final couple. Hence it is Bob who is going to the prom with Gina. Incidentally, logic puzzles typically make use of other bits of commonsense knowledge to make the puzzle more interesting. Instead of saying "with someone other than Gail" in the first clue, it might say something like "with Gail's sister." Rather than "with someone other than Brad" in the second clue, it might say "with Brad's best friend." This would not change the reasoning above: Bob is still going with Gina.

This leaves open the interesting question as to what common sense should actually do with incomplete information of this sort—that is, before any puzzle solving is even attempted. Arguably, given something like (4) above, we ought to be able to determine that Alice, Mary, or Jill is in John's basement, without having to first identify who that individual is. (More on this in the bonus chapter.)

In considering knowledge about individual things, what does it mean in general to have identified one? In the prom puzzle above, it meant being able to attach a name to the individual going with Gina to the prom: Bob,

Brad, or Bill. But there is more to it than this. We suggested above that we should understand a sentence such as (1) as if it meant something like this:

Someone whose name is "Mary" is in John's basement with a flashlight.

This is not so different from saying something like this:

Someone whose hair is brown is in John's basement with a flashlight.

Why should we think of the first sentence as having identified the individual in question but not the second? If we were imagining a world where many people had the same name, knowing the name would not be sufficient to identify one of them. Nor is it necessary; if we read a murder mystery, and it reveals at the end that it was the butler who did it, we would say that we finally know who the murderer is, even though we might not know the butler's name.

What does seem to be involved in these examples is something like this: there are a number N of individuals under consideration, presented in some way, with descriptions $d_1, d_2, \ldots d_N$, each considered to refer to a distinct thing. We then say that we know who a new description refers to if we can identify which d_i refers to the same thing. For the prom example, the individuals were presented as Bob, Brad, and Bill, so we needed to identify Gina's prom date by name. For the murder mystery, the individuals might be presented as the butler, the estranged wife, and the visiting professor, and so it might be sufficient to associate the murderer with one of those descriptions.

A common case is when the group of individuals under consideration are presented *indexically*—that is, by using phrases that make reference to the here and now: "five seconds from now," "two blocks straight ahead from here," "the watch I am wearing," or "the sign on the door to my left." This is because actions performed by agents involving other things depend on the agents knowing where those things are relative to their current coordinates rather than where they are in some more global, absolute sense. If you need to be at a certain precise location, it is not enough to find out what that location is in a global sense if you don't know where you are; it is both necessary and sufficient for you to know how to make that location become where you are (for instance, by walking ahead two blocks). Similarly, if you need to do something at a certain precise time, it is not enough to find out what that time is in a global sense if you don't know the current time; again, what you need to know is when that time is now (say, by waiting five seconds).

This indexical idea carries over to names. Suppose, for example, that you would like to shake hands with the richest person in the room. Finding out something of the form

The richest person in the room is Thurston Howell III.

may be of no help at all. You are still left wondering which person in the room has that name. On the other hand, if you come to know something more indexical like

The richest person in the room is the person to your immediate right.

you will then be in a position to shake that person's hand.

Factual Information about Kinds

Much of the factual information we care about is clearly about individual things and the properties they have. When we ask something of the form "How many *P*'s are there?" or "Is there a *P* that has property *Q*?" we are asking a factual question. How many people attended the wedding? Is there a baseball game on Tuesday? Are there any prime numbers between twenty-four and twenty-eight? The answers depend on the things we believe there to be and the properties they have.

Sometimes, however, we seem to be looking for factual information not about things but instead about kinds of things. We might ask,

How many kinds of dogs are there?

In one reading, this question is somewhat odd. If we take it to be about our conceptual structure, we might expect answers like this:

According to the way I think of the world, there are guard dogs, racing dogs, cartoon dogs, lap dogs, mongrels, snarly dogs …

This is almost certainly not what was intended. But there is a more sensible question lurking here—one not about concepts but rather about the world:

How many breeds of dog are there?

This is now a factual question, not so different from asking how many people attended a wedding. As it turns out, the World Canine Organization has the number of dog breeds currently at 339 (at the time of this writing), including ones like Bichon Frise and West Highland White Terrier, divided into ten major groups.

So distinct from the dogs themselves and the various concepts of dogs (like guard dogs, say), there are things in the world called dog breeds with properties such as origin, history, related breeds, and so on. A factual question that seems to be about the kinds of dogs is actually a question about a different sort of abstract thing altogether. Similar considerations apply to questions about the kinds of cars made by Ford, cereals produced by General Mills, and corn at the grocery store.

Once we admit the existence of things like breeds, it is natural to think of them as properties of dogs. Just as dogs can have a certain color, they can have a certain breed. (Many dogs are of mixed breed, but we ignore that complication here.) Just as we can talk about dogs whose color is brown, we can talk about dogs whose breed is Pug (one of the 339). Yet there is a difference between the two properties. What we know about a brown dog is that it is a dog and has a certain color, and it stops there. But what we know about a pug is more than that it is a dog and has a certain breed; we also know that it has distinctive wrinkles, bulging eyes, and a curly tail. (Or to be more precise, people who know dogs know this.) Where does this knowledge come from?

First of all, note that curly tails and the rest are properties of dogs, not of breeds. Furthermore, the fact that these dogs have curly tails is not some property they just happen to have like the dustiness of the paint cans in John's basement mentioned in the previous section. We might imagine saying something like

All the dogs whose breed is Pug have curly tails.

the same way we might say

All the dogs at the dog show were wearing red dog collars.

but the emphasis is wrong. The curly tails are somehow inherent in the breed. (Information about ad hoc collections, like the paint cans in the basement or dogs at the dog show, is interesting in its own right. See the bonus chapter for more.) This suggests that what we have in mind is something more like the concept of a pug. Just as birthday parties have birthday cakes, pugs have curly tails:

A pug is a dog that has wrinkles, bulging eyes, a curly tail, …

The description would go on to mention its flat nose, short hair, size, and so on. Presumably, we would want to say something about its breed too:

A pug is a dog whose breed is Pug.

This is correct, but misses the fact that if you have a dog and its breed is Pug then that is enough for it to be a pug, regardless of any other property it may or may not have. The *sufficiency* of this property is something that might be expressed using the word "any" as follows:

A pug is any dog whose breed is Pug. It has wrinkles, bulging eyes, a curly tail, …

This is similar to how we might present other concepts with a sufficiency condition, such as

A quadruped is any animal that has four legs.

as opposed to

A horse is an animal that has four legs.

So to recap: factual questions about kinds of things are best understood as questions about certain abstract things like breeds of dogs, brands of cereals, models of cars, and varieties of corn. These abstract things (call them types) can have properties in their own right, such as when they were first introduced. Properties of the underlying things (that is, the dogs, cereals, cars, and ears of corn) are then expressed in the usual way as part of a conceptual structure, with the extra stipulation of a sufficiency condition in terms of the corresponding type.

A Challenge to Conceptual Structures

In bringing this chapter to a close, we do not mean to suggest that we have exhausted the sorts of issues that arise. There are many topics where even the simplest forms of commonsense knowledge are quite challenging to put into words. To conclude this chapter, we want to consider this challenge one last time, but from a slightly different perspective.

In thinking about factual knowledge concerning the world, it is tempting to think of a statement like

1. *There is a red boat on the lake.*

as being similar to a statement like

2. *There is a prime number between twenty-four and twenty-eight.*

They both talk about what things there are and what properties they have. But a belief in something like (1) has to take into account what we mean by "red," "boat," and "lake." These terms are vague, and as already noted, people can legitimately disagree on their boundaries. Just what do we mean by the word "red" anyway? Is red wine really red? And what does it mean to be of a certain color? Does the entire surface of the object have to be of that color, or just a good part of it? How much? And what do we mean by "boat"? Are we including toy boats? Rafts with some sort of seating arrangement on them? Finally, what do we mean by "on the lake"? Can we believe that (1) is false while believing there is a red boat tied to a dock near the shore?

This kind of hairsplitting might seem laughable, only of interest to somebody like a lawyer trying to win an argument on a technicality. (It brings to mind the famous Bill Clinton line, "It depends on what the meaning of the word 'is' is.") But behind it there is a serious challenge to the whole idea of commonsense knowledge.

The challenge is this: perhaps what we think of as commonsense knowledge is something that cannot be expressed in words after all. Maybe we are fooling ourselves when we use ordinary English words like "red," "boat," and "lake." Perhaps what we have is a collection of ideas connected to a range of actual experiences in a way that does not carve the world into discrete nameable categories like "red," "boat," and "lake" at all. Brian Cantwell Smith puts it this way:

Yes, we may talk as if the world were ontologically discrete; and yes, too, we may believe that we think that way. It seems increasingly likely, however, that such intuitions reflect the discrete, combinatorial nature of language and articulation more than any underlying ontological facts, and also more than the patterns of tacit and intuitive thinking on which our articulations depends.

So categories exemplified by words like "red," "boat," and "lake" might be more about how we *talk*, not how the world is, nor how we *think* about it.

If this were true, then what would we actually believe in this case involving the red boat? Here is one way to put it. Imagine saying something like

(3) below while pointing to some nearby boats, some color swatches, and a lake:

> *3. There is something like these things, having a color like this or this, located on the surface of a region similar to this one here.*

We are still using words in (3), of course, but without assuming an underlying conceptual structure involving the color red, boats, and lakes.

This way of thinking about commonsense knowledge has the nice advantage of making a direct connection to past experiences. Instead of thinking of something as being "red," we think of it as being similar (in some way) to a collection of previously perceived hues that may or may not have a label. No prototypes; only a raft of undifferentiated perceptual exemplars. (This could have important ramifications in building AI systems that perform low-level perceptual learning and still exhibit common sense.)

Is the challenge itself correct, though? It is no doubt true that we have knowledge we never expect to be able to put into words: how to ride a bicycle; in what way Jimmy looks like his cousin Sammy; the taste of lime as distinct from lemon. But when we do manage to put things into words, such as (1), are we just fooling ourselves in thinking this is how we think about it?

As we have tried to argue here, our view is that a conceptual structure is indeed much more than a way of talking about the world. It has a direct bearing on what an intelligent agent uses in deciding what to do.

Go back to the example at the start of this chapter: baseball. Do we really want to claim that a *double play* is just a way of talking about baseball, not a way of thinking about it? When a shortstop makes a decision to throw the ball to second base rather than to first base, are there no baseball concepts involved in that decision, like how many are *out* in the inning, but only a collection of past experiences of people running around, throwing balls, and swinging bats? Similarly, when we decide to say "Happy Birthday!" to one particular child in the room yet to none of the others, are there no birthday concepts involved in that decision, but only past experiences of being among groups of animated children wearing party hats? This all seems highly unlikely, contrary to what Smith says.

Not to minimize the importance of perceptual learning in a game like baseball, but learning that a shortstop ends up throwing to first base the vast majority of the time is neither here nor there. What matters are the *reasons* to act one way or another, and these, it seems to us, involve baseball concepts. In baseball, there are some crucial considerations such as how many are out that players are expected to know and take into account, but are not determined by or recoverable from the immediate perceptual field of play. AI scientist Rodney Brooks's antirepresentation maxim, "the world is its own best model" (roughly, "if you need to find out something, look to the world itself, not to models of it"), may be at least plausible for activities like soccer and Go (or for some part of them, anyway), but clearly not for baseball, nor for birthday parties, nor, we submit, for many of the commonsense situations we find ourselves in.

In the end, the challenge might best be thought of as an empirical issue. Smith feels that symbolic AI failed to produce systems that behaved intelligently in part because they were shackled to an overly simplistic breakdown of the world—that is, into nameable things and properties. Our sense is different: they failed because they did not give commonsense knowledge and commonsense reasoning their proper due. Time will tell.

7   Representation and Reasoning, Part I

All knowledge is connected to all other knowledge.
The fun is in making the connections.
  —Arthur Aufderheide, quoted in "The Mummy Doctor," by Kevin Krajick

Having spent the last two chapters elaborating on the idea of commonsense knowledge, it is time to look at what it might mean to actually put such knowledge to use in a machine. This begins our transition from discussing knowledge in informal English terms to how that knowledge can be captured in a machine and processed. (We are not going to try to cover everything raised in previous chapters, but only some of the main ideas.)

As already noted, the KR hypothesis implies that the story we need to tell in the next two chapters will be a *symbolic* one: an agent will represent some of its commonsense knowledge in symbolic form and then perform computational operations over those symbolic structures for purposes related to the actions it might need to take. In this chapter, we sketch how commonsense knowledge might be represented in connected symbolic structures we call *models* and some of the basic processing over those models. In the next chapter, we discuss how to represent *propositions* in symbolic form and how to reason with models in a more complex way.

In this chapter and the next, we will be proposing a variety of symbolic structures that can be used for commonsense representation and reasoning, based on our own experience in this area of research. But there are many ways of doing this, and other AI researchers have worked with quite different forms of symbolic representation and reasoning. For this book, we have made the symbolic structures look a lot like English expressions to make them somewhat easier to read, yet it is worth remembering that they are nonetheless symbols intended for machine consumption. What matters is not really how easily we humans can read and interpret them but rather what machines will be able to do with them.

In trying to understand how common sense can be built on a foundation of symbols and symbol processing, it will be necessary to peel back the familiar outer shell of common sense and look closely at the workings of the machinery underneath. We believe this to be a critical stretch of the road to common sense, but it is also a more demanding one: the topics are drier, less intuitive, and, admittedly, less commonsensical. Once we make it to chapter 9, the road will be easier going again, as we see where the symbolic machinery we have examined can be put to use in making more familiar commonsense decisions about how to behave.

World Models

In considering how to represent commonsense knowledge, it is useful to separate what needs to be represented into two distinct realms. As suggested in the previous chapter, two different types of knowledge need to be accounted for:

- knowledge of individual things in the world (like "John" and "Boston") and their properties, which make up a state of the world;
- knowledge of the concepts in a conceptual structure (like "hospital" and "birthday party"), which are general ideas about the kinds of things there can be and the kinds of properties they can have.

Correspondingly, a representation of commonsense knowledge will have two parts: a world model to represent a state of the world, and a conceptual model to represent a conceptual structure—a framework of generalizations that can be used to classify items in the world.

In the simplest possible terms, a world model is a symbolic structure intended to reflect in a direct way a fragment of some world state under consideration. Because we are imagining a world made up of things with properties, the world model will be made up of symbols standing for those things and symbols standing for properties of those things, all connected in a certain way.

This is easily seen with an example. Suppose we are considering a world with two people, John and Sue, where Sue is John's birth mother. A representation of this world would be one where there would be a symbol standing for John—we'll use John for now—and a symbol standing for

Sue—we'll use Sue. (In general, we'll use this font to show symbols in a world or conceptual model.) Next, we will need a symbol representing the concept of a person—person—and a symbol representing the birth mother relationship—birthMother—that holds between John and Sue. Finally, we need a way of grouping these symbols to represent the connections among them. The simplest such grouping is as a sequence of symbols:

```
John is a person.
Sue is a person.
John has Sue as a birthMother.
```

This is really all there is to a world model: it is a collection of expressions of the same form as these three sentences. The content symbols—the John, Sue, person, and birthMother—will change from sentence to sentence; the other symbols—the is, a (or an), has, and as—will always be the same. In fact, we could have left those out and used something more like

```
(John person)
(Sue person)
(John Sue birthMother)
```

to similar effect, but the symbolic structures would have been harder for people to read. (To further help in the reading, we are capitalizing the names of individual things, while leaving the names of properties to start with lowercase letters.)

Before moving on, however, it is worth making a few changes to the three sentences above. First, we are better off not using names like John and Sue directly in the world model, since many entities can have the same names. Instead we will use numbered symbols with a special "#" character in them to represent individual things in the world, with separate properties connecting them to identifying strings (within quotation marks) or numbers. So for John and Sue, we might have something like this:

```
Person#17 is a person.
Person#17 has "John" as a firstName.
Person#16 is a person.
Person#16 has "Sue" as a firstName.
```

Second, instead of directly representing John as having Sue as his mother, we might want to analyze this property further and say that the property actually derives from an underlying event involving both of them: the event of John's birth. Besides indirectly representing the relationship

between John and Sue, this allows us to consider additional properties of
the event itself, such as where and when it took place.

Using this idea, the following would replace the `birthMother` sentence
above. First, a representation for the city of Boston, `City#18`:

```
City#18 is a city.
City#18 has "Boston" as an englishName.
```

Next, a representation for a spatial point somewhere in Boston, `SpacePt#25`:

```
SpacePt#25 is a pointInSpace.
SpacePt#25 has City#18 as an enclosingCity.
```

Then, a representation for a time point in 1979, `TimePt#24`:

```
TimePt#24 is a pointInTime.
TimePt#24 has 1979 as an enclosingYear.
```

And finally, a representation for the specific event in question, `Event#23`,
John's birth to Sue somewhere in Boston sometime in 1979:

```
Event#23 is a birthEvent.
Event#23 has Person#17 as a baby.
Event#23 has Person#16 as a mother.
Event#23 has TimePt#24 as a time.
Event#23 has SpacePt#25 as a location.
Person#17 has Event#23 as a birth.
```

So rather than representing John as something that has Sue as a birth
mother directly, we represent him as being part of a (human) birth event
where Sue is the mother involved. With these symbolic structures, we no
longer use the `birthMother` symbol itself. In the next chapter, we will see
how to reintroduce that symbol to represent a *derived property*: a person will
be considered to be a birth mother of another precisely when there is an
associated birth event with the right properties. (At a deeper level of detail,
we might want to further analyze the birth event itself, casting it, on the
one hand, as a complex series of subevents with other individuals involved
like nurses and midwives, and on the other hand, as the culmination of
a reproductive process, with still other individuals involved such as the
father, and possibly donors and surrogates.)

The basic structure of a world model is summarized in the first item of
figure 7.1. (The remaining two items of the figure, the conceptual model
and derivation clauses, will be discussed later.)

World Model:

- a link from an individual to a concept.
    Person#17 is a person.

- a link from an individual to another individual via a role.
    Person#17 has Event#23 as a birth.

Conceptual Model:

- *Concept*: a category linked to a more general one.
    A person is a kind of animal.
    A birthEvent is a kind of event.

- *Role*: a basic property associated with a concept.
    Having a duration is a property of an event.
    Having a mother is a property of a birthEvent.

- *Restriction*: a limit on the number or category of a role filler.
    nr#29: A birthEvent has 1 associated baby.
    vr#26: A mother of a birthEvent is a woman.

- *Annotation*: a cancellation or a default filler for a role.
    ann#504: The restriction nr#29 is canceled
              for a multipleBirth.
    ann#702: A duration defaults to 1 for an event.

Derivation Clauses: (presented in chapter 8)

- an expression using "when" and a formula from the language $\mathcal{L}$,
  used to represent a derived property.
    Person:x has Person:y as a birthMother
              when
    there is an Event:z where
        Person:x has Event:z as a birth and
        Event:z has Person:y as a mother

Figure 7.1
The components of a knowledge base

While using short sentences like those above in a world model is quite sufficient for the computations to follow, as the models get larger, it becomes increasingly difficult for a human reader to get insight into what is going on. For this reason, a world model is often displayed as a graph with nodes and edges that can be much easier for people to look at and absorb, as in figure 7.2. (To orient yourself, notice that the leftmost circle represents Sue and the rightmost one represents Boston.)

So what do these sentences in a world model mean exactly? What would a computational system having a model like the one above believe about its world? We are not fully ready to answer that question since we have not yet discussed propositions, and as already noted, propositions are the things that are believed. The question will be answered in detail in the next chapter, but we can give a rough summary here. An agent using a world model to represent a state of the world believes that in that state, a certain number of things exist with a certain number of properties. (As discussed before, an agent can also use a world model to represent counterfactual states of the world, such as ones that are in the past or future, ones that other agents believe in, and other imagined ones.) The names like Person#17 and SpacePt#25 will turn out not to matter at all as long as they are kept distinct from each other. Names like person and enclosing-City, on the other hand, actually refer to elements of the agent's conceptual model, the categories the agent uses to think about the world, which we will get to in a moment.

And what are the reasoning operations to perform on a world model? The main ones will be discussed in the next chapter since they too involve propositions. Still, we can already imagine some interesting operations that do not involve propositions directly, but rather connections among individuals, as in the following:

In what way is John connected to Sue?

He has a birth event where Sue is the mother.

In what way is John connected to Fenway Park?

He was born in a city that has Fenway Park as a local baseball stadium.

In what way is John connected to Pennsylvania?

He was born in the year when there was a major nuclear accident near Harrisburg ("Three Mile Island"), which is the capital of Pennsylvania.

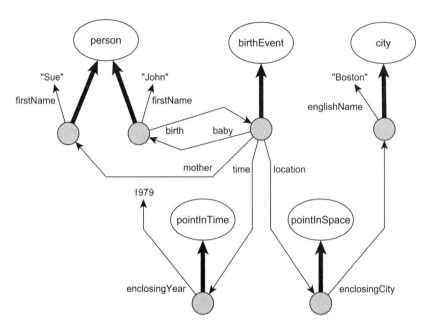

Figure 7.2
A graphical version of a world model

To determine these connections, we can imagine a computational operation, **FIND-PATH**, that would take as its arguments (that is, as its input parameters) two symbols representing individuals in the world. For example, we might invoke **FIND-PATH** with the symbols representing John and Sue. **FIND-PATH** would use the world model to compute a path connecting the two. Such a path would be a sequence of symbols representing relationships and other individuals. (See the appendix of the book for how this operation might be defined.) We will have nothing further to say about this reasoning operation here except to note that something like it would be useful for what is sometimes called *associative thinking*, such as finding individuals brought to mind by other individuals.

Conceptual Models

Let us now turn to conceptual models. We can think of a conceptual structure from the previous chapter as something like a world. It's not a world of things and properties, however, as in the previous section; it's a world of *ideas*: general concepts of things, their parts, and their relationships with other ideas. These can be represented in a symbolic structure similar to a world model—a conceptual model.

For our purposes, we can think of concepts as having three kinds of parts: *roles, restrictions,* and *annotations*. Roles are the properties and essential relationships associated with the concept, restrictions are constraints on the fillers of the roles associated with the concept, and annotations concern how to interpret various other parts of the concept. (See the second part of figure 7.1.)

Let us look at some examples. Consider the concept of a birth event and the mother relationship, as used in the previous section. A conceptual model might contain the following:

```
A birthEvent is a kind of thing.
Having a mother is a property of a birthEvent.
```

So for concepts and roles, we have expressions in the conceptual model like the two sentences above. The content symbols in these sentences are birthEvent, thing, and mother; all the other symbols are just there to make readable sentences expressing the essential connections among the content symbols. Other concepts like person and city, and other roles like baby and enclosingYear, would be handled in an analogous way. (From now on, for ease of wording, we will sometimes use a symbol representing a concept as a way of referring to the concept itself. So when we say, "Other concepts like person and city," what we really mean is, "Other concepts like the ones represented by the symbol person and the symbol city.")

Let us now turn to restrictions. A *value restriction* is used to constrain the kind of things that can be fillers of a role. Here is an illustration:

```
vr#26: A mother of a birthEvent is a woman.
```

In this case, we use the symbol vr#26 to represent the restriction on the kind of filler expected for the mother role for the birthEvent concept. (Just as concepts and roles have names, the restrictions have names so that later annotations can refer to them directly.) The content symbols here are vr#26, mother, birthEvent, and woman.

A *number restriction* is similar to a value restriction and is used to constrain the number of things that can be fillers of a role. Here is an example:

```
nr#28: A birthEvent has 1 associated mother.
```

The symbol nr#28 in this case is used to represent the restriction on the number of fillers expected for the mother role for the birthEvent concept. The content symbols are nr#28, mother, birthEvent, and the numeral 1. (Had the number been larger, we would have wanted to pluralize the mother symbol for readability.) Note that the number of roles that are associated with a concept is not the same as the number of fillers; a single role like the parent role might have two fillers, and conversely, a company might have a CEO and president, but those two roles might be filled by the same person.

Conceptual models (or some parts of them anyway) are often displayed in a graphical form analogous to that for world models, as seen in figure 7.3. Note that the links in this diagram now involve value restrictions: for the concept birthEvent, the mother role is restricted to be a woman; and for pointInSpace, the enclosingCity is restricted to be a city. (The broad link between woman and person will be discussed in the next section.)

Before diving into other aspects of conceptual models, let us briefly review how they are connected to world models. We saw that things in the world could have properties involving other things. For instance, in the previous section, we had

```
Event#23 is a birthEvent.
Event#23 has Person#16 as a mother.
```

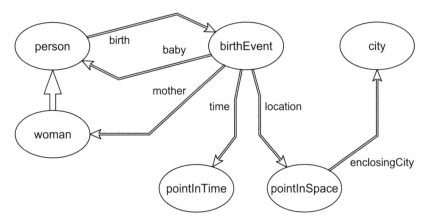

Figure 7.3
A partial conceptual model

This was a way of representing a specific birth event where Sue was the mother involved. This fragment of the world model is clearly related to a fragment of the conceptual model above:

    A birthEvent is a kind of thing.
    Having a mother is a property of a birthEvent.

In other words, the idea that Event#23 is a birth event where Sue is the mother is contingent on the more general notion that birth events are the kinds of things that have associated mothers. Had Event#23 been a baseball game instead of a birth, we would not have expected to see this mother relationship in the world model. Furthermore, because of the number and value restrictions above, we expect the mother (in this case, Sue) to be a woman and the sole filler of that role. In general, the fillers of roles in the world model respect the restrictions specified in the conceptual model. (But we will see later how exceptions can occur.)

We can also imagine other sorts of restrictions associated with concepts beyond the number and value restrictions seen above. These would be other properties that the fillers of the roles might be expected to jointly satisfy, expressed perhaps using the formulas presented in the next chapter.

Taxonomies

In addition to having parts like roles and restrictions, concepts can be related directly to each other. The most important such relation is that of one concept being a *subconcept* of another, meaning that as ideas, the former includes the latter. For example, we might have

    A person is a kind of mammal.

This declares a person to be a kind of mammal rather than just a thing. Besides identifying the relationship between the two concepts, the upshot is that anything in the world identified as a person can be thought of as a mammal too. Displaying subconcept/superconcept relationships like this graphically results in the familiar sort of taxonomic diagram shown in figure 7.4. The broad link in figure 7.3 between woman and person is an instance of this kind of relationship.

Related to the birthEvent examples in the text above, our conceptual model might contain the following:

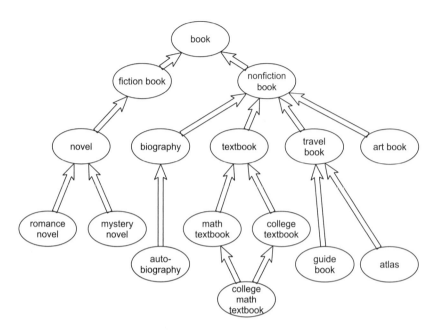

Figure 7.4
A taxonomy of concepts about books

```
A birthEvent is a kind of liveMammalBirth.
A birthEvent is a kind of medicalProcedure.
```

(This is of course for those births that are handled by medical personnel.) Then, any roles, restrictions, and annotations that are part of liveMammal- Birth or medicalProcedure would be considered to be parts of birthEvent as well. As we will see in the next section, these parts are said to be *inherited*— unless they are explicitly canceled with an annotation.

As already noted, organizing concepts into a taxonomy of subconcepts and superconcepts is a powerful way to organize a large collection of them in a modular way. For instance, the idea of a human birth involving a mother, baby, and other things is actually something inherited from the more general notion of a mammalian live birth (as opposed to births from eggs). So we imagine the concept liveMammalBirth having roles for the mother and baby as well as value and number restrictions. The birthEvent concept would then inherit all of this structure, with only two local restric- tions of its own, ensuring that the fillers of these two roles are persons and not just mammals. (A concept can have or inherit many restrictions pertaining to the same role. These should be understood as all applying simultaneously.) Similarly, the time and location roles for birthEvent used in the world model of the first section might be inherited from the more general concept of an event. The medicalProcedure concept would also inherit these two roles since it is a kind of event, and perhaps restrict the location to be within a hospital—a restriction that birthEvent would then inherit as well.

Inheritance and Cancellation

While it is generally useful to be able to say that one concept is a sub-concept of another, this utility would be severely diminished if we had to commit to believing that every instance of the former had to have all the properties of the latter. To take a famous example in AI, we might think of birds as animals that get around by flying, and penguins as birds, but we do not want to be forced into thinking that penguins get around by flying. It is true that by and large, birds fly, and that is certainly part of the idea of a bird, yet there are many exceptions, including penguins, ostriches, kiwis, and others. Birds also have a fairly standard size, but as noted before, bee hummingbirds and royal albatrosses have sizes that are exceptional.

What this suggests is that in addition to roles and restrictions, concepts can have annotations of the sort discussed before to override the parts of a superconcept that do not apply. Annotations within a conceptual model will be represented with sentences similar to those for restrictions. To see an example, first consider a number restriction on the baby role for the birthEvent concept:

    nr#29: A birthEvent has 1 associated baby.

This reflects the expectation that under normal circumstances, a birth event will involve only a single baby. Since this is not always the case, we might have the following in a conceptual model to account for multiple births:

    A multipleBirth is a kind of birthEvent.
    ann#504: The restriction nr#29 is canceled for a multipleBirth.

The first sentence says that a multiple birth (for twins, triplets, and so on) is a kind of birth event; the second one says that for a multiple birth, there is an annotation (ann#504) that cancels the restriction on the number of babies involved (nr#29). The content words in the annotation are ann#504,

nr#29, and multipleBirth. Subconcepts of multipleBirth (like twinBirth)
are then free to add new number restrictions of their own. Value restrictions
and other parts of concepts can be overridden analogously.

With this notion of cancellation, we can now be specific about what
it means for a concept to inherit a part from another concept and in a
defeasible way. We imagine a procedure **GET-PARTS** that operates on the
symbolic structures in a conceptual model. **GET-PARTS** takes as argument
a symbol representing a concept, and returns as value the symbols representing all the roles, restrictions, and annotations that the concept has or
inherits according to the current conceptual model. The idea is this: one
concept is a subconcept of another if there is a (perhaps empty) chain of
"is a" links from one to the other (for example, from person to mammal to
animal to livingThing, and so on). Then **GET-PARTS** will return a part (such
as a number restriction, say) if the given concept is a subconcept of another
that is directly associated with the part (within a number restriction sentence in the conceptual model) and there is no annotation inherited for the
concept that cancels that part. Of course, for this cancellation annotation
to be inherited, it must itself not be canceled by a second annotation that is
not canceled by a third, and so on. (See the appendix for the exact details.)

Note that although we still have not talked about propositions, we can
already see that the **GET-PARTS** operation is a form of reasoning. It will allow
us to conclude, for example, that border collies have four legs from that
property of dogs in general. By the time we get to the bottom of the taxonomy, concepts will inherit a rich structure of roles, restrictions, and annotations from all their superconcepts. Moreover, the **GET-PARTS** operation can
be expected to be readily computed even in large conceptual models. We
would expect a taxonomy to be a structure where each concept is below
only a small number of more general concepts, making it quite feasible
to search up these "is a" links even in extremely large taxonomies. (The
inheritance would be considerably more complicated if these links could
themselves be canceled. See the next section.)

Defaults and Other Annotations

Perhaps the most useful annotation for a concept is that of a *default filler* for
a role. Consider, for example, a representation for the generic concept of an
event, which might include the idea that it has a duration in seconds. (As

already discussed, we might prefer a more elaborate representation of this duration as a quantity that maps to different numbers for different units of measure, but we are taking the simplified view here.) We can specify a default filler for this durationInSeconds role by adding an annotation like this:

```
ann#706: A durationInSeconds defaults to 1 for an event.
```

This says that for the event concept, there is an annotation (ann#706) that provides a default filler of 1 for the durationInSeconds role. What it stipulates, in effect, is that if we are looking for a filler for the role and have no reason to prefer any other value, we can use the default value, understanding that it may be dislodged by other considerations. So if we have no reason to believe otherwise, we will assume that the duration of an event is one second.

The notion of a default value for a role is a powerful idea and makes an enormous difference in how the representations will be used.

Here is one application. The idea of canceling subconcept/superconcept relationships has been proposed in the AI literature to allow, for instance, penguin to be a subconcept of bird, and bird to be a subconcept of flyingAnimal, without requiring penguin to be a subconcept of flyingAnimal. As mentioned above, that proposal leads to considerable complications in the definition of inheritance (compared to the **GET-PARTS** defined in the appendix), so much so that determining if a property is inherited can end up looking more like a logical puzzle. But that flies in the face of our view that commonsense reasoning should be fast and easy.

Some of these complications can be avoided by using default values. We start by representing categories with strict sufficiency conditions like flyingAnimal not as concepts to be further specialized but rather as derived properties. (We will see how to do this in the next chapter.) In other words, something is considered to be a flying animal precisely when it is an animal whose mode of locomotion is flying—no more, no less. Then instead of saying that bird is a subconcept of flyingAnimal, we say that the bird concept has Flying as its *default* mode of locomotion. The penguin concept can then be a subconcept of bird as desired, but cancel this default with another annotation.

There is one final piece of the puzzle left to consider in how these representations will be used, and that is the idea of the *importance* of a role as well as the *strength* of a restriction or annotation.

If we were to explicitly represent in a world model everything that was required to exist according to the conceptual model, each person would have a birth event, and each birth event would involve a mother—a person older than the baby. That person would in turn have a birth event involving a mother and so on. This implies a world model with an infinite number of people!

But when representing a person, we may choose not to represent explicitly their birth, even though we know there must be one. It may or may not be important to think about the birth when thinking about the person. This importance is determined by an annotation indicating how central the role is (a priori) to the concept in question:

```
ann#501: A birth has an importance of 0.6 for a person.
```

Taking these importance numbers to be between 0.0 and 1.0, we can think of annotation ann#501 as saying that the birth of a person is a fairly important (0.6) property, but not be overly concerned about ignoring it. So it's not that Sue did not have a birth; it's that we judged the event to be less important than other things in the model. To the point, we did not expect her birth to be the subject of the sort of reasoning operations considered in the next chapter. As our attention changes, though, we may need to extend the model and consider her birth; we discuss this in the next section.

The idea of the strength of a restriction or annotation is similar. Consider birthEvent again. While we want to allow for a birth involving multiple babies, we should certainly be much more surprised (or rather, shocked) to see a birth involving multiple birth mothers. This suggests that the restriction on the number of mother fillers (nr#28 above) in a birthEvent is much stronger than the one on the number of baby fillers (nr#29 above). We could introduce new annotations for this, but it is easier to assume that restrictions and annotations can have an extra part in the sentence indicating an (a priori) strength. So the two number restrictions above might be specified as follows:

```
nr#28: A birthEvent has 1 associated mother (strength 1.0).
nr#29: A birthEvent has 1 associated baby (strength 0.9).
```

Here we are insisting categorically (1.0) that the number of mothers is as given—that is, one. But our belief about there being exactly one baby is not quite as strong. Similarly, the typical duration of an event might be specified by something like

```
ann#706: A durationInSeconds defaults to 1 for an event
        (strength 0.1).
```

which says that the default is quite loosely attached; it's a weak default. A subconcept of event like moviePerformance or birthdayParty can cancel this default duration, and propose a different default with a much higher strength.

Incidentally, it might make more sense to use order of magnitude numbers to capture wide gradations in the strengths. The strength of the restriction on there being one baby in a birth might be 2 (all but one birth in a few hundred, say), but on there being one birth mother, it might be more like 11 (all but one birth in a hundred billion), allowing that the restriction could still be violated in principle, such as for mothers who happen to be conjoined twins.

We can imagine other varieties of annotations. Here we mention three. First, we might use annotations to record *similarities* among concepts. For instance, whales are similar to fish, wagons are similar to cars, and hospitals are similar to churches. Analogies offer additional examples: Rutherford atoms are like solar systems, arguments are like war, and time is like money. A similarity annotation would connect a concept to a mapping from some of the parts of the concept to some of the parts of another. Among other things, this would be useful in doing the sort of differential diagnosis mentioned before (and below).

Second, we might want to annotate the properties of individuals in a world model. In the model about John's birth in the first section, we had

```
Event#23 is a birthEvent.
Event#23 has SpacePt#25 as a location.
```

Here, Event#23 stood for his birth, and SpacePt#25 stood for a location in Boston. We might want to record in an annotation about how we came to believe that the event took place there. If this was a default assignment, say, we can record how strongly we feel about this use of the default. If we then draw additional conclusions from this assignment, we will want to record their sources as well. These annotations will have a role to play if we end up having to reconsider where John was born.

A third possible application of annotations concerns metalevel concepts and roles. We can treat a number restriction sentence in a conceptual model like this

```
nr#29: A birthEvent has 1 associated baby (strength 0.9).
```

as if it were an abbreviation for a collection of smaller sentences as follows:

```
birthEvent has nr#29 as a PART.
```

```
nr#29 is a NUMBER-RESTRICTION.
nr#29 has baby as a SUBJECT.
nr#29 has 1.0 as an OBJECT.
nr#29 has 0.9 as a STRENGTH.
```

The other sentences in conceptual models, for annotations, concepts, and roles, can all be expanded analogously. These expansions make a conceptual model look exactly like a world model, but at a metalevel: the individuals are represented by symbols like birthEvent, location, and ann#706; the concepts are represented by symbols like NUMBER-RESTRICTION and ROLE; and the roles are represented by symbols like PART and SUBJECT. We might take this opportunity to replace symbols like birthEvent and location with ones like Concept#19 and Role#58, as we did for the symbols representing individuals in world models, to allow for the fact that more than one idea can have the same English name.

Figure 7.5 shows a portion of the earlier figure 7.3 as a world model at the metalevel. (To get one's bearings, note that the upper-leftmost individual

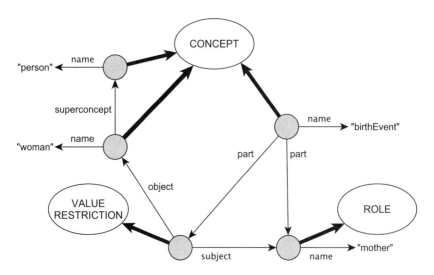

Figure 7.5
Metalevel world model for a portion of the conceptual model of figure 7.3

represents the concept person and the upper-rightmost individual represents the concept birthEvent. The bottom-center individual represents the value restriction vr#26.) The metalevel individuals could then be annotated as above. For example, the OBJECT role of a number restriction could have a default value of 1, and the STRENGTH role of an annotation could default to 0.4. These typical values could then be used if no others can be found, and could themselves be further annotated.

Adding to a World Model

As remarked above, as our attention shifts, we may need to extend our world model to include additional things and properties. Thinking about Sue as a person in her own right and not just as John's mother, for example, we would want to look at other properties we expect to see in a person. To do so, we can use the **GET-PARTS** procedure mentioned above to find the roles for the person concept. In this case, the birth role (perhaps inherited from mammal) might be deemed important enough at this point that we would want a symbol in the model standing for its filler, just as we had for John. According to a value restriction on this role, the filler should be a birth event. So there needs to be a new birth event for the birth of Sue in the model. (It is possible that there is already a symbol standing for this event. See below.)

So we would need to instantiate the birthEvent concept. We look at all the roles for this concept (via **GET-PARTS** again), and decide which ones are important enough to have their fillers represented. We see, for instance, that the baby role should be filled by a person. We may also find, however, that there is a relevant restriction from the person concept: the baby of a birth of a person should be that person. (These sorts of restrictions are known as role-chain equalities.) So the newly minted birth event would have Sue as the filler of the baby role. The birthEvent concept has other roles like mother, time, and location that might be left unfilled for now, and other inherited roles (such as for duration) that are even less important.

What are the conditions that would compel us to engage in extending a world model in this way? The main thing is that for one reason or another, we want to shift our focus away from the things we were previously thinking about.

This could be a bottom-up impetus. Perhaps we observed something new in our immediate surroundings; perhaps we were told something that mentions some new things or properties. But there could also be a top-down impetus. Perhaps we decided to perform some sort of perceptual action like looking into a box to find out what new objects it contains. Perhaps we need to consider some new objects to achieve a goal of interest; maybe we need oven gloves to pick up a hot pot or boots to go outside in the snow.

Whatever the reason, we are pushed toward extending the world model to include new things and properties. We would expect the impetus to be more or less specific about what new things and properties ought to be included. If we are told that Sue's mother is a person whom we did not know about before, then we would extend the model to include her, and a new birth event with Sue as the baby and that person as the mother. We might also include annotations to the effect that this elaboration of the model was the result of something we were told.

But if we need to think about John's mother and grandmother with no additional information, we would not have much to go on in deciding whether the people involved were already represented in the model. A reasonable guess would be that they are new, and we would change the model accordingly. Similarly, if a role has a high enough importance, we want to represent its filler, even with no definite idea about who or what that filler is. This is the primary job for defaults: they are values to use when no other information is available. In all such cases, however, we would want to annotate the fact that assumptions are being made that might need to be corrected later. (See the last section of this chapter.)

The process would be much the same if we were to find out that the birth city of Sue was Phoenix. We might expect to leave out all the properties for the new location item other than its enclosing city, as we did for John.

Yet a much more complex situation arises if we were to learn somehow that Sue's birth city was either Phoenix or Tucson without finding out which. We might choose to use one of the two cities (chosen at random) as above, perhaps with an annotation saying that it was picked randomly, in case the choice was later found to be wrong. Or we might prefer to treat the information about Sue's birth city as some sort of clue to a puzzle to be solved later, like Gabby's date for the prom in the puzzle of chapter 6. It might be tempting to simply generalize the world model representation to include a special new notation for this case, but this does not really resolve the issue. The world model would no longer represent the enclosing city as it did before, but only some *information* about that city. That information is challenging to reason with, whatever notation is adopted. (This is taken up in the bonus chapter.)

A more sophisticated approach is also possible. We might ask ourselves, What do we know about the two given cities in question? We can look at our conceptual model and find the most specific concept that includes both cities. We might know, for instance, that they are both cities in the state of Arizona. We can then expand the model to record the enclosing state: instead of using an enclosingCity property as before, we would use an enclosingState property. We lose information in doing this—and a lot of information when we are given two cases that have little in common such as Tucson and Timbuktu—but there is a clear advantage: we get to add some relevant information about the location to the world model without having to solve a logic puzzle or make unwarranted guesses.

Adding to a Conceptual Model

We've now introduced enough technical machinery to imagine building a sizable knowledge base in a computer with richly textured concepts that describe individual things that the computer might encounter in its world. In the previous chapter, we focused on the kinds of things and properties we might want to represent. If we go back to our observations about common sense in humans, we are reminded that it is largely about everyday things and events, remembered in order to support drawing quick, plausible conclusions. When we see a few examples in the world of what feels to be the same kind of thing, we are quick to generalize and start to simplify how we remember those things; we are inclined to form a new concept capturing some of the more salient properties.

Imagine the first time we encounter cars. We might see a black one, white one, and silver one, and then many other silver ones. We might see a convertible or two, but mainly sedans. As we notice their many perceptual similarities, we are likely to automatically imagine a new concept of which they could all be said to be instances. As a result of the distribution of the examples we observe, we might be inclined to build our concept of a car to mimic the common case of a silver four-door sedan. As we know, there are many exceptions, but the easiest way to remember that might simply be to have the color of our car concept have silver as a default, though with weak strength. So seeing a red car doesn't cause any consternation (as we will see in the next section), simply the abandonment of silver as the default color. On the other hand, generally our defaults of cars having four wheels and windshields will be much stronger, since we almost never see cars with fewer wheels or without windshields.

This notion of creating a concept that reflects the most common characteristics of members of a class not only makes sense in terms of the ease of constructing new concepts and remembering new things but has been commonly observed by psychologists about human memory too. We remember specific representative exemplars or perhaps constructed prototypes of a concept rather than the details about every member of a class we encounter. As mentioned in chapter 2, psychologists like Sir Frederic Bartlett observed that much of human memory appears to be based on such prototypes and a form of reconstruction as opposed to an exact memory of the details observed. People often make poor eyewitnesses unless the person (or crime) they observe has some remarkably unusual aspect that does not match our generally quite-generic remembered prototypes. Bartlett suggested that memory may work by remembering not photographic representations of individual things observed but instead generic versions of what is observed plus salient exceptions—differences between how the item we've observed *ought* to have appeared and how it actually appeared. The more unusual the exceptions, the easier they are to remember.

We see exactly the same phenomenon when it comes to our memory for sequences of events or procedures. Classic illustrations in AI involve things like a visit to a doctor's office, meal in a restaurant, or birthday party. Once we've encountered a few of these, we construct concepts that capture the ordinary cases as scripts involving sequences of smaller events, with participants playing various generic roles. In order to represent these temporally sequenced activities, we would need more apparatus than introduced here, particularly more elaborate mechanisms for representing sequencing in time and the effects of events. We'll see some of that in the next chapter.

In a moment we'll say more about what might happen when our prototypical expectations are not met, but generally we seem to get along quite well calling to mind general concepts including scripts that we can follow almost on the kind of autopilot we talked about earlier. Here is a good place to remember what we introduced from Minsky regarding frames in the previous chapter. All the technical machinery above is in order to represent ordinary things in a way that can guide a rapid, almost-reflexive interpretation of a new situation and a determination of what to do next.

Reconciliation in a World Model

We conclude this chapter with a quick note on what might happen when things go wrong. (Recall our earlier observation about common sense regularly coming into play when something unexpected happens.) We can think of the computational operations in this chapter and the next as purely inward-looking processes: our attention is focused solely on internal representations and making use of them as best we can. What might snap us out of this reverie is the realization that there is a problem, such as that new information we want to incorporate in the model conflicts with something already there.

Of course, major contradictions in what is believed are expected to be problematic and may never be fully resolved. The big ones often deal with the boundaries between antagonistic ideas. For example, we may have strong beliefs about the need to protect free speech and equally strong beliefs about the need to prohibit hate speech. But just as we might judge a certain body of flowing water to be a river sometimes and too small to be a river at other times (see the discussion in chapter 5 on naive physics), we may well be inconsistent about cases on the boundary between free speech and hate speech. Sorting out conflicts like these in a satisfactory way is a lifetime job and not what is at issue here.

What we have in mind are more modest contradictions like this: the world model we have of the hospital we are about to visit is that it will by default, say, have six floors. As we approach the building in question, however, we observe that it has only five floors, contradicting the model. Or here is another example mentioned above: we are told that Tweety is a bird and draw the conclusion that it gets around by flying, only to learn later that Tweety is in fact a penguin and cannot fly. We would expect violations of expectations like these to be quite common and something that should be reconciled in a world model without any major disruption.

In the easiest case, the conflicting value in the world model is something like a loosely held default value. We would need to examine annotations to see the strength of the assignment. As long as no additional conclusions were drawn from the default value, we can dislodge the default, change the world model appropriately, and be done with it.

Yet not all reconciliation will be quite this easy. For instance, if we enter a building we expect to be a hospital only to find a large high-ceilinged room where a crowd of people are gathered, apparently singing and praying, we will want to reconsider the premise that we are in a hospital. This is where the similarity annotations mentioned above might be useful, allowing us to see that we might be dealing with something more like a church. This can involve reinterpreting things that were previously understood as parts of a hospital and reassigning them to the corresponding parts of a church. All of this seems to be essential as part of everyday commonsense reasoning.

8 Representation and Reasoning, Part II

Reading furnishes the mind only with materials of knowledge;
it is thinking that makes what we read ours.

—John Locke, quoted in "Hand Book: Caution and Counsels,"
The Common School Journal, by Horace Mann

In the previous chapter, we looked at world models and conceptual models as representations of commonsense knowledge. But in terms of what is actually needed for common sense, a large piece of the representational puzzle is still missing.

To see this, imagine an agent with common sense deliberating about what to do. It might believe that a certain door is open, for example, and be thinking about whether or not to close it. Notice that to be able to think along these lines, the agent has to be able to entertain the idea of the door being closed even though it actually believes it to be open. Ideas like that of a door being open or closed are what we called *propositions* in chapter 5. So we are presuming that an agent with common sense will be able to think about propositions being true without necessarily believing them to be true in the current state.

If a computational system is going to be able to deal with propositions in this way, it will need a symbolic representation of them. Its knowledge of the world might still be represented in the world and conceptual models of the previous chapter. These are the materials of its knowledge, to use Locke's phrase. But the propositions it will want to think about for one reason or another will have to be represented in a third realm distinct from these models. Indeed knowledge itself is a propositional concern. An agent might represent a door as being open in a world model, but the actual belief it has will be a proposition: it believes *that the door is open*, among other things.

In this chapter, we will discuss symbolic representations of propositions and show how a cognitive agent can make use of them in concert with its world model to deal with questions like "Is *P* true now?," "Would *P* be true if I took action *A*?," and "What actions could I take to make *P* true?"—all of which are essential components of commonsense thinking.

A Representation Language for Propositions

To represent propositions symbolically, we will use an artificial language called *L*. Technically, *L* is an English-like variant of what is called the first-order predicate calculus (mentioned in chapter 4). The main difference from ordinary English is that it uses special symbols called variables. So the expressions of *L*, called *well-formed formulas* (or *formulas* for short), will be English-like except that there will be two ways to refer to individuals: as before, symbols like `Person#17`, which we will henceforth call *constants*, and symbols written with a special : character in them like `Person:x`, which we will call *variables*. (We will see how variables are used in a moment.) The constants and variables of *L* together are called *singular terms* (or *terms* for short), and play the role of noun phrases in English.

In this section, we lay out the language *L* in detail and then say what the formulas are supposed to mean—that is, which ones are intended to represent true propositions and which ones represent false propositions. (From now on, for ease of wording, we will say that a formula of *L* is true instead of saying that it is a symbolic representation of a proposition that is true.)

Let us begin with the structure of formulas. There are three types of formulas of *L*: *atomic formulas*, *equalities*, and *composite formulas*. The atomic formulas of *L* are just the symbolic expressions that appear in world models, but allowing for variables in addition to constants. So for example,

```
Person#17 has Event#23 as a birth.
```

is an atomic formula, but so is

```
Person:x has Event#23 as a birth.
```

The equalities of *L* are formulas consisting of two terms separated by the word "is." So for instance,

```
Person:x is Person#16.
```

is an equality formula.

Finally, the composite formulas of $\mathcal{L}$ are those that have other formulas as parts: a *conjunction* is made by putting the word "and" between two formulas; a *disjunction* is made by putting the word "or" between two formulas; a *negation* is made by putting the words "it is not the case that" in front of a formula; and finally, an *existential quantification* is made by putting the words "there is a," a variable, and the word "where" in front of a formula. Here then is an example of a composite formula:

```
There is a Thing:x where
    Thing:x is a person and
    it is not the case that Thing:x is Person#16.
```

This is the entire language. The components are summarized in figure 8.1. There are also a few special-purpose extras in $\mathcal{L}$ that have nothing to do with world models for dealing with numbers and sequences. These are described in the appendix, which can be consulted later. Note that we are ignoring the fact that the language $\mathcal{L}$ is syntactically ambiguous: formulas with multiple "and" or "or" words can be grouped in different ways. We will use indentation on the page to disambiguate as necessary.

There are a few abbreviations we can use to make the formulas somewhat easier to read. When we have multiple formulas joined by "and" words, we will leave out all but the last "and" and use commas instead as separators. Similarly, when we have a "there is" nested inside another "there is," we will group the variables together, and separate them with commas and a final "and." So for example,

```
There is a Person:x and an Event:y where
    Person:x is a person,
    Event:y is a birthEvent, and
    Person:x has Event:y as a birth.
```

is an abbreviation for

```
There is a Person:x where
    there is an Event:y where
        Person:x is a person and
        Event:y is a birthEvent and
        Person:x has Event:y as a birth.
```

Term:

- *Constant*: a name for an individual in the world.
    `Person#17`

- *Variable*: a placeholder for an individual, used like a pronoun.
    `Person:x`

Simple Formula:

- *Atomic formula*: a world model sentence, but allowing for variables.
    `Person#17 has Event#23 as a birth.`
    `Person:x is a barber.`

- *Equality*: a formula with "`is`" as a connective between two terms, meaning the two terms refer to the same individual.
    `Person:x is Person#16.`

Composite Formula:

- *Conjunction*: a formula with "and" between two formulas, meaning both embedded formulas are true.
    `Person#17 has Event#23 as a birth and`
    `    Person#17 has "John" as a firstName.`

- *Disjunction*: a formula with "or" between two formulas, meaning at least one of the embedded formulas is true.
    `Person#17 has "John" as a firstName or`
    `    Person#17 has "James" as a firstName.`

- *Negation*: a formula starting with "`it is not the case that`", meaning that the embedded formula is not true.
    `It is not the case that`
    `    Person#17 has "James" as a firstName.`

- *Existential quantification*: a formula with "`there is`" and "where" to indicate the existence of something with properties.
    `There is a Person:x where`
    `    Person:x is a barber and`
    `    Person:x has Event#23 as a birth.`

Figure 8.1
The language $\mathcal{L}$

These abbreviations add nothing of any substance to the language, but they do make the formulas less wordy.

The whole point of having a symbolic representation language like $\mathcal{L}$ is to consider computations that process the symbolic structures. We will get to those reasoning operations starting in the next section. But let us first go over what the formulas are supposed to mean, beginning with formulas with no variables. Intuitively, these formulas should be understood as true or false according to a world model.

Atomic formulas with no variables should be read as they were before. The ones that appear exactly as is in the world model are considered to be true; all the others are considered to be false. So for instance, for the world model from the previous chapter, the formula

```
Person#17 has "John" as a firstName.
```

is considered to be true, but the formula

```
Person#17 has "James" as a firstName.
```

is considered to be false. An equality formula with no variables is true exactly when the two terms are the same constant. This means that the formula

```
Thing#237 is Thing#238.
```

is considered to be false no matter what there is in the world model. For composite formulas without variables, the rules are the usual: an "and" formula is true exactly when both conjuncts are true, an "or" formula is true exactly when at least one of the disjuncts is true, and a "not" formula is true exactly when the negated formula is false.

The truth of a "there is" formula that mentions a variable is slightly more complex. It is considered to be true when there is a constant such that the formula embedded within the "there is" can be made true by replacing the variable involved by that constant.

Suppose, say, we have a world model like the one in the previous chapter that contains just the following seven items:

```
Person#17 is a person.
Person#17 has "John" as a firstName.
Person#17 has Event#23 as a birth.
TimePt#24 is a pointInTime.
TimePt#24 has 1979 as an enclosingYear.
```

```
Event#23 is a birthEvent.
Event#23 has TimePt#24 as a time.
```

Then the following formula is true according to this model:

```
There is a Person:x and an Event:y where
  Person:x has "John" as a firstName and
  Person:x has Event:y as a birth.
```

This is true because we can replace the variable Person:x by the constant Person#17 and the variable Event:y by the constant Event#23 in the embedded formula, and end up with

```
Person#17 has "John" as a firstName and
Person#17 has Event#23 as a birth.
```

which is considered to be true. This formula represents the proposition that John has a birth, or more literally, that there exist two things, where the first thing has "John" as its name and the second thing as its birth.

Finally, what are we to make of a formula like

```
Person:x has "Harry" as a firstName.
```

which contains a variable? This is a formula that is neither true nor false; it has no truth value. It can be read as something like "It has 'Harry' as a first name"—that is, as a sentence with a pronoun. The formula only gets a truth value when it appears within the scope of a "there is" quantifier such as

```
There is a Person:x where Person:x has "Harry" as a firstName.
```

which can be read as "There is a thing, and it has 'Harry' as a first name," or better, "Something has 'Harry' as a first name," which is false according to the model above (since there is no substitution for the Person:x variable to make the embedded formula true). A variable that is not within the scope of a "there is" quantifier is called a *free variable*, and only formulas of £ without free variables are intended to get a truth value.

Answering Factual Questions

Now we are ready to talk about reasoning. As mentioned at the start, the primary use of the formulas of £ is to express questions about the world that a reasoning agent might want to consider for some purpose. The answer to the question will be found in the world model, but the question itself will be represented as a formula. Questions in $\mathcal{L}$ are *about* the world that the model represents, but they are not *in* the world model.

Overall, there are two sorts of factual questions to consider. A *wh-question* (say, "Where was John born?") expects an answer to be a symbol representing something in the world—in this case, a location. A *yes-no question* (say, "Were any of Sue's children born in Toronto?") expects a binary answer. Wh-questions can also have multiple answers (for instance, "Who are the people born in Boston?"), in which case the answer will be a finite set of symbols. Questions about how many things have a certain property (for example, "How many beekeepers are chemists?") can also be answered by counting the number of answers to an appropriate wh-question.

We can use formulas of $\mathcal{L}$ to express these questions. We imagine two operations on formulas:

- For yes-no questions, the operation **TEST** will return one of the symbols TRUE or FALSE depending on whether the given formula is considered to be true or false according to the current model.

- For wh-questions, the operation **FIND-ALL** will return all combinations of constants such that the formula would be true if its free variables were replaced by those constants.

Note that for the **TEST** operation, the argument must be a formula with no free variables; otherwise it will not have a truth value. So for example, **TEST** will be able to compute the truth value of the formula

```
Person#17 has "Jim" as a firstName.
```

as FALSE; but the formula

```
Person:x has "John" as a firstName.
```

has no truth value. **FIND-ALL**, on the other hand, would be able to interpret this second formula as the wh-question "Who has 'John' as a first name?" and compute the answer as Person#17.

Both the **TEST** and **FIND-ALL** operations work by breaking apart the given formula into its pieces, and then looking for atomic formulas in the world model. Because the language $\mathcal{L}$ is constructed recursively—formulas can appear as parts of other formulas—the **TEST** and **FIND-ALL** procedures are similarly recursive. The full definitions of the two procedures are given in the appendix; the precise details are not important.

Note that the answers to wh-questions may not be informative. For example, suppose we want to find out when John was born. The single answer returned by **FIND-ALL** would be TimePt#24, which indeed represents the correct time point for John's birth according to the world model above, but does not *identify* it in any way. In some cases, we might not need an identification—for instance, we may just want to check if two returned results are the same. But if we do, we will want a follow-up wh-question to go from a symbol like TimePt#24 to an identifying string or number. For a time point, we might want the year and name of the month (and maybe more details); for a person, we might want a first and last name, or maybe a phone number or email address, depending on what we are trying to do. Even in cases where indexical identification is required for subsequent action (as discussed before), we will still want identifying strings of characters and numbers: How many seconds from now? How many quarter turns clockwise from the current heading? What string is written on the sign directly ahead?

It is also worth noting that the **TEST** and **FIND-ALL** operations perform a kind of logical reasoning. (We spell out the details in the bonus chapter.) Importantly, however, what **TEST** does is much easier than dealing with a collection of deductive rules as in classical logic. We are using ideas from the field of database retrieval, with little in the way of logical machinery. In fact, using off-the-shelf database technology, it should be possible to run these reasoning operations on gigantic world models having hundreds of thousands of symbols. It is the computational tractability of these operations that makes this simple form of logical reasoning so well suited for common sense.

Deriving New Properties

Just because we are using world models to represent knowledge does not mean that the formulas of $\mathcal{L}$ can only be used for questions. We can think of a world model as representing the *basic* properties of things in the world, and then use formulas of $\mathcal{L}$ as a way of dealing with additional properties to be derived from them.

Here is the idea. Consider the world model about John and Sue presented in the previous chapter. We can see that the person named John is linked to a birth event, which is then linked to a location somewhere in

Boston. In other words, we have represented John as having Boston as his birth city. And yet we cannot ask an easy question like "What is the birth city of John?" since the birth city is not a property expressed anywhere directly in the model. Using formulas of $\mathcal{L}$, though, we can extend our conceptual vocabulary to treat a birth city as a property of people to be derived from other, more basic ones.

To do this, we imagine that in addition to world and conceptual models, a knowledge base will contain symbolic expressions called *derivation clauses* (or *clauses* for short). (See the third part of figure 7.1 in the previous chapter.) These are made up of three parts: an expression that uses some variables, the word "when," and a formula of $\mathcal{L}$. The idea is that the expression at the start of the clause is a new formula that is considered to be true whenever the formula of $\mathcal{L}$ at the end of the clause is true. It is an easy matter to extend **TEST** (and therefore **FIND-ALL**) to allow for a collection of derivation clauses of this sort. (The details are in the appendix.)

To see this in action, we might imagine characterizing the birth city of a person as the enclosing city of the location where the person was born:

```
Person:x has City:c as a birthCity
    when
there is an Event:e and SpacePt:s where
  Person:x has Event:e as a birth,
  Event:e has SpacePt:s as a location, and
  SpacePt:s has City:c as an enclosingCity.
```

This defines a new, derived role relating a person to a city. The `birthCity` relationship holds if there is some event and point in space, such that (1) the event is the birth of the person in question, (2) the location of the birth event is the point in space, and (3) the enclosing city of that point in space is the city in question.

With this derivation clause in place, whenever something like

```
Person:z has City#65 as a birthCity
```

appears within a formula, **TEST** will interpret it as if the formula embedded in the clause above had been used instead. The `birthMother` property mentioned in the previous chapter would be handled analogously.

If it wasn't obvious before that **TEST** was a reasoning operation, the case is much more evident now. For example, assume the world model includes the following:

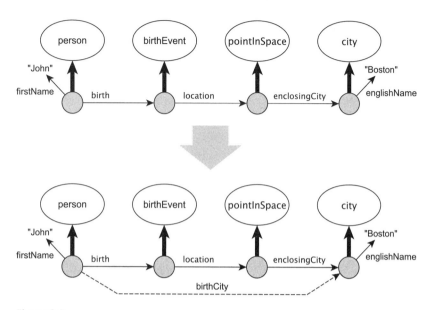

Figure 8.2
Application of a derivation clause

```
Person#17 has Event#23 as a birth.
Event#23 has SpacePt#25 as a location.
SpacePt#25 has City#18 as an enclosingCity.
```

The **TEST** operation would then conclude that

```
Person#17 has City#18 as a birthCity.
```

is true as well. The operation assembles some basic properties about four
individuals to derive a new conclusion relating John (`Person#17`) to Boston
(`City#18`), as illustrated in figure 8.2.

The use of derivation clauses as above allows us to introduce derived
properties with any number of arguments, not just derived roles. For example, we might want to think of a native Torontonian as any person born in
Toronto:

```
Person:x is a nativeTorontonian
    when
there is a City:y where
  Person:x has City:y as a birthCity and
  City:y has "Toronto" as an englishName.
```

Note that these derivation clauses involve what we previously called *sufficiency conditions*. What we are saying is that it is sufficient to have a birth city with the name "Toronto" to be considered a native Torontonian. If we wanted to allow a richer notion of Torontonian, we would need a concept for it in our conceptual model with additional parts, as seen in the previous chapter. Other properties involving sufficiency conditions such as flying-Animal or quadruped would be handled analogously. (See the appendix for how to handle the dog breed illustration from the end of chapter 6 as a derived property.)

As mentioned in the previous chapter, derivation clauses give us a nice way to handle typical properties without the complications involving defeasible subconcept and superconcept relationships. Here's the idea: the derived flyingAnimal property will hold whenever the animal in question has the right locomotion property. If by default, individual birds are instantiated with Flying as their mode of locomotion, then by the same token, they will be classified as having this flyingAnimal property. So birds end up being flying animals by default without requiring any relationship in the conceptual model between the general concept of a bird and the flying-Animal property.

We can also derive properties about pairs of things that are seemingly unrelated in the world model (such as pomegranates and laundry baskets, say). Consider the property of one thing being larger in volume than another. (For simplicity, we treat the volume of something not as a quantity but rather as a number in some unspecified units, just like we did for duration in the previous chapter.) The property might be encoded as follows:

```
Thing:x1 is larger in volume than Thing:x2
    when
there is a Number:v1 and a Number:v2 where
  Thing:x1 has Number:v1 as a volume,
  Thing:x2 has Number:v2 as a volume, and
  Number:v1 > Number:v2.
```

The > here is a special symbol in $\mathcal{L}$ for numbers and has its usual arithmetic interpretation. So for example, if the **TEST** operation can determine that

```
Thing#656 has 3 as a volume.
Thing#474 has 7 as a volume.
```

are both true (perhaps using other derived properties), it would then be able to derive that

```
Thing#474 is larger in volume than Thing#656.
```

is true too. Properties that hold to a degree (like being rich or fond of something) can be characterized using arithmetic in a similar way. Using these ideas, we can also have properties that involve more than two things—something that cannot be represented in a world model at all, such as the property that John might have of being closer in age to Bill than to Sue.

As a final consideration, we can allow for properties that are *recursively* defined. Imagine, for instance, that we already have a (basic or derived) property of being a parent. Then we can have this derivation clause:

```
Person:x has Person:y as an ancestor
    when
there is a Person:p where
  Person:x has Person:p as a parent and
  Person:p is Person:y or Person:p has Person:y as an ancestor.
```

In other words, one person has a second as an ancestor if the first person has a parent who either is the second person or (recursively) has the second person as an ancestor. (Using an item within its own definition is what makes this recursive.) Then, if there is a chain of parent relationships between two individuals in a world model, **TEST** will correctly conclude that one is an ancestor of the other. (There are some caveats discussed in the bonus chapter.)

Simulating Change

The idea of using formulas of $\mathcal{L}$ to characterize properties that can be derived suggests a natural way of dealing with change—or at least simple forms of change. Recall from chapter 5 that not only is our commonsense world made up of things with properties but these properties also are assumed to change over time as a result of events that occur in the world. (Events can cause things to start or stop existing as well, but we put aside that part of the story here.)

Let us consider doors again. We might expect a world model to represent a door as being in a certain state, open or closed, perhaps using something like this:

```
Door#58 is a door.
Door#58 has "open" as a doorState.
```

But we also need to represent how things will be different after events take place, such as the opening or closing of doors. (We will be ignoring the locking of doors here for simplicity.)

To simplify matters, it will be convenient to assume that we have representations in the world model for events that may or may not occur so that we can ask hypothetically what would be true if they were to take place. So for our purposes, a symbol like Event#427 in a world model will represent an event (such as a wedding, the purchase of a bicycle, or the closing of a door) without assuming that the event has occurred or will ever happen (unlike Event#23, which in the previous chapter, represented an event assumed to have occurred in 1979).

To talk about what would be true if an event like Event#427 were to happen, we can use the language $\mathcal{L}$, with one additional feature: we will allow atomic formulas to include the word "after" followed by a sequence of terms at the end. This will only make sense when these terms represent events. The idea is that this extended atomic formula says that the embedded formula is true *immediately after* the given sequence of events has taken place. In fact, we will treat an atomic formula without a sequence term as an abbreviation for one with the empty sequence:

```
Door#58 has "open" as a doorState.
```

should be understood as an abbreviation for

```
Door#58 has "open" as a doorState after [].
```

(The term [ ] here denotes the empty sequence, and a term with a | in it can be used to represent a nonempty sequence, as presented in the appendix.)

But then how should the **TEST** reasoning be modified to interpret atomic formulas of this sort? The answer is that we can treat a changed door state as a derived property. For an atomic formula that uses the empty sequence, the **TEST** procedure can handle this exactly as before, looking for the formula without the after [] in the world model. This can be thought of as the *current* state of the door, as represented in the world model. But for something where the sequence of events is not empty, the **TEST** procedure can look for a derivation clause characterizing what the door state will be after the sequence of events.

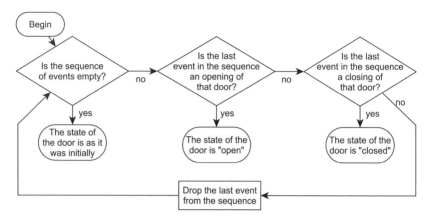

Figure 8.3
Flowchart for determining the state of a door after a sequence of events

Inspired by our discussion of doors from before, we might want to reason about how the state of a door will be different after a sequence of events, if it changes at all, along the lines of the flowchart depicted in figure 8.3.

In other words, we can characterize the changing state of a door using something like this:

The state of a door immediately after any sequence of events is as follows:

- *If the last event in the sequence was an opening of that door, then the door state will be "open" (regardless of what came before).*

- *If the last event in the sequence was a closing of that door, then the door state will be "closed" (regardless of what came before).*

- *Otherwise, the door state is unaffected by the last event in the sequence (door related or not) and will be whatever it was just prior to that last event.*

Here is the same thing now written as a derivation clause:

```
Door:d has State:z as a doorState after Seq:s|Event:e
      when
if Event:e is a doorOpeningEvent and
      Event:e has Door:d as an object
   then State:z is "open"
   else if Event:e is a doorClosingEvent and
           Event:e has Door:d as an object
        then State:z is "closed"
           else Door:d has State:z as a doorState after Seq:s.
```

(The "if-then-else" used here is an abbreviation for a disjunction: either the "if" part is true and the "then" part is true, or the "if" part is false and the "else" part is true.) This somewhat complex recursive clause actually embodies a rather simple idea: the commonsense law of inertia from before. It says that the state of a door remains unchanged except for certain special events: openings and closings of that specific door. Using this clause, **TEST** can read off from a world model not only the current state of the door but the state of the door after any given sequence of events too.

To see how this works, let us suppose that our world model contains a symbol, Event#017, representing the closing of Door#50. Again, we are not assuming that this event has occurred or will occur. Then, using the derivation clause above, **TEST** would determine that the formula

Door#58 has "closed" as a doorState after [Event#817].

is true—that is, that the door will be closed immediately after the given event. Furthermore, the operation would determine that

Door#58 has "closed" as a doorState after [...].

is false for any sequence of events that did not involve Door#58, such as humming a tune or reading a book. (The appendix has examples with other sequences of events.) Also note that we can find out what single event will make the door be closed using **FIND-ALL** with

Door#58 has "closed" as a doorState after [Event:u].

and receive the door-closing event Event#817 as an answer. While we are getting close to enabling the system to do planning, we are not quite there yet, since an agent has no way of knowing whether this Event#817 can be made to occur. We will get to that in the next section.

One subtlety in this scheme for dealing with change concerns the passage of time. Some properties can be changed by events that are seemingly unrelated as a result of their duration. For example, if a bathtub is full of water, then it remains so immediately after the sequence of pulling the plug from the drain, turning off the light, and closing the door. The bathtub, however, would be empty after the sequence of pulling the plug, baking a cake, and closing the door. One way to understand this is that pulling the plug causes the bathtub to enter a draining state, and in this state, the water level is changed according to the duration of any subsequent event, including humming a tune, baking a cake, or reading a book. Similar temporal considerations are involved in things like the cooling of hot objects or falling of unsupported ones.

The expectation is that our knowledge base will include derivation clauses like the one for doorState above for any basic property that can be changed by events (like marital status, the water level in a bathtub, the location of objects, and so on; these are called *fluents* in the AI literature). If a clause like this is not present in the knowledge base for some basic property, the **TEST** procedure can simply assume that the property is unchanged by any occurrence of events. For a property that is not basic, on the other hand, in particular for one characterized by a derivation clause, **TEST** can assume that the property changes in accordance with how the properties mentioned in the embedded formula of the clause change.

This way of understanding change allows us to simulate the change produced by any sequence of events. The idea is that we start with a world model having something like this

```
Door#58 has "open" as doorState.
```

and imagine some sequence of events taking place. Now we construct a new world model where the door state is as determined by the doorState derivation clause above. For example, if the door is determined to be closed after the events in question, then the new world model instead contains

```
Door#58 has "closed" as doorState.
```

Now assuming we update every basic property we care about in this way, we end up computing a new world model that takes into account how each basic property changes as a result of that sequence of events. The derived properties will change automatically as underlying basic ones change. We can, if we so desire, think of this new model as our "current" model of the world. We only have to go back to the original model if we want to consider how things were before, or how things might have turned out differently had the events not happened.

Planning for Change

As we have emphasized from the beginning, an essential aspect of common sense is using reasoning to make effective use of certain types of knowledge to achieve practical goals, so determining what an agent can do to make things true in the world is critical for common sense.

In the previous section, we saw how to compute the changes produced by an event. All that is left is how to reason about whether an agent can actually cause the event to occur. It is typical to say that there are these things called *actions* that agents are able to perform. For our purposes, we will interpret the idea of an agent performing an action as a way of saying that the agent is somehow causing an event to occur. So saying that an agent pushed a button, for example, is a way of saying that the agent made a certain button-pushing event take place.

In the previous section, we saw how door-closing events cause the state of the world to change. But this does not mean that an agent will always be able to make such an event occur. An agent who is nowhere near the door may be unable to close it, for instance. As discussed before, we expect that actions performed by agents will have *prerequisites*—that is, conditions that must be true for an agent to be able to cause the event to happen.

For primitive events—that is, events that are not thought of in terms of simpler component events—we can represent their prerequisites using a property that we call possible. This derived property can be characterized by clauses like this:

```
Event:e is possible for Agent:x
     when
Event:e is a doorClosingEvent and
  there is a Door:d where
     Event:e has Door:d as an object,
     Agent:x is near Door:d, and
     Door:d has "open" as a doorState.
```

In other words, a door-closing event can be made to occur by an agent if the agent is near the door in question and the door is open. The expectation is that our knowledge base will include a possible derivation clause like this for each type of primitive event. So as far as this clause is concerned, John can cause Event#817 to occur if he is near Door#58 and that door is open. This is a somewhat crude characterization that might be further qualified or annotated. For example, John might be unable to close the door if he is near the door but paralyzed, the door has been jimmied open, or the door is too massive for one person to move. Note that this is a completely different consideration from what the effect of the action would be. Here we are asking if the agent can cause the event to take place, should the agent so choose, rather than what the event will change.

For nonprimitive events—that is, events made up of other subevents—we still would like to know if the agent can cause them to take place. Let us make the simplifying assumption that such events are characterized as *sequences* of primitive events only. In this case, we would need to characterize when it was possible to cause a sequence of primitive events to occur. As it turns out, this property, which we call possibleSequence, can be defined from possible as follows: it must be possible to perform the first action in the sequence; then in the state that results from having performed that first action, it must be possible to perform the second; then in the state that results from having performed those first two actions in sequence, it must be possible to perform the third, and so on. (See the appendix for the exact details.)

To see how this would all work, suppose that in the current world model, Door#58 is open and Person#17 (John) is not near that door, but that there is some sort of motion event, Event#357, that John can make happen in the current state and that would put him near the door. The **TEST** operation can then determine that the following two formulas are true:

[Event#357,Event#817] is a possibleSequence for Person#17.

(John can move near the door and then close it.)

Door#58 has "closed" as doorState after [Event#357,Event#817].

(The door will be closed after that sequence of events.)

The state of affairs resulting from this sequence of events is depicted in figure 8.4. (There are other examples of possible and possibleSequence in the appendix.) This is precisely what is needed for planning: there is

Figure 8.4
A sequence of two events involving Person#17 and Door#58

a sequence of actions that can be performed by the agent, and after that sequence, the goal of having the door closed will be satisfied.

With this in mind, we can imagine a basic form of planning. We would have a procedure **PLAN** that takes as arguments an agent and a goal formula. The **PLAN** procedure would return a sequence of actions that the agent can perform starting in the current state to make the goal formula true. For example, John might want to plan for the following goal,

```
Door#58 has "closed" as a doorState.
```

and hope to receive the answer [Event#357,Event#817]. In other words, to achieve the goal of the door being closed, John can move to be near the door and then close it.

At first blush, we might think of computing **PLAN** for John by using **FIND-ALL** over the following:

```
Seq:s is a possibleSequence for Person#17 and
  Door#58 has "closed" as a doorState after Seq:s.
```

But this idea does not quite work. **FIND-ALL** looks for *constants* in the world model, and we cannot expect to see constants for all the (infinitely many) potential sequences of events that might need to be considered.

On the other hand, if we knew that we were looking for a plan with exactly two actions in it and there were constants in the model for each individual event we might want to consider, then we could use **FIND-ALL** over the following formula:

```
[Event:u,Event:v] is a possibleSequence for Person#17 and
  Door#58 has "closed" as a doorState after [Event:u,Event:v].
```

In other words, find two primitive events such that John can cause them to occur in sequence, and after doing so, the door will be closed. This should correctly return the combination Event#357, Event#817. As we will see in the next chapter, this more limited memory-based notion of planning will be enough for commonsense purposes.

Answering Generic Questions

To conclude this chapter, let us return to answering questions, but ones of a different sort. The questions for which we considered using **TEST** and **FIND-ALL** above were about specific things in the world and their properties. But when people talk about common sense, what first comes to mind are more generic questions that are not about specific things at all:

- *Is a bird a flying animal?*
- *Can a baby drive a car?*
- *Will a haircut take longer than a birthday party?*
- *Does a grizzly bear weigh more than a wheelbarrow?*

While these questions are not about specific individuals, there are indeed related ones that are about individuals. For the first question above, for instance, we might ask if *all* the birds are flying animals. Assuming we already have properties for bird and flyingAnimal, we can use **TEST** over the following formula:

```
It is not the case that
  there is a Bird:x where
    Bird:x is a bird and
    it is not the case that Bird:x is a flyingAnimal.
```

This **TEST** operation will return TRUE if it is not the case that there is a bird that is not a flying animal, or removing the two negations, if every bird is a flying animal. But this is clearly not the same as the generic question above.

So we might start by asking, What exactly is the difference between the following two English questions?

1. *Is a bird a flying animal? (or, Are birds flying animals in general?)*

2. *Is every bird a flying animal? (or, Are all the birds flying animals?)*

There are two main things. First, (1) might be considered to be true even in cases where (2) is false. We may want to believe that birds fly (in general) even if we know some exceptions, like Chilly the penguin who does not fly. Second, something like (1) might be considered to be false even in cases where the corresponding (2) is true. For example, suppose that the only birds we know about happen to be exceptional ones like Chilly. Then we might believe that all of these birds live in the Antarctic and do not fly, even though we may not want to believe that birds in general are like this. As an obvious consequence, even when the *majority* of the birds we know about have some property, we may not want to believe that birds have the property in general.

As we saw above, (2) is a question about the birds represented in a world model, and so is a question that **TEST** can deal with. But how then to answer a question like (1)? What exactly do we mean by birds "in general" as distinct from those represented in a world model?

In a sense, the answer to a generic question like (1) involves a conceptual structure: When you consider your *idea* of a bird, what sort of properties do you have in mind? Properties of the particular birds you happen to know about will not determine the answer one way or the other. The complication here is that the properties we associate with a concept like `bird` are subject to a complex array of restrictions and annotations, including defaults and cancellations, at various levels of strength and importance, as seen in the previous chapter. We do not really want to probe the structure of the conceptual model (as in, How many restrictions on this role? What is the strength of that annotation?), but we do want to make use of all of this structure in answering the question.

One way of making sense of a question like (1) is as follows:

Imagine (hypothetically) a world state where there is a new bird you've never thought about before. Is *that* thing a flying animal?

In other words, we can imagine doing something like what was done in the previous chapter: we extend the world model by instantiating the `bird` concept using all the properties associated with it in the conceptual model, either directly or through inheritance. This will produce a new symbol like `Bird#247` representing this hypothetical bird and having a variety of properties. When this is done, we can then use **TEST** to determine if the formula

```
Bird#247 is a flyingAnimal.
```

is true according to this world model.

This is much closer to the answer we are after for (1), although it still does not tell us whether the flying property is due to a default (and how strongly that default is applied) or a restriction more fundamental to the concept (which might still be canceled, of course). In the former case, we might be tempted to answer a question like (1) with "Yes, typically"; in the latter case, we might answer with something like "Yes, as a rule." In either case, we might even include a number representing the strength of the default or restriction.

9   Common Sense in Action

Just because you make a good plan, doesn't mean that's gonna happen.
—Taylor Swift, quoted in *Taylor Swift: The Platinum Edition*, by Liv Spencer

Common sense, as we have been saying, is the ability to make effective use of ordinary background knowledge in deciding what to do in everyday situations. In the previous two chapters, we examined symbolic representations of commonsense knowledge and general reasoning operations defined over these representations. The purpose was to make that knowledge available for computation. In this chapter, we complete the picture by showing how these computations can be put to use in deciding what to do. Specifically, we focus on one clear manifestation of common sense first described in chapter 2: being jolted out of a familiar routine by something completely unexpected. We look at a concrete example of a plan going awry (just as Taylor Swift says), investigate in detail what common sense ought to be able to make of it, and then show how this can emerge from the sort of symbolic representation and reasoning seen in the previous two chapters.

Note that we are not going to try to address all forms of what might be considered common sense. We are going to take a somewhat utilitarian view, where common sense is only for immediate *action*. We are putting aside other less active uses of commonsense knowledge, like daydreaming, reminiscing, or even reading a book or watching a movie. The whole point will be to end up with a suitable answer to the question, "What should I do now?" The possible answers we have in mind are common, mundane actions, about which we expect to have common, mundane knowledge. For a person, the actions might be things like saying something, picking up an object, or heading off somewhere. They would not be things like controlling internal organs or engaging muscles, even though biological activities like these will clearly be involved.

From this utilitarian point of view, there are really only two modes of commonsense reasoning first mentioned in chapter 2—top-down and bottom-up:

- Top-down reasoning occurs as the result of agents needing to use what they know to achieve goals they are working on. Its purpose is to answer a question like "What should I do to make proposition P true?"

- Bottom-up reasoning occurs as the result of agents needing to use what they know to make sense of something perceived. Its purpose is to answer a question like "How should I react to proposition P being true?"

As we will see, both of these will contribute to answering the "What should I do now?" question.

Also recall that when we talk about commonsense reasoning, we have in mind something more limited than figuring out everything that might follow from what is known. It may well be that a person has all the necessary information to be able to determine whether they should open door number one or door number two, but for one reason or another cannot determine which. This inability need not be a failure of common sense. What we have in mind for common sense will clearly include drawing appropriate conclusions from what is known, but not necessarily being able to draw all of them.

Before we get to using common sense, we begin by reexamining a kind of rote behavior with no common sense—one that uses a simple form of condition-action rules. We then consider how to incorporate knowledge into the process and why.

Rule-Based Behavior

Let's begin with the notion of a *routine*. As we said in chapter 2, most of what we humans deal with in day-to-day life is not too surprising. We spend almost all of our time in situations that are at least somewhat familiar to us. We run into the same sorts of things over and over, and learn ways of dealing with them. It might be things like wanting to cross a street, open a paint can, or buy a cup of coffee, or it might be things we observe like the sight of an approaching storm, smell of burnt toast, or sound of an approaching ambulance. In its most basic form, here is what happens: we recognize the familiar situation, recall from memory a routine that deals with it, and follow the steps prescribed.

To behave in such a way, we need at a minimum two things:

1. The ability to recognize certain common conditions, and do so in a context-free way, independently of any goals or expectations.
2. The ability to follow a routine (and any subroutines it calls on), again in a context-free way, independently of any goals or expectations.

Overall, we can think of this basic behavior as rule based: we have a collection of rules of the form $[X{\rightarrow}Y]$, where each X describes a condition in the world, and each Y describes a routine to perform. In its most primitive single-purpose form, there is just one rule in the collection—a single routine to perform on cue. The more general behavior is some sort of *observe-decide-act* loop: we repeatedly observe the world, and among the rules $[X{\rightarrow}Y]$ whose condition X we determine to be satisfied, we decide (in some way) on which routines Y to enact, and we go ahead and act on them. (As it turns out, if a rule-based system of this sort also has access to an unbounded working memory that it can write to and read from, the resulting architecture will be general enough to emulate any other computational system.)

Once we have decided to perform a routine, the process is somewhat like cooking from a recipe. The job is to follow the steps in the specified order; it is not to question why we must do certain steps, or what would happen if we did otherwise. The steps can be thought of as small rituals to perform. If the routine says to push a button three times, we perform those steps as if the actions themselves are what mattered rather than any effect they might achieve. Similarly, when a drill sergeant orders a private to clean a floor with a toothbrush, it is those specific actions that count; it would be gross insubordination for the private to propose some better way of getting the job done.

The step-by-step execution of a routine can be quite mindless and mechanical—something that can be performed by a suitably programmed automaton. The automaton need not be simple, however; it might be an entire chess-playing machine or a sophisticated infection-diagnosis machine. But the execution is expected to be context free, which is to say that broad, commonsense knowledge about the surrounding environment is not a factor in the execution. We expect a chess-playing automaton to play the same in the middle of a tornado or during a global war. The only real connection to the world beyond the inputs to the program is in the invocation of the routine itself.

As already noted, we expect the invocation of a routine to be based on an ability to recognize certain common conditions in the world, and without any expectations about what to be looking for. It is clear that humans have such an ability, acquired through some sort of learning process. If we are watching a baseball game and something totally unexpected happens, such as a fire truck suddenly appearing on the field, we can still recognize the thing as a fire truck even though we did not expect anything like it. Similarly, we can recognize the first few notes of Ludwig van Beethoven's *Symphony No. 5* even in contexts where we do not expect to hear anything musical. This is not to say that perception in its most general form can take place without top-down expectations. In a blurry image of a street scene, we might recognize a certain blob in the image as a car only because it occupies a position in the depicted scene that we expect to be filled by things like cars.

Because the action and perception we are imagining will be context free in this way, the parameters that are relevant for the overall behavior can be circumscribed in advance. In other words, a rule-based system of this sort is what we previously called a *closed* system: a system with a set of parameters that can be listed in advance. While the parameters are predictable, the values those parameters will take need not be. You will know what a chess move is supposed to look like, for example, even if you do not know which one your opponent will choose. You will know that a certain amount of force will be required to open a refrigerator door even if you do not know in advance what that force will be. As long as things are going well, we never step back and question what we are doing, or whether we should be doing something else. This notion of a closed system can, of course, be quite powerful. We already talked about closed AI systems and their impressive achievements. For many practical applications, this will be enough. But as we will see, in many cases, it is not.

Breaking the Rules

Where a closed system will not be enough is when a system must be able to work properly in an environment that cannot be circumscribed in advance—that is, in one where events that are totally unanticipated may occur. We only really need to step back from a fixed collection of rules and use common sense when there is an incongruity—something that violates our expectations.

Maybe something completely unexpected happens. Maybe we are crossing the street and the ground suddenly gives way; maybe we enter our hotel room and smell bacon cooking; or maybe we are trying to open a paint can with a screwdriver and somebody shouts, "Don't use that screwdriver!" It need not be something major. Maybe we spot a toy giraffe at the bottom of the pot we are going to use to make linguini. Or maybe things go the other way: something that is supposed to happen does not. Maybe the water in the pot on the stove never reaches a boil; maybe the person we are greeting with a handshake does not move to shake our hand; or maybe the coffee we just ordered at our favorite coffee shop never arrives. In cases like these, we need to break out of our routine and reconsider what to do next.

Of course, a rule-based system might be flexible enough to deal with some of these unanticipated situations. A chess-playing program may be able to find an appropriate move to make even when the opponent moves in outlandish and surprising ways. A routine for crossing the street may be able to cope quite well with a sudden unanticipated flow of water from a nearby fire hydrant. A rule-based system might be general and flexible enough to deal with a number of such variations.

In a truly open environment, however, sooner or later something will happen that lies outside the parameters of the system. We simply cannot expect to have a fixed collection of rules that deals sensibly with everything that might actually happen in real life. Furthermore, as already mentioned, although each of these unanticipated events might be extremely rare individually, because there are so many of them—so many different bizarre things that can happen—the chance of encountering one of them in real life is actually high. As we said, extremely rare events are quite common.

So what has to happen when a routine we are following is unable to cope with the current situation? We need to reconsider what we are doing. But to allow this, a routine has to do more than just specify steps (and subroutines) to follow. The execution needs to be much more deliberate, and so the routine needs two additional components:

1. For each step where some action is called for, the routine needs to make clear what the step is intended to accomplish so that it will be possible to

ascertain if the step was successful and allow the agent to consider other ways of getting there should the step prove to be unsuccessful.

2. For each step where the routine says to wait until some condition holds, the routine also needs to make clear about how long it makes sense to wait and how often it would be appropriate to check for the condition.

In other words, to deal with variations and breakdowns, we need a symbolic representation that emphasizes conditions in the world being achieved by the steps in the routine. Let us use the word "plan" to describe a routine of this sort. (It is not our intent to discuss the symbolic representations needed. They would be analogous to what was seen before. For instance, a plan could use formulas of the language $\mathcal{L}$ to represent conditions in the world.)

The inattentive (or mindless) execution of a plan would be just like the step-by-step execution of a routine described above, oblivious to anything other than the actions involved. The deliberate (or mindful) execution of a plan, on the other hand, would also be monitoring conditions in the world, standing by to interrupt the execution when certain conditions are not met.

So the role of common sense in action is twofold: first, we need to watch what we are doing to confirm that conditions we care about are being satisfied as they should and notice when unexpected things happen; and second, on failure, we need to be able to reconsider how we are achieving these conditions, and whether there might be other ways of doing so, taking into account the structure of the current plan we are working on, what we have discovered about the current situation, and our general commonsense knowledge of the world. In the rest of this chapter, we will be concentrating on what common sense should dictate when expectations are not met in the deliberate execution of a plan.

But clearly still another story needs to be told: What exactly triggers a shift from a mindless to a more mindful execution of a plan? (A related question is the shift in the other direction: How does the mindful but somewhat plodding execution of a novice become, with enough practice, the mindless but smooth execution of an expert?)

In our opinion, the shift from mindless to mindful is itself not the product of common sense. Consider something like an alarm. It's not as if you decide to listen for an alarm and that's why you hear it. An alarm will grab your attention in a context-free way, whatever your beliefs and goals happen to be. Yet its purpose is only to put you into a state of mindfulness, where you must now ask yourself, "What's going on? Is there something I should be doing?" Deciding on what you should do *after* you have been jolted in this way is where common sense enters the picture.

The difficulty with this story is that it relies on strong signals that are detected unambiguously, such as loud sounds, bright flashing lights, sharp smells, firm touches, or people saying alarming things like "Be careful!" or "Pay attention!" But it is possible to be shifted into a state of increased mindfulness by something much weaker, like the unexpected toy giraffe in the pot mentioned above or even an unusual passage of time such as water refusing to come to a boil. And yet it is not as if *all* unexpected things grab your attention in this way. If you happen to spot a squirrel holding a thimble somewhere on your bicycle path, you do not immediately pause to reconsider what it is you should be doing and why. Similarly, the passage of time might be completely ignored if you are engrossed in a conversation. Exactly what should or should not trigger a more deliberate reappraisal of your current situation is a thorny problem that awaits a clear solution.

Goals and Plans

Where do agents' goals come from? The easy answer is that they mostly come from other goals! The goal of crossing a certain street might come from a goal of getting to a specific restaurant, which comes from a goal of eating out, which comes from a goal of obtaining food (and socializing). This is not to say that obtaining food entails crossing that street. There are many ways of getting food, including cooking at home. But what we know is this: one way to get food involves eating out, one way to eat out involves getting to that specific restaurant, and one way to get to that restaurant involves crossing that specific street. Use a certain plan often enough to obtain food, and it becomes routine—something we later recall in its entirety as a way of achieving the goal.

What about the goal of eating? Where does that come from? Some goals are not just ways of achieving other goals but instead are more fundamental drives. The need to eat is not something we have much choice over. We can choose not to eat, of course, but not for long. Every system, biological or not, will have drives like this that it is compelled to deal with, and about which it has little or no control. A simple computer system, for example, can be driven to execute its program. A more complex robotic assistant might be given a standing order to do whatever it is told to do—subject perhaps to something like author Isaac Asimov's three laws of robotics—from which all sorts of subgoals will then emerge.

This is not to suggest that goals only change when we discover other ways of achieving the higher-level goals they derive from. Our values can change as well. We may acquire a goal because we come to realize over time that the goal is worth having. We may have no desire to read the classics, for instance, but aspire to be the kind of person who does. In a sense, our goal would be to eventually become the kind of person who has certain other goals. Goals are also affected by the choices and commitments we have already made. Once we have decided to enroll in a college program, for example, all our subsequent goals will be filtered by that commitment.

When it comes to commonsense behavior, the main question we ask ourselves is this: Given what I know and what I want, what should I do now? Expanding on this, the question is more like the following:

According to my current knowledge and goals, what plan of action do I think is best, and what does it have me doing next?

And here it is in much more detail:

According to everything I know, allowing for the fact that there is a lot I do not know but may be able to find out, and according to all my goals, including all my needs and desires, preferences and inclinations, and aspirations and ambitions, and given all the choices I have made so far and the commitments I intend to respect, among all the plans of actions that I know are currently available to me, are there any that stand out? In other words, do I know of a plan for which there is no other that I can say is better?

What then does it mean for one plan to be *better* than another in this context? The answer involves some sort of commonsense cost-benefit analysis: the benefit of achieving a goal against the cost of the actions in a plan for doing so. You may have goals like getting to San Francisco that are all-or-nothing; there is no benefit to you with respect to this goal unless you make it there. But you may also have goals like enjoying a vacation or keeping the house clean, which may be satisfied to varying degrees. On the other hand, each action you are considering in your plan may have costs—that is, negative effects on resources you care about (like money, time, or social capital). Moreover, we want to include in this cost things like effort and inconvenience as well as the degrees of risk and danger. Risky actions like skydiving are not inherently negative, but may end up incurring a high cost.

So the easy answer to the question above is this: one plan is better than another if it is expected to have a higher benefit to you at the same cost or an equal benefit to you at a lower cost. A slightly more nuanced answer allows that one plan can be better than another even if it has a slightly higher cost as long as its benefit is significantly higher as well (and similarly for actions with slightly lower benefit at significantly lower costs).

All of this suggests that a representation for a plan should include not only what conditions are being achieved by each step (its benefit, in other words) but also what costs are being incurred. (Again, we will not discuss the symbolic representational details.)

This is not to suggest that benefits and costs can all be compared on some uniform scale; some costs and benefits are quite plainly incomparable. Although common sense is not expected to be able to resolve all the pairwise comparisons, it is expected to handle the easy ones, and even some less obvious ones, perhaps using something like the order of magnitude reasoning discussed before. For example, although we know that it would be safer never to cross a busy street, we cross the street anyway because we know that the benefit of getting to the other side far outweighs the risk of not making it.

Planning Reconsidered

When it comes to planning as a form of commonsense reasoning, we suggested in the previous chapter that it was asking too much to be able to assemble entire sequences of actions on the spot that might achieve a goal under consideration. This might be fine as a puzzle-mode activity, but it is too demanding for ordinary common sense. (This issue comes up again in the bonus chapter.)

What we proposed instead is that when an agent needs to find a plan, it would go looking in its world model for actions it already knows about. These actions may of course be complex ones involving a number of steps—*premade plans*, in other words. The agent must be able to perform the (possibly complex) action in the current state since it will not be looking for additional preparatory actions that could make any prerequisites true. The executability of an action is what we considered in the previous chapter using the possible property. Furthermore, for each property that is part of a goal to be achieved, we would expect to be able to determine how that property can be affected by actions, just as we did for door states in the previous chapter. So overall, the sort of memory-based planning that will be required here will make use of the **FIND-ALL** and **TEST** operations along with the rest of the symbolic machinery seen before. Using those operations, we should be able to compute a tentative list of the executable actions that can make a goal condition true, sorted perhaps with the most familiar ones first.

The idea of looking for a *single* action to achieve a goal might seem like an overly strong restriction. For example, it might appear to rule out using a phone to contact someone since that might require first picking up the phone, with prerequisites of its own. But one way of thinking about this is that phoning someone is in fact one (somewhat complex) action involving a number of steps, one of which is picking up the phone. So for the purposes of memory-based planning, the *real* prerequisites of phoning someone are having a working phone nearby and knowing the number to call. Other less critical issues, such as needing to put down the coffee cup you are currently holding to be able to pick up the phone, would be sorted out in the actual performance of the action, not in the planning.

One major complication we are sidestepping here concerns actions that are knowledge requiring or knowledge producing. The former are actions that have knowledge conditions in their prerequisites such as phoning someone, which requires knowing the number to call. The latter are perceptual actions like consulting a telephone directory, peering into a room, or dipping a toe into a lake, which do not change the world so much as change what is known about it. To represent and reason about actions like these, the representation language $\mathcal{L}$ would need to be augmented since while it can talk about what is or will be *true* in the world, it has no way of talking about what is or will be *believed*.

One additional complication is the notion of cost. It is important to keep an eye on the side effects of an action—that is, we should simulate the changes produced by the action as in the previous chapter, and then look for conditions affected by the action that are not related to the goal under consideration (especially for actions that have multiple steps) to ensure that there are no hidden snags or costs that are too high (including of course the time required).

To go a bit further, let us briefly consider what should happen if you are faced with a novel goal condition, where you have not yet contemplated individual actions that might be able to achieve it. All is not lost. You may still be able to find a plan in your world model that deals with something *analogous*. The planning process would then need to be able to take one of these existing plans and use it to construct a new one.

How would this form of analogy actually work out in computational terms? It's complex, and as far as we know, a completely satisfactory story has yet to be told. In the simplest case, we imagine taking an individual action we know about and using it to instantiate one that is identical except with different things playing the roles in question—the object, the instrument, and so on. This involves constructing a new symbolic representation, as discussed in chapter 7. The value restrictions on these roles from the conceptual model would guide which of the things at hand might be able to play the roles in question. You may have never paid the bill at *this* restaurant before, for example, but you have done so at other similar establishments. You see a video of someone repairing a toaster and now consider the analogous action of *you* repairing the toaster in front of you.

More generally, this analogy process would involve finding correspondences between individual actions in some source domain and those in a target domain. These might be connected in advance by something like a similarity annotation, as discussed before. Analogues to a source activity can then be constructed by mapping its parts onto the new target domain. For example, as a toddler, you might have learned the idea of crawling around an object (going right, left, left, and right, say) as a way of getting past a sofa or avoiding a scary uncle. By analogy, this same maneuver can then be mapped onto other modes of locomotion, such as getting around obstacles when you first learn to walk, swim, ski, or ride a bicycle.

An Example: The Interrupted Journey

To see how these ideas might actually work out in practice, it is worth looking at a concrete everyday case in detail. We are going to imagine following a plan, having our expectations violated in an unanticipated way, and then using common sense to figure out what to do.

Of course, we are not expecting magic here. Although the unanticipated situation will be outside the behavioral parameters of the system, it should not be totally foreign to the system. That is, we expect there to be relevant commonsense knowledge of the sort already considered to use in deciding what to do. What makes the situation new and unexpected is that there will be no direct connection between this background knowledge and the behavior in question. The knowledge we have is simply information about the way the world is, not tied to any particular application or behavior, and certainly not to the plan we are following. Similarly, the plan we are following will not be tied in advance to all the considerations that may turn out to be relevant when something goes awry.

Consider now this scenario, first seen in the preview at the start of the book:

You set off late one holiday morning to do some grocery shopping for an afternoon barbecue. As you drive toward Jones's Grocery Store, you approach an intersection at Bradford and Victoria that you normally drive through on your way there. The traffic light happens to be red, so you stop and wait for it to turn green. This is all routine. Something strange now happens, however. Three minutes go by, and the light stays red. Five minutes go by, and the light is still red. You know that at some busy intersections, a light can stay red for a long time—longer than five minutes. But you also know that this is not one of them. Something is wrong.

What should you do?

In what follows, we will explore a range of contingencies and figure out what common sense should tell you in each case. But one might ask, Could these contingencies not be part of the original plan? With enough experience, could we not have learned from situations like this before? Might we not have said to ourselves, "Aha! The old traffic-light-stuck-on-red business. I'm on it!" for which we already have workable plans? The answer is clearly *yes.* But we are imagining an open system, and no matter how much experience we have, and no matter how much learning has taken place, sooner or later we will run into situations that have not been considered in advance. For the purpose of this example, let us imagine a traffic light being stuck on red as one of those unforeseen eventualities. (If this seems too routine, it is easy to come up with even less likely situations.)

So what should a person do with a stuck traffic light like this? The answer, of course, is *it depends!* There is no single right course of action; context is everything. This is precisely why common sense is needed. The best we can say in general terms is that you need to consider the particular situation you find yourself in and let common sense be your guide. As we will see, depending on the circumstances, there is an open-ended list of factors that might be relevant.

Let's get started. To get one's bearings in the discussion to follow, consult figure 9.1, which shows the relevant streets and grocery stores, the troublesome traffic light, and even a possible source of some distant brassy music coming from the east. Perhaps the most obvious thing to consider doing in the case of a stubborn red light is to put on the right turn signal, make the right-hand turn at Victoria (when it is safe to do so), and then find an alternate way to get to Jones's store, perhaps taking Barrie Street. In many cases, this will be the final commonsense response.

But it is easy to imagine circumstances where common sense should tell you otherwise. For example, if you believe that the light is staying red because there happens to be a parade on Victoria (as in the preview), common sense should certainly not encourage you to turn right. Similarly, if you know that Victoria is a busy one-way street going in the wrong direction, common sense again should not be telling you to turn right. In some jurisdictions, a right turn on red is not even legal (although it might still end up being your best option). And even if the turn is legal, when the traffic coming from the left on Victoria is fast and heavy, you may be unable to make the turn safely while your signal is red. And there are other reasons for avoiding a right turn. For example, you might know that Victoria is the on-ramp to a freeway (this is not the case in our figure, but it could be). It might take considerable time to get off the freeway and wind your way back to the grocery store. If other options are exhausted, however, you might still need to take that right turn and make do.

If the right turn on Victoria is a bad choice, then common sense might suggest some other options. Going straight through the red light is clearly illegal, but may end up being your best bet, especially if Victoria has little or no traffic, such as on a quiet rural street. A left turn at Victoria is also a possibility, but a left on red is almost certainly worse than going straight and somewhat of a last resort. Otherwise, turning around on Bradford will be the better choice (unless it happens to be a busy one-way street or divided highway). If there is a driveway nearby on your right (as in the figure), it would be a reasonable place for the maneuver. Otherwise you will have to turn around on the street itself, which means that there could be trouble

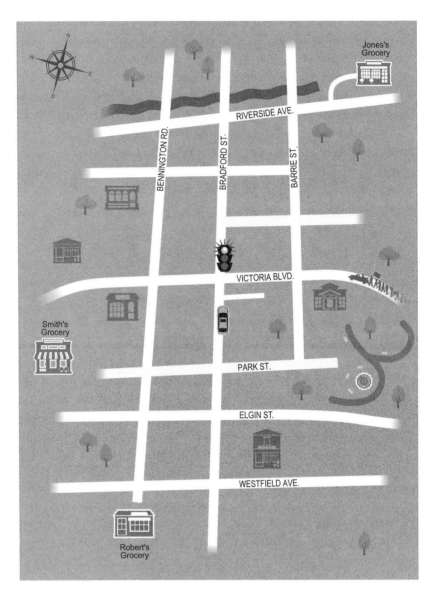

Figure 9.1
Stuck traffic light at Bradford and Victoria

from other cars, especially cars coming quickly off Victoria. Having turned around, making a couple of quick lefts onto Park and then Barrie might work, unless there is a parade coming, in which case the intersection at Barrie and Victoria would likely have the same problem. Turning right at Park is also an option, but for a much more roundabout route. In the end, you may want to go to a different grocery store (like Smith's or Robert's), or if things are really dire, give up shopping altogether at this time.

Of course, there are many other factors that might enter into deciding what to do. Is there a person, say, standing in the middle of the intersection directing traffic and signaling you to wait? Is it a police officer, or more like a ten-year-old child? Is there a car ahead of you? Does that car stay put even with a polite toot on the horn? Are there cars behind you as well, boxing you in? Does Bradford on the other side of Victoria appear to be blocked off? If not, what are drivers on the other side of the intersection doing? How much longer is the grocery store going to be open? How much gas (or charge) is there in the car? Is there a child onboard in a car seat? When is that storm-of-the-century supposed to hit? But maybe we have seen enough.

What does this example tell us about common sense? The main thing to observe is that there are both top-down and bottom-up considerations in using common sense in a situation like this. The top-down ones deal with the goals being pursued: driving to the store as part of a plan to get groceries as part of a plan to obtain food. The bottom-up ones deal with what was detected at the scene: the inoperative red light, the traffic on the cross street, a parade, what nearby cars are doing, somebody directing traffic, and so on.

In the next two sections, we will go over these top-down and bottom-up issues in a more systematic way, and suggest how commonsense knowledge gets to be applied using the machinery of chapters 7–8 to make commonsense decisions like those outlined above.

Common Sense from the Top Down

Let us start with the top-down reasoning. We might think of asking ourselves,

Is there a way of getting to that grocery store without going through that troublesome intersection?

This is not the right question, though. If there is indeed another way to get to the store but it will be closed by the time you get there, then common sense should not favor that choice. The point of the trip, after all, was not to get to the store; that was only in service of other, higher-level goals.

So maybe the real question to ask yourself here is more like this:

In light of my current situation, how should I go about achieving what I was originally setting out to do—that is, getting food for the barbecue?

If you will settle for nothing less than the best way of obtaining the kind of food you want given the new circumstances you now find yourself in, then there is really no alternative but to reconsider all of your options and construct an entirely new plan for food from scratch. But again, this kind of first-principles reasoning is rarely practical and not really what common sense should be aiming for either.

So what does common sense do here? This is the critical question. How does common sense come to tell you to turn right in some cases, but to give up on going to this grocery store altogether in others? What we want to suggest is that there is a commonsense reasoning procedure that builds on the symbolic operations from before and provides answers to questions like this. We will call this procedure **MODIFY-PLAN** and sketch how it works.

Let us imagine that when we encounter the stubborn traffic light, we are in the process of following a plan structured somewhat as shown in figure 9.2. (As noted above, we are assuming a symbolic structure for a plan that contains the sequences of actions to be performed as well as the goals and subgoals to be achieved, and some measure of the cost of each action.)

Here, presented informally, is the **MODIFY-PLAN** procedure for making a change to an existing plan like the one above:

- Look at the given plan and consider the *most specific* subgoal that failed. In this example, it was the goal (1.B.4) of getting through the intersection at Bradford and Victoria that failed because of the stubborn red light. Find the best way of achieving just this subgoal given what is now known about the current situation. Use memory-based planning via **TEST** and **FIND-ALL** as described above for doing this.

- Now assuming you found a plan in the previous step, maybe one that involves first turning right at Victoria, look at its cost. If the cost is not much higher than what you had for this subgoal in the plan

Obtain food for this afternoon's barbecue:

  1. Get to a grocery store with good steaks:

    A. Get in the car.

    B. Drive to Jones's Grocery Store on Riverside:

      1. Head west on Elgin toward Bradford.

      2. Turn right on Bradford.

      3. ...

      4. Go through the lights at Bradford and Victoria.

      5. Continue on Bradford.

      6. ...

      7. Turn right on Riverside.

      8. Continue on Riverside for 200 m.

      9. Turn left into the parking lot at 178 Riverside.

    C. Get out of the car.

  2. Purchase the necessary groceries inside the store.

  3. Get back home.

Figure 9.2
A plan for getting groceries

originally, change the overall plan to incorporate this new subplan, and you're done.

- But if no plan was found in the previous step or if the difference in cost is too high, go back to the given plan again and consider the goal that gave immediate rise to that subgoal. In this instance, it was the goal (1.B) of driving to Jones's Grocery Store. (We were trying to get through the intersection because we were trying to drive to Jones's.) Find the best way of achieving just that goal in the current situation. Again, use memory-based planning. This might now involve a different route. If this new route has a cost that is not much higher than what you had for the original route, incorporate this new subplan, and again you're good to go.

- If not, look at the plan again and consider the next higher-level goal. In this case, it was the goal (1) of getting to some grocery store that sells good steaks. (We were driving to Jones's because we were trying to get to a store with good steaks.) See how that goal might now be best achieved in the current situation and at what extra cost. This might now involve driving to a different grocery store. Again, if the cost of getting to this new store is reasonable, then adopt the new subplan, and away you go.

• Continue like this as necessary or until the top-level goal is reached.

This **MODIFY-PLAN** procedure replaces an existing plan with a new one, but it looks for plans that are similar in a certain way to the original one. In the worst case, you might end up having to reconsider the entire top-level goal, yet in most situations, you will only deal with much more specific subgoals like alternative ways of getting through the troublesome intersection.

To avoid having to reconsider the top-level goals in a plan, it makes sense to acquiesce to ever higher costs during the execution of **MODIFY-PLAN**. For example, we might initially reject the cost involved in making a right turn as a way of getting through the intersection, but then, later in the procedure, decide to accept that same cost higher up in the plan when we come to realize that making that turn will be the best way of getting to any grocery store.

In the grocery shopping illustration, the **MODIFY-PLAN** reasoning procedure above would first ask if there was some other way of getting through the intersection (step 1.B.4). As it turns out, most drivers with a modicum of experience will indeed know a second (legal) way of achieving this goal. The maneuver has no name, but it goes like this: make a right turn, then a U-turn, and then another right turn. (Impatient drivers sometimes use this move to avoid waiting for long red lights.) Even inexperienced drivers would be expected to know about getting around obstacles—going right, left, left, and right—as we saw before. This move gets you past the intersection, but puts you farther down the road. So assuming memory-based planning can find actions like these in the world model, the only remaining issue is the cost.

For this right-U-right maneuver, each right turn will have a cost, but let us ignore those and consider just the U-turn. (It is an interesting question in itself as to how we calculate and remember the costs of these actions, but it is clear that regular, unimpeded right turns happen so frequently that they become mindless or low cost, whereas U-turns require more careful perceptual activities, concerns about legality, and paying attention to traffic going in two different directions.) What can we be expected to know in advance about the cost of making a U-turn? The effort, time, and inconvenience are all negligible; the real issue is the risk. If we are close to another intersection on the right and in a jurisdiction where U-turns at intersections are welcomed, the risk of a U-turn will be low; otherwise, if we can perform the turn at a nearby intersection with a left turn traffic signal (so that no traffic will be coming the other way), the risk is low; or otherwise, if the U-turn is to be made in the middle of the cross street, the risk is somewhere between medium and extremely high according to the traffic on that street.

Depending on the current situation, there may of course be other ways of getting through the intersection at a lower cost. Yet in the end, if the cost of achieving a particular subgoal is too high, common sense dictates that we will need to reconsider higher-level goals, as sketched above.

Common Sense from the Bottom Up

Let us now turn to the bottom-up reasoning needed for common sense. Certainly there are times when you need to react to a situation immediately without much additional thought. If a rock smashes through your windshield or the car in front of you suddenly bursts into flames, then this is not the time to ponder the fine points of getting to a grocery store. To a certain extent, this is also true when a police officer on the road points at you and directs you to drive somewhere. In cases like these, you will not really be making reasoned decisions about what to do. Your reaction—or at least your immediate one—would be controlled less by common sense and more by something like a reflex, or perhaps a condition-action rule.

But not all reactions are like this. In less urgent cases, you will want to make a thoughtful decision about what to do. It is a mistake to think that reactions to new situations must always be immediate knee-jerk ones, or that common sense is only used after the fact to rationalize or reconstruct the behavior that took place. The ability to make use of what you know on the spot is what allows you to choose how to react in a sensible way.

In the grocery shopping example above, the original plan to get the groceries failed because something expected did not happen. But beyond that, there may have been nothing out of the ordinary at the scene. In that case, the bottom-up reasoning would be (relatively) straightforward. In deciding what to do, you will mainly need to use the knowledge you had before you arrived at the intersection and some specific details about the scene around you: how many passengers are in your car, the traffic on the cross street, which way other cars are facing, which ones are parked, and so on, all of which should be reflected in your current world model.

Some of what you knew in advance concerns basic facts about your world. You will know how to get to the grocery store, for instance, but probably also how you would get there if you had to turn right. In other words, assuming this is a familiar route, you will have a mental map of where you are and how to get to where you are going. This is not to suggest that you need some sort of two-dimensional Cartesian representation in your head such as the image in figure 9.1. What you need is a world model that will enable you to orient yourself: what roads are connected to what intersections in what directions. This part of a world model acts like an analogue of your locale, just like a two-dimensional map would. If this is not a familiar route, you may need to consult a map or navigation aid to build some sort of internal map. Your world model would probably come with additional information about the roads, freeways, one-way restrictions, and trouble spots.

Where bottom-up reasoning gets more involved, however, is when something unexpected takes place at the scene. In that case, there may well be new things in the immediate surroundings that end up determining what to do next. To sort this out, you need to be able to recognize a thing not just as being of some fundamental type, like a goat, bandage, or truck, say, but also in terms of what it suggests for subsequent action, or what psychologists call its *affordances*: something you can sit on, something to throw, or something to write with, and more generally, something you can make use of, something to ignore, or something to actively avoid.

How does this bottom-up reasoning take place? In broad terms, what needs to happen is that the thing in question needs to be classified and understood in terms of a conceptual structure. This is one place where the conceptual model presented in chapter 7 (as distinct from the world model) gets to play a direct role. Overall, you will need to make sense of the thing according to the collection of concepts you have to work with. For each such concept, you ask yourself, Could the thing in question be one of those? And if it is one of those, does that suggest the presence of something else to watch for? If it's an adult duck crossing the road, might there be baby ducks not far behind? If it's an overturned pickup truck, might its contents have spilled on the road just out of your line of sight?

This process is driven by the hierarchical organization in the conceptual model. For any given concept, we can look through the conceptual model for related concepts: in one case, we want to know if instances of one concept might also be instances of another (the taxonomic "to be" part of the conceptual model); in the other case, we want to know if instances of one concept might have a role to play in instances of another (the "to have" part of the conceptual model). There may be other useful connections among concepts that are similar or related somehow, as suggested in chapter 6 in the context of Minsky frames.

In the grocery shopping situation, suppose that while waiting for the light to turn green, you observe—in a context-independent way perhaps—a person walking on the cross street who happens to have a round red nose. What to make of that? In asking yourself what kind of person you are dealing with (looking through subconcepts in your conceptual model), you might conjecture that the person is a clown, and then confirm this by looking for and finding other things like big floppy shoes. But you don't stop there. You might wonder what a clown is doing on this cross street, and ask yourself whether it is part of something else on the scene. You might then conjecture (using your conceptual model again) that the clown is part of a parade—something whose presence might be confirmed by distant music from an as-yet-unseen marching band. You might then continue by asking what kind of parade this might be, and whether the parade is playing a role as part of something else, and so on.

This sort of bottom-up classification has a direct bearing on the top-down plans being considered. Once you recognize the presence of a parade on the cross street (and incorporate this into the world model), some of the potential plans for getting to the grocery store will end up being rejected. Similarly, recognizing the presence of other things (like a switch on a nearby telephone pole for manually changing the traffic light) will allow you to consider top-down plans that might have been judged unsuitable otherwise. In the end, this is how to answer the question: What kind of thing is this, and on that basis and given what I'm trying to accomplish, what should I be doing next?

How Common Sense Works: Recap

Having looked at both the top-down and bottom-up aspects of common sense, let us step back and summarize the story we have told about the computation of common sense in this chapter as well as those that preceded it.

Our position has been that common sense is a certain ability—specifically, an ability to make use of certain background knowledge in deciding what to do. Commonsense knowledge is about the things in the world and the properties they have, mediated by what we called a conceptual structure, a collection of ideas about the kinds of things there could be, and the kinds of properties they could have. Knowledge would be put to use by representing it symbolically and performing computational operations over those symbolic structures. The commonsense decisions about what to do would amount to using this represented knowledge to consider how to achieve goals and how to react to what has been observed.

In chapter 5, we argued that the story above presupposed a certain worldview: we had to be able to think of the world in terms of things and properties that change as a result of events, where some of those events were actions performed by agents. In chapter 6, we recognized that a conceptual structure had to deal with concepts with indistinct boundaries, and both typical and exceptional cases. In chapter 7, we looked at building symbolic models of states of the world and conceptual structures as representations of knowledge. In chapter 8, we looked at what it would take to compute if a formula was true according to this represented knowledge, whether it would be true after some events took place, and whether it was possible for the agent involved to make those events occur.

Finally, in this chapter, we returned to the analysis of common sense itself. We argued that with enough experience, it is often possible to make do without anything like common sense. When something unanticipated happens, however, we need to be able to make use of what we know in both a top-down and bottom-up way. The top-down reasoning involves looking through the actions we know about, including those in analogous areas, to find other reasonable ways of achieving goals that have been stymied; the bottom-up reasoning involves looking through the concepts we know about to see if something observed could have a bearing on the goals we are trying to achieve. Both of these forms of reasoning need to function expeditiously and in tandem to make effective decisions about what to do, and we saw how the symbolic representation and reasoning of chapters 7–8 provided the necessary ingredients.

Of course, there is more to common sense than being jolted out of a routine. But for that part of it at least, this, in our estimation, is how common sense works.

Notice that this account does not lay out a computational architecture for a cognitive agent, with common sense somewhere near the top in a position of honor. In fact, it does not explain at all how the overall behavior of an agent would be managed and controlled by common sense. The reason is simple: in our opinion, this is not the right way to think about it. An agent with common sense does not turn into some sort of philosopher of action, constantly asking itself, "According to what I know and what I want, what should I really be doing next?" Instead, we imagine that the agent would continue to be governed by habits and routines, or perhaps an evolving collection of rules of the sort discussed at the start of this chapter. An appeal would be made to common sense only when this breaks down: something new happens, something expected fails to, or something presents itself that suggests extra care or mindfulness is called for. This is when we would expect to see a much more deliberate form of behavior, an agent asking itself what its goals are, what it knows about its current situation, and so on, as seen here. If this picture is at least roughly right, then there is no overall cognitive architecture for common sense. Common sense has only a subordinate role to play in the mental life of an agent, making habits and routines much more flexible, versatile, and robust—more intelligent—than they would otherwise be.

10   Steps toward Implementation

Walking on water wasn't built in a day.

—Jack Kerouac, "Some Western Haikus"

As we begin to wind down our study of common sense, it is a good time to pause for a moment to reflect on topics that were either bypassed or given only a passing glance. In this short chapter, we want to focus on one specific question that we did not really spend any time on at all: What would it take in practical terms to actually build an AI system with common sense? Even after everything considered so far in this book, we are not going to pretend that what is left is just more of the same or a few days of routine work. If it were that easy, somebody would have done it by now. But we do want to survey briefly what we think is involved.

Our view, repeated throughout this book, is that common sense is an ability to put what we called commonsense knowledge to good use. We talked about the kind of knowledge involved, how this knowledge could be represented in symbolic form, and how putting it to use really meant processing the symbolic structures in a certain way for certain purposes, which we called commonsense reasoning. So to actually build an AI system with common sense, we need to think about building two things: a commonsense reasoner, and a commonsense knowledge base for it to work on.

Building a Commonsense Reasoner

Let's take the reasoning first. We might ask, Where does commonsense reasoning come from in humans? For example, if we are told that Jack is looking at Anne, we immediately come to the conclusion that Jack is looking at somebody, without having to be told how to figure this out. If we are told that Babar is an elephant and already know what elephants are like, nobody has to tell us how to apply that elephant knowledge to draw tentative conclusions about Babar's color or the size of his ears. The reasoning that humans perform in cases like these is logical, but it is logic of a basic form that does not need to be learned in a classroom or from a textbook.

But where does this logic come from? In the case of humans, this is a complex subject for developmental psychology. It is clearly not an ability acquired by learning some specialized procedures to follow, like how to solve a system of linear equations or make Baked Alaska. The real question is whether the reasoning is something we all just get by virtue of being human (unless something goes wrong) like the ability to grow hair, or whether it is something we get only in rudimentary form, but then have to develop, such as the ability to throw a football. Can people actually get better at commonsense reasoning? There is an entire self-help industry that seems to be geared to helping people be more effective at it: better organized, better focused and attentive, better at separating the relevant from the irrelevant, and less prone to mental flubs. (Curiously, books like *The Seven Habits of Highly Effective People* appear to be aimed mainly at corporate managers, as if this effectiveness was less of a concern for, say, sheet metal workers.)

In the case of machines, however, we see no alternative but to roll up our sleeves and code all these forms of reasoning by hand. Yes, it would be nice if all the necessary reasoning procedures could emerge spontaneously through some sort of machine learning process. But at this point, this is a tough bet to take. There are some results indicating that certain specialized neural net architectures can actually learn procedures (such as the multiplication of binary numbers), but these currently look more like a tour de force demonstration than a practical methodology for building systems.

On the positive side, our sense is that there should only be dozens of reasoning procedures to implement rather than the thousands suggested by systems like Cyc. These procedures would be of the kind discussed or alluded to in previous chapters. We gave fairly detailed accounts of procedures like **GET-PARTS**, **TEST**, and **MODIFY-PLAN**. But we only sketched what might be involved in things such as instantiating concepts, simulating change, dealing with inconsistencies, or making use of annotations like strength or importance. And we said almost nothing about bottom-up invocation, the use of analogy and similarity, the recognition of situations, and the overall position and coordination of common sense in a larger cognitive architecture. Much hard work remains to be done on these things and their integration.

Building a Commonsense Knowledge Base

Let us now turn to commonsense knowledge. Here we cannot expect there to be only dozens of items to consider. If knowledge about hospitals counts as one, and knowledge about birthday parties counts as two, then we should expect tens or maybe hundreds of thousands of items to be involved. Where is all of this knowledge going to come from?

In terms of humans, it is much clearer. As stated in chapter 1:

In some cases, we get our understanding through repeated experience (like how to eat a melting ice cream cone on a hot summer day); in some cases, we get advice from friends (such as what to wear—and not wear—for a party); and in other cases, our understanding may well come from something like a guide or manual (like how to set up a home printer).

In other words, for humans, some of the knowledge comes firsthand from personal experience, and some of it comes secondhand from the language of other humans (spoken or written).

And for machines? Since we cannot really expect deep learning to deliver the goods (at least not in any obvious way), do we have to resign ourselves to building these enormous knowledge bases by hand, in the spirit of Cyc? Maybe some of this knowledge will have to be handcrafted by people, but let us explore the possible alternatives.

For knowledge that humans get through language—that is, knowledge that has been written down or recorded somewhere for humans to use—it would certainly make sense to try to find a way to get machines to avail themselves of that information, and we will talk more about that prospect below.

But for knowledge that humans get through personal experience, should we expect machines to have similar experiences and learn from them in a similar way? If this takes many years for humans, will it be the same for machines? In a wonderful science fiction story called "The Lifecycle of Software Objects" by Ted Chiang, we find this:

There are no shortcuts; if you want to create the common sense that comes from twenty years of being in the world, you need to devote twenty years to the task. You can't assemble an equivalent collection of heuristics in less time; experience is algorithmically incompressible.

Maybe this is true. Even if experiences themselves are incompressible, though, some of what needs to be learned from them might still be compressible. Let us try to be more specific about the kind of knowledge involved.

Knowledge from Experience

The key observation when it comes to personal experiences is this: they are mediated by the senses. You cannot experience something in the physical world unless you see it, touch it, smell it, and so on. For simplicity, let us restrict our attention to visual experiences. (Humans also experience things internally without sensing them, but we will ignore that at this point.)

By focusing on the senses and vision in particular, we do not mean to suggest that our experience of the world is primarily *passive*. Consider the sense of touch, for example. We can certainly touch an object like a trumpet, say, but more important, we can pick it up and act on it. We feel its weight, rigidity, and texture. We turn it over, see its sheen from different angles, rap it with a fingernail, and then hear the metallic ring. We can move the valves but fail to move the mouthpiece. We blow a kind of raspberry into the mouthpiece and hear the result. This is how we get to know trumpets. The experiences are sensory or maybe even sensual, but they are also part of an *active* engagement with the physical world.

One thing we clearly expect to acquire from a lifetime of visual experiences is the ability to recognize things. You see enough fire trucks (or images of them) to be able to reliably recognize one in a context-free way, as suggested before. This might well be done through something like deep learning. With this learning in hand, you would then be in a position to connect the set of perceptual parameters acquired to a symbol in a world model representing a fire truck—say, Truck#95—and from there to symbols for conceptually related things like ladders, hoses, firefighters, and fire events. (This would allow you to conjure an image of a fire truck whenever you were thinking about one too.) It is worth noting that this form of *symbol grounding* only works for symbols that represent what we earlier called medial macro-objects. Symbols standing for the other things we think about, like political parties and property taxes, cannot be grounded in this way.

But there appears to be more to learn from visual experience than how to recognize or visualize things. What about learning with your own eyes that people wear warm clothing in the winter? Acquiring this kind of knowledge through visual perception is tougher to account for. As we saw in chapter 4, visual images do not lend themselves to this kind of thinking for the simple reason that they do not make clear what is germane in the image, other than what it looks like (and how it aggregates with other images that look similar).

To get a glimpse of what is involved, however, it is useful to consider one clear case of humans learning about the world through personal experience—a case where human language must necessarily play a much less prominent role: the learning experiences of *toddlers*.

When a person is young enough, we expect them to learn primarily from their personal interaction with the world (generally guided by an adult, but not always). What a child gets in preschool, before first grade, is what is usually called *early childhood education* (ECE). We expect ECE to be mostly about social and emotional development, but some of it concerns knowledge of the world.

There is a book by Judy Herr called *Creative Resources for the Early Childhood Classroom*. It is interesting to look at the range of "themes" it considers suitable for inclusion in an ECE classroom:

Ants	Apples	Art
Birds	Blue	Breads
Brushes	Bubbles	Buildings
Camping	Caring for our earth	Cars, trucks, and buses
Cats	Chinese New Year	Christmas
Cinco de Mayo	Circus	Clothing
Communication	Construction tools	Containers
Creative movement	Dairy products	Dentist
Diwali	Doctors and nurses	Dogs
Easter	Eggs	Fall
Families	Farm Animals	Feelings

Feet	Firefighters	Fish
Flowers	Friends	Frogs
Fruits and vegetables	Gardens	Halloween
Hanukkah (Chanukah)	Hats	Health
Homes	Insects and spiders	Kwanzaa
Mail carrier	Mice	Music
Numbers	Nursery rhymes	Occupations
Pets	Plants	Puppets
Purple	Rain	Ramadan
Red	Safety	Scissors
Shapes	Sports	Spring
Summer	Thanksgiving	Trees
Valentine's Day	Water	Wheels
Winter	Worms	Yellow
Zoo animals		

For each of these seventy-six themes, the book presents ideas on how to organize a curriculum appropriate for a preschool child. For example, for the "construction tools" theme above, the author suggests a number of classroom activities for preschool children:

- Cut out silhouettes of the tools and place them on a bulletin board.
- Sing "This is the way ..." for each tool.
- Practice pounding with small hammers.
- Explore a display with various tools on it.
- Visit a shoemaker's store, or an arts and craft store
- Dip a small tool into paint and print it on paper
- Discuss safety rules for tools
- Participate in tool cleanup

For each theme, the book also presents the vocabulary a child might be expected to pick up. For the "construction tools" theme, it's this:

tool: an object to help us

drill: a tool that cuts holes

wrench: a tool that holds things

screwdriver: a tool that turns screws

saw: a cutting tool with sharp edges

hammer: a tool used to insert or remove objects such as nails

pliers: a tool used for holding

clamp: a tool used to join or hold things

ruler: a measuring tool

wedge: a tool used for splitting

plane: a tool used for shaving wood

Finally, but most interesting for our purposes, for each theme, the book presents the main ideas that a child can be expected to learn from the curriculum activities. (The author calls these ideas "concepts," but maybe "propositions" is a better name.) Here is what the book says are the ones for the "construction tools" theme:

1. Tools can be electric or hand-powered.
2. Tools are helpful when building.
3. Pliers, tweezers, and clamps hold things.
4. Drills, nails, and screws make holes.
5. Planes, saws, and scissors cut materials.
6. Hammers and screwdrivers are used to put in and remove nails and screws.
7. Rulers are used for measuring.
8. To be safe, tools need to be handled with care.
9. Goggles should be worn to protect our eyes when using tools.
10. After use, tools need to be put away.

So it seems that a good part of what the children are expected to acquire from their experience in an ECE classroom is ordinary commonsense knowledge that can be stated quite clearly in English. The implication here is intriguing: although preschoolers may not be able to make much sense of a sentence like "Goggles should be worn to protect our eyes when using tools," it is expected that they will be able to learn what that sentence says through experience.

Here is another example, for the "camping" theme above, with the following ideas to be learned:

1. A tent is a shelter used for camping.
2. We can camp in the woods or at a campground.
3. We can also camp in a park, at a lake, or in our backyard.
4. Hot dogs, fish, marshmallows, and beans are all camping foods.

5. A camper can be driven or attached to the back of a car or pickup truck.

6. Lanterns and flashlights are sources of light used for camping.

7. A sleeping bag is a blanket used for camping.

8. Some people camp by a lake to water ski and go boating and fishing.

Here is what is to be learned for the "winter" theme:

1. Winter is one of the four seasons.

2. Winter is usually the coldest season.

3. It snows in the winter in some areas.

4. People wear warmer clothes in the winter.

5. Some animals hibernate in the winter.

6. Trees may lose their leaves in the winter.

7. Lakes, ponds, and water may freeze in the winter.

8. Sledding, skiing, tobogganing, and ice skating are winter sports in colder areas.

9. To remove snow, people shovel and plow.

10. December, January, and February are winter months.

What this early learning suggests is that what is acquired from personal experience comprises two distinct things: (a) the ability to recognize and name certain categories of mundane physical objects like fire trucks, pliers, tents, and sleds; and (b) some additional ideas that can be expressed in language (even if a young human may be unable to make much sense of the language involved). So leaving (a) for something like deep learning, let us now turn to (b).

Knowledge from Language

While it would certainly be convenient for AI systems to be able to learn from texts the way humans do, there is a serious impediment noted in chapter 3: the need to make sense of that text. Massive amounts of unanalyzed English text might be just what is needed for certain tasks like retrieval ("Find me all the medical articles about Ebola outside Africa") or basic forms of translation ("How do you say 'What time is it?' in Portuguese?"). But for common sense, we want to construct symbolic representations amenable to reasoning procedures of the sort already seen. This means we need to figure out from the text what kinds of things are claimed to exist and what kinds of properties they are claimed to have. This is what commonsense knowledge wants, and what the declarative sentences of a language like English purport to offer.

The problem with this is that there is a large gap between declarative sentences (linear strings of words, in other words) and these sorts of symbolic structures. Even putting aside metaphoric and poetic text, the English sentences of ordinary expository text express ideas in a dense and complicated way, leaving many of the necessary details to be filled in by a knowledgeable language user. This is worth examining closely since it has a tremendous impact on how AI systems will be able to make use of online textual resources.

Consider a simple example: the English phrase "a small dog." Observe that you cannot really construct a symbolic representation of the desired sort unless you figure out that this involves the property of size. But "size" is not mentioned in the phrase. We can see this sort of omission even more clearly in what is called noun-noun modification. Consider "a wood table" versus "a coffee table." One has to do with material composition and one has to do with purpose, but nothing in either phrase spells this out. If we want to build a symbolic representation, we cannot just conjoin the idea for "coffee" and the idea for "table" the way the words are conjoined in English. And once we resolve the whole liquid issue for "coffee table," we will need to think again for something like a "water table." Similarly, we need to know that "plant food" is food for plants, while a "food plant" involves food from plants (so be careful which one you decide to eat!). In some cases, the properties left unspecified demand a complex story. It's clear that an "old family recipe" is not like an "old goulash recipe," but it's less clear what kind of thing a recipe has to be for it to have a property involving families. Sometimes English phrases are no more than a jumble of nouns, with all the analysis of properties left to be done, like a "truck stop diner Thursday night hamburger platter special." (Is there such a thing as a "diner Thursday" or "night hamburger"?)

The need for prior knowledge is even more evident in the case of ambiguity. Suppose we are trying to construct some sort of a symbolic representation for the sentence used before:

The large ball crashed through the table because it was made of steel.

All the word senses here are reasonably clear. We would want to construct a world model where, among other things, there were two things, a ball and table, and the ball had the property of being made of steel. As noted before, however, nothing in the individual words of the sentence points to the ball as the thing made of steel. And isn't it more likely that a table would be made of steel than a large ball?

So yes, it is quite remarkable what can be done with massive amounts of text (in applications like Google Translate, say) without any sort of systematic analysis of what the sentences mean or how they are being used. For many purposes, the differences between "plant food" and "food plant" are just not worth worrying about, except in terms of the texts they appear in. But if English text is to be used as the basis for a commonsense knowledge base, it will need to be converted into a form that is suitable for commonsense reasoning, and this does seem to require much closer attention to what the declarative sentences are actually declaring.

In sum, what we have here is a quandary: we want to build representations of commonsense knowledge from English text, but to do so, we need to be able to make sense of the text, which requires commonsense knowledge!

How do we break out of this loop? Some current AI efforts to build large knowledge bases just ignore it. Projects like the previously mentioned NELL or the crowdsourcing ConceptNet effort out of MIT seek to produce a multitude of commonsense facts and rules without too much concern for the things and properties involved. Yet as clearly shown in the Marcus and Davis book *Rebooting AI*, the resulting symbolic representations tend to be somewhat chaotic. Not only do the projects not spend nearly enough time on the reasoning aspects, it is far from clear that the resulting knowledge bases are internally coherent enough for reasoning procedures to work on them in a fully automated way.

This issue of coherence arises in knowledge bases handcrafted by people as well, especially if the various parts of the system are assembled by different people. One person's view about how to break the world into categories of things and properties might not fit well with another's. From a practical engineering point of view, there needs to be some sort of *curation* to resolve the clashes and misunderstandings that naturally arise in big distributed projects.

How then to deal with the quandary above in a more principled way? One idea is to take seriously the fact that for humans, the ability to make sense of English text is not a single monolithic skill that arrives at age eighteen, say; it comes in stages. You can understand and use language without understanding it all. Teenagers, even advanced ones, may not be able to make much sense of the writings of philosopher Immanuel Kant. Eight-year-olds might not be able to make heads or tails of some ordinary adult conversation.

And the same is true even for two-year-olds. Consider these lines from the famous reader *Goodnight Moon* for young tots:

> In the great green room
> There was a telephone
> And a red balloon
> And a picture of
> The cow jumping over the moon.

The connection between some of these words and parts of the accompanying illustrations will be meaningful even for two-year-olds. But the language skills in play are obviously quite limited. And there is no possible connection to illustrations when it comes to words that that cannot be shown in pictures, like these:

> account, act, addition, adjustment, agreement, amount, amusement, answer, approval, argument, attempt, attention, attraction, authority.

This is not a random list of *A* words; these are the first 14 nouns of the 850 words that make up what is called Basic English (invented by philosopher Charles Ogden in the 1930s). These particular nouns are said to be "nonpicturable." Even though they are not really technical terms, an extra degree of sophistication beyond what a two-year-old can muster is needed to make use of them.

What all of this suggests for AI is that we should perhaps be willing to treat the problem of extracting knowledge from text as something to be developed in stages. The system can start by making sense of simple expository texts that use English in a basic way. With this done, it can then use the knowledge acquired (and any additional knowledge acquired by other means) to help make sense of the next round of slightly more demanding texts. And the process iterates.

While this bootstrapping idea may turn out to be a bust in practical terms, there are a couple of factors that give it credence. The first is that we already talked about building world and conceptual models in a staged way. As we said in chapter 6, we should expect to begin with blunt, simple-minded versions of concepts like hospitals and birthday parties, and be prepared to refine and annotate them in subsequent rounds. So it's not as if we expect complex notions to enter conceptual models only in some sort of final, definitive form. Indeed, it is perhaps a mistake to think of preliminary versions of concepts as being *superseded* by more sophisticated ones; they both have roles to play. Going back to hospitals, sometimes we do want to think of them as physical buildings, and at other times we want to think of them as social institutions that are merely housed in those buildings. This explains how something can have both a third floor and a board of trustees.

The second factor is that there already exist rich textual resources that do not presume the full language abilities of human adults—and are worth briefly looking into.

An Online Resource

There is a version of Wikipedia called KidzSearch that has been designed to be read and understood by children. The collection is said to contain two hundred thousand articles written in a simplified English that is more suitable for children (of what age is not clear, but not toddlers). The sentences tend to be short and direct, with jargon kept to a minimum.

Here, for example, is the start of an article on gophers:

Gophers are small, burrowing rodents. There are over 100 kinds of gophers in America. Gophers have long front teeth, tiny features, and short tails. They live in very complex tunnels underground. They live by themselves and feed on roots and shrubs. They are known to be pests and ruin people's lawns and gardens.

In contrast, here is the start of the Wikipedia article on gophers (for older readers):

Pocket gophers, commonly referred to as just gophers, are burrowing rodents of the family *Geomyidae*. There are about 35 species, all endemic to North and Central America. They are commonly known for their extensive tunneling activities and their ability to destroy farms and gardens.

To see a second example, here is part of an article on opera. First, the KidzSearch version:

An opera is like a play in which everything is sung instead of spoken. Operas are usually performed in opera houses. The singers who sing and act out the story are on the stage, and the orchestra is in front of the stage but lower down, in the orchestra pit, so that the audience can see the stage.

Then the Wikipedia one:

Opera is a form of theater in which music has a leading role and the parts are taken by singers, but is distinct from musical theater. Such a "work" (the literal translation of Italian word "opera") is typically a collaboration between a composer and a librettist and incorporates a number of the performing arts, such as acting, scenery, costume, and sometimes dance or ballet. The performance is typically given in an opera house, accompanied by an orchestra or smaller musical ensemble, which since the early 19th century has been led by a conductor.

There are some obvious differences, but they are not dramatic. The KidzSearch text is not as elaborate as Wikipedia's, but it is still full of information. If you are able to make sense of KidzSearch articles and have access to all two hundred thousand of them, you can learn a lot. More to the point, if you were able to make effective use of all the knowledge contained in those KidzSearch articles, you would be well on your way to having what you need to make sense of the next round of more demanding text.

Of course, as a way of making use of online textual resources, this staged approach leaves open two major questions. What would it take to develop AI systems knowledgeable enough (and linguistically capable enough) to make appropriate sense of something like the KidzSearch article on gophers above? And what else does an AI system need to know beyond all of those KidzSearch articles to make sense of more demanding text aimed at adults? Neither of these have easy and obvious answers.

The Lesson

What all of this suggests is that from the point of view of building machines with common sense, there needs to be a much closer connection between researchers interested in representation and reasoning, and those interested in linguistic analysis and particularly the analysis of simple forms of expository language. There was indeed such a connection in the past. But the area of computational linguistics has changed in the last few decades to play down the traditional subareas of syntax, semantics, and pragmatics, and play up the use of massive amounts of English text as a resource for things like information retrieval and summarization, capitalizing on the remarkable success of the statistical methods seen in deep learning. If English text is to be used as the basis for commonsense knowledge, though, it will need to be mapped onto symbolic representations geared to commonsense reasoning, and this does seem to require much closer attention to the issues of the syntax, semantics, and pragmatics of conventional linguistics.

11 Building Trust

With great power comes great responsibility.

—Peter Parker, *Spider-Man*

Our presentation so far has been primarily descriptive: we discussed how common sense appears in humans (chapter 2), how it does not show up in current AI systems (chapter 3), and how it seems to work (chapters 4–9). In this chapter, we are going to step back and take a somewhat broader, more prescriptive point of view. We are going to propose a certain vision for AI systems of the future and the role to be played there by common sense. We will not be talking about how future AI systems should be engineered but instead more about what we think this engineering should be aiming for so as to end up with AI systems with that most important of features: trustworthiness.

Autonomous AI Systems

Let us first remind ourselves of the kind of AI we have in mind. We are imagining highly advanced AI systems that work in unconstrained real-world settings, making decisions for themselves about what to do and how to deal with what comes up in real life. Future AI systems with full-fledged intelligence are sometimes called "artificial general intelligence" systems, but we prefer the term "autonomous" to "general" as it emphasizes that the systems will not be able to rely on the intelligence of others to make decisions for them. This is not to say that such systems must be working alone. We can easily imagine autonomous AI systems working in close collaboration with humans and other AI systems.

So we will have nothing to say here about AI systems working in artificially defined domains, where the range of inputs that the system can be expected to deal with can be circumscribed in advance. As we have stressed, this applies to almost all existing AI systems—the successful ones anyway—from systems that play games like chess and poker, to blood-infection-diagnosis programs, to face recognition systems, to movie recommenders, and so on.

Closely related to this, we will also not be concerned in this chapter with AI systems where the ultimate decisions about what to do are taken to be the responsibility of somebody else. The term "autonomous" is often used to describe any system that runs without direct human control. But what we care about here, and what is part and parcel of our imagined future general AI systems, is that they will be held *responsible* for their actions and are making decisions that are their own responsibility. If a more conventional machine in a shop is running without human intervention after being given initial parameters, and it hurts or kills a worker, it is just an accident, and the machine can't be blamed the way a human can. But we are imagining a future in which autonomous AI systems will be held accountable for their actions in the same way humans are held accountable—like the human who sets the machine parameters. So when we use the term "autonomous AI systems" here, we mean AI systems that indeed have responsibility for their actions in the world and are not merely running unattended.

To clarify this notion, consider something like a thermostat. Once a thermostat is set, it certainly runs unattended and decides for itself when to turn on the furnace. It also operates in the real world. All sorts of unanticipated things can happen there, such as a cold spell in the middle of summer, a window suddenly breaking and letting in the outside air, an unexpected elderly visitor who likes the room temperature hotter than usual, and so on. What makes the thermostat a *closed* system, however, is that the full set of parameters that will determine its behavior has been decided in advance. For a basic thermostat, the only things that matter are the ambient temperature near the thermostat (as determined by a sensor) and its relationship to the setting on the thermostat. So the thermostat can be thought of as working in a closed, artificially defined environment where there is a single numerical input to contend with. Its responsibility is extremely narrow: turning on the furnace when that input is lower than the setting and turning off the furnace when it is higher. It is decidedly not responsible for the overall temperature in the room nor the comfort of the people there. When something unanticipated happens in the real world, it is the responsibility of the people there to change the thermostat setting as necessary (or perhaps even to call a contractor to fix the furnace if it's broken). The same is true for the much more elaborate "smart" home control hubs (under the guidance of things like Amazon Alexa and Google Home)—with many more sensors and actuators, of course, but the same reliance on people for all the high-level decisions.

Now consider self-driving cars. These are cars where an AI system of some sort is controlling the vehicle. In the most advanced cases, the system takes little human input, and decides on its own how to follow the road, where to turn, what speed to maintain, and when to stop. Everyone certainly recognizes that if the system gets in a fix, fails to see or hear something, or otherwise miscalculates, it will be up to a human to take control, somewhat like an airline pilot turning off the autopilot. (It remains a thorny ongoing challenge to find reliable ways of keeping a person who is not controlling an automobile attentive enough to be able to assume control quickly when necessary.)

But quite apart from the car making mistakes, human decision-making can be involved in other, more significant ways. We considered a situation in chapter 9 involving a traffic light stuck on red. We saw that there was an open-ended set of factors that might be relevant in deciding what to do next—whether to turn right, go straight, or turn around. Common sense was needed to make the right decision, but that common sense did not have to come from the car. Even a top-of-the-line self-driving car of the future might not be asked to make that kind of call. Like the thermostat, it can defer to the humans there.

It might well be asked, Will we ever want to build AI systems that do *not* defer to humans in this way? Maybe we will judge the risk of autonomous AI systems to be too great. If there is anything about AI that animates science fiction books and movies, it is the idea of a system that acts on its own, makes decisions for itself, and in the worst cases, makes decisions at odds with the wishes of humans. Technology running amok in this way is not what is behind science fiction about nuclear or biological disasters. In those cases, what we have is either the willful misuse of the technology by evil-minded humans or perhaps accidents involving negligent humans.

Science fiction about AI disasters is more like the Frankenstein story, where the creature decides for itself to misbehave.

The usual rationale for autonomous AI systems is that we may wish to consider applications where intelligent decisions might be required, but where for one reason or another, no human will be available to make them. Think, for example, of an unmanned rover on a distant planet where communication delays with Earth are long. Or consider robots working where the available personnel and communication is limited, like in emergency recovery after a massive earthquake, especially underground or in dense structures. Having a human in the loop to watch, supervise, and supply all the necessary intelligence may be the most desirable option, but may not be practical. A much more common justification involves situations where there are people who could do the job, but where it might be safer, cheaper, or more convenient to have it done by machine.

There is another, more fanciful reason we might want to consider autonomous AI systems—one favored more by futurists than by AI researchers themselves. At some point in the future, we may be able to envisage autonomous AI systems that will be *better than humans* at dealing with what comes up in real life. Superintelligence and all that. In other words, we may want to consider autonomous AI systems because of the extra capability that may offer us.

But how strong are these justifications? Are the benefits really worth the risk? To be clear, what we will be talking about in the rest of this chapter is a direction for autonomous AI technology if—and this is a big if—we were to decide to pursue it. The question about what technology a society ought to aim for should be informed by technical considerations, of course, but does not stop there. As the old saying goes, just because something *can* be done doesn't mean it *should* be done. And we need to be ever mindful that technology of any kind may not be used as it was originally intended, no matter how laudable those intentions. Who would have thought, for example, that Facebook could be used so cheaply and effectively to spread disinformation and divisiveness? As venture capitalist Roger McNamee puts it, it is all too easy to confuse "easy success with merit, good intentions with virtue, rapid advances with value, and wealth with wisdom." This appears to be especially true for AI technology.

In the end, our opinions on what can be done in AI technology are based on our technical experience and what we have learned throughout our careers in AI research. Our opinions on what ought to be done to best serve the needs of humans are no more authoritative than anyone else's.

Specifications for AI Systems

Let us step back for a moment from possible AI systems of the future and look at them as no more than a certain software technology, not so different from other computer applications such as those for preparing income tax returns or playing simulated soccer. (We are putting aside the hardware considerations in things like robots.) It is useful to think of a computer system in two different ways: the actual *implementation* of the system that users interact with on their devices, and the *specification* of the system—that is, the understanding the engineers have about what the system is supposed to do.

Of course these days as a result of market pressure, software systems are often assembled with only the vaguest idea about what the system will ultimately be able to do. Initial releases of the software might be weak—and buggy. Yet to have a chance of competing in the marketplace, it is essential to get them there quickly and correct problems on the fly. New features are continually being considered and incorporated into new releases. This is not an ideal way to build technology of any kind, but for better or worse, "move fast and break things" has become the norm in the software business.

But let us take a somewhat idealized point of view and imagine that the time to market is less of a concern, and AI system builders of the future will have time to think hard about the specifications of their system, with the goal of carefully building software products that work as intended. To most consumers, this might seem far from their experience with commercial software, but it is precisely what is already attempted in certain mission-critical software, like the software found in aircraft guidance systems, or systems controlling complex devices such as planetary rovers or nuclear power plants. In cases like these, there is only one chance to get the implementation right. It's not to say that there are no mistakes; it's that the mistakes cannot be shrugged off like some new whizbang feature of Microsoft Word that is not yet working as advertised. They can be fatal to the entire mission—and people.

The way computer professionals approach this problem for some mission-critical software is as follows: they write a specification for the system in a formal language, they write the computer code that they hope will satisfy the specification, and then they try to prove mathematically (with the help of computers, of course) that the code satisfies the specification. To the extent that this approach to software development is practical—and it is becoming increasingly so—it results in computer systems that are guaranteed to meet their specifications. This does not mean the resulting systems will be free of errors; it simply means that the errors will almost invariably lie in the specifications of the system, not in their implementations.

Now think of a future AI system from this point of view. If it is going to be making decisions autonomously, and these decisions will be life changing or mission critical, we need to be as clear as we possibly can about what the system is supposed to do.

Here, though, we can see that there is an immediate problem when it comes to autonomous AI: How can we possibly specify what the system is supposed to do if it will be working for itself in the real world? That is, if we cannot predict in advance what the system will have to contend with, how we can stipulate what it should do? The system will not only have to cope with the unknowns we can anticipate in advance; it will also have to cope with unknowns that we have not yet thought about—the "unknown unknowns," in the famous words of former US secretary of defense Donald Rumsfeld.

Making Hard Choices

And the problem goes beyond this. It's not just that there will be situations we have not thought about; there will also be situations we may have thought about where we ourselves are unsure about what should be done.

Consider, for instance, what are called *trolley problems*. These are little thought experiments that help us visualize life-and-death choices and how to make them in a reasonable way. Here is an example lifted from Wikipedia:

You see a runaway trolley moving toward five tied-up (or otherwise incapacitated) people lying on the tracks. You are standing next to a lever that controls a switch. If you pull the lever, the trolley will be redirected onto a side track, and the five people on the main track will be saved. However, there is a single person lying on the side track. You have two options:

1. Do nothing and allow the trolley to kill the five people on the main track.
2. Pull the lever, diverting the trolley onto the side track where it will kill one person.

What should you do?

What makes situations like these so troubling is that there appear to be no good guiding principles for making decisions about what to do. Is it always better to save five people, even if one has to die? What if the five people are convicted murderers, scheduled to receive the death penalty the next day? What if saving the five people actually requires pushing an innocent person to a certain death on the tracks? Is that any different, and if so why?

It is far from clear how to resolve dilemmas like these, and they have been the subject of considerable attention in moral philosophy (and criticism too). But they do serve to remind us that we cannot expect a specification for an AI system to invariably result in decisions about what to do that everyone would immediately agree with. There will be troublesome cases that have no easy answers for people or AI systems.

It might be tempting to say the following: an AI system should just do what it is told, no more, no less, and simply act like it was not there in cases where it is unsure of what to do. This has some advantages. It limits the unintended or unknown side effects caused by actions taken by the system. It takes the AI system out of the loop on the really tough decisions and transfers all the responsibility to people.

Yet notice that in the trolley example above, it would insist on the "do nothing" option (1), for better or worse. Is that really what we want? And it has other drawbacks as well. If an AI system is directed by somebody to cause death to other people (in a trolley-like situation, say), should that be enough for it to do so? Alternatively, if the AI system does what it is told, but subject to restrictions like Asimov's laws of robotics about causing harm to people, will that be enough? (There are many stories by Asimov himself about how his own laws fall short.) In the end, an AI system that stays out of the fray as much as possible is actually embodying a moral choice, just as it would be for people. In some cases, it will be a reasonable choice; in other cases, not so much. AI systems that are overly wary to act will end up being as problematic as those that are overly eager to do so.

Given these seemingly insurmountable ethical problems, how can we possibly go forward? What ought we to expect of autonomous AI systems operating in the real world, facing situations that we have never thought about or situations where reasonable people will disagree about what ought to be done? Again, a case can certainly be made that we should not even contemplate a technology where these issues arise. But let us go through the intellectual exercise and consider what it might be sensible to aim for.

Behaving for a Reason

What we want to suggest is that the specification for autonomous AI systems should not even try to pin down the right decisions about what to do. In many cases, we will simply not know in advance what those are. Instead, we will set the bar quite a bit lower. What we will argue is that these imagined AI systems of the future should be designed and built *to have good reasons for what they do*—reasons that we can understand, even when we disagree with them.

If you were to listen to AI researchers talking about the history of the field and what AI systems have been like over the years, you would certainly hear a wide variety of opinions. Among the AI researchers behind the recent developments in machine learning, however, there is a certain broad agreement, somewhat along the following lines:

AI systems of the past focused very much on symbols and symbolic representations. But that symbolic approach (a) did not work at all well, and (b) was mostly due to the misapprehension that intelligence was somehow tied to words and *language*. To be intelligent meant being able to converse the way people did—the Turing test and all that. Modern AI systems have taken a quite-different route, where embodiment in the world is what matters, not words and symbols. Why should a rover alone on Mars have to worry about dealing with the fine points of language, like when to use the word "acquaintance" versus "friend," or what the "it" refers to in "The large ball crashed through the table because it was made of steel"? There's nothing wrong with questions of language, of course, but they are just that: questions of language, not of intelligent behavior more broadly.

Along similar lines, it might be argued that the kind of common sense we have been talking about, where knowledge expressible in ordinary language was the focus, would really only be of concern for systems that had to deal with a language like English.

We think this argument is understandable but wrong. It is true that human language ability leans heavily on commonsense knowledge. Yet as we have contended, common sense transcends the use of language. The reason we want AI systems to exhibit common sense of the sort we have discussed here is not because we want to communicate with them in English or any other natural language. The reason is much more fundamental. We want AI systems to have common sense so that they will have good reasons for what they do—reasons that we humans will be able to understand.

Why would we need to understand AI systems at all? We will take this up in the last section of this chapter. For now, let us simply assume that we do want this. For a future AI technology that may be making life-altering decisions or operating for us in a remote environment, we will want to be confident that what it is doing makes sense. If something goes wrong, for example, we will want to be able to find out why it went wrong in terms we can understand.

Now think of how we go about understanding people. We might say something like "Johnny opened the refrigerator door because ..." and then try to complete the sentence using only true statements about Johnny's central nervous systems, sensory organs, muscles, and so on. Someday this might be possible, but even if it were, we would never attempt to formulate such an account. The details would overwhelm us, and in the end, not help us understand why Johnny did what he did. We need reasons we can deal with. Maybe he opened the refrigerator door because he wanted to cool off. Maybe he thought there was a Popsicle inside. Maybe it was because he wanted to show the babysitter that he didn't have to listen to what he was told to do. Maybe he knew there were no Popsicles inside, but he wanted his sister Mary to think there were some. These are the kinds of reasons we can get our heads around.

When talking about sufficiently complex things like people, we describe them as agents, as acting on, among other things, their beliefs and goals (as we saw in chapter 5). Philosopher Daniel Dennett calls this *taking an intentional stance* toward the thing in question. Johnny did *A* because he believed that *P* and wanted *G*. We know that it might be possible someday to talk about Johnny's behavior in other terms, but it is unlikely that we will ever give up this intentional way of thinking. We seem to be wired that way.

This will apply to complex things like AI systems as well. It might be possible in principle to describe them in physical, electrical, or computational terms. Maybe the computer code behind the AI system is open source and available for inspection; maybe we could get a detailed report on the weights on all the neural net connections. But those descriptions would overwhelm us, just as a neurological description of Johnny would. We will need to take an intentional stance for a complex AI system for the same reason we take one for Johnny.

Getting the Beliefs and Goals Right

So if the behavior of a sufficiently complex AI system is going to be understandable at all, it will be in intentional terms: the system did action A because it believed that P and wanted G. But we have not yet said anything about what those beliefs and goals ought to be.

What if the AI system has the goal of making as much money as it can, all other considerations being secondary? Or perhaps it has the goal of making as many paper clips as it can, in the more whimsical example from philosopher Nick Bostrom. Or maybe it's the goal of relentlessly making copies of itself, as in "Autofac," the chilling 1955 story by writer Philip K. Dick. This is clearly not what we would ever want. Similarly, an AI system that acts on beliefs that are mostly false and consistently misinterprets what it learns (either willfully or by incompetence) will surely be more trouble than it is worth.

Getting the beliefs and goals right will be a nontrivial concern for AI systems as much as it is for people. First off, who gets to decide what the right ones are when there is no clear consensus? Should an AI system believe that an elephant is bigger than a dog? Of course. Should an AI system believe that society would be safer overall if more of its law-abiding citizens carried firearms? It seems to depend on who you ask.

For humans (or mentally fit adults anyway), we might say that they get to see the evidence and decide for themselves what to believe. But as a society, we are not totally consistent about this. You can be put in jail for acting on beliefs that are far enough from what is generally accepted, even if your actions are perfectly rational given those beliefs. You can also be taken to task if you fail to act on what a "reasonable person can be expected to know"—that is, when you fail to show common sense, as we have described it. There are situations where negligence can be as serious an infraction as commission.

In our opinion, while it will be possible to specify *necessary* conditions on the acceptable behavior of an AI system, it will never be possible to specify *sufficient* conditions for the same reason we do not expect to be able to specify them for humans. Observe that laws for people only specify what it is necessary to do (or not do); they do not spell out what would be sufficient. We recognize that we will want people to behave appropriately even in cases we have never really thought about before. We will add new laws as new cases arise, but until then, our hope is that people will follow the spirit of the existing laws in dealing with them.

This is what we would want for our AI systems as well. It is easy enough to imagine an AI system following all the conditions we specify, but only to the letter, and causing us no end of grief. Imagine the following sort of justification (spoken with a smirk): "Ah! But you said *A*! You didn't say anything about *B*. So I was just doing exactly as I was told, wasn't I?" An AI system with a disobliging attitude, one that has been programmed to look for ambiguities and loopholes, will surely be able to find them even as it does what it's told. And we probably don't want to design AI systems to act like passive-aggressive humans on their worst days.

So we need AI systems that not only act according to their beliefs and goals but have largely the right beliefs and goals too, and the right attitude about those things not explicitly covered. We may not be able to make any of these considerations much more precise than this. This is related to the sort of nonspecific directives parents give to their children: play nice, mind your manners, and follow the golden rule. While the intent of these is clear in general terms, deciding whether or not the rules have been violated in specific situations is harder to substantiate. An obliging attitude is expected.

There is something we *can* insist on, however. Assuming we have an AI system acting for reasons we understand, we can insist on the system being capable of change when we disagree with those reasons. If the system chose to do action *A* because it believed that *P* and wanted *G*, we need to be able to look at this and see why we disagree. Perhaps the problem is *P*; maybe *P* is false. We ought to be able to change the behavior of the system by correcting this mistaken belief. "Why did you think that *P* was true? Did you not know that *Q*?" So we might not be able to insist that the behavior of an AI system will always be right. But we ought to insist that we can always make it better.

The Vision: Two Fundamental Requirements

Let us now summarize the specification we are proposing for autonomous AI systems of the future. Overall, this involves two high-level requirements:

1. We will only build systems that have reasons for what they do. They will have knowledge and goals we can understand, and their actions will be the result of applying this knowledge in pursuit of those goals.
2. We will only build systems that can accept advice. When their knowledge or goals are not quite right, we will be able to engage in a corrective dialogue with them without having to reprogram them.

So in the end, our insistence that AI systems of the future have commonsense reasons for their decisions is not really just for them; it's for us too. What they do needs to make sense to us. It has nothing to do with wanting them to use a language like English.

If words and language are not necessarily part of the system requirements, though, might it not be possible to have AI systems whose behavior is describable in terms we can understand, but that are built in a way that is nothing at all like what we talked about in the middle part of this book? Why would we need symbolic representations of knowledge, for instance? Why not numerical weights on links between neuron-like units, say? This is a good point. What we are talking about here is a specification for an AI system. There's really no a priori reason here that it has to be implemented one way or another. Whatever works, works.

Nevertheless, there is a complicating factor coming from the second requirement above. However belief is realized in the system, the architecture of the system will need to be such that it will be possible to isolate a mistaken belief or goal from the rest of the system and change it. This, perhaps more than anything, is what favors a story based on symbols— although admittedly it still does not entail one.

On a related note, the second requirement also makes it clear why it would not be enough to have some sort of "explanation module" tacked onto an otherwise-inscrutable system. Even if such a module could somehow explain the behavior of the system in terms of commonsense beliefs and goals, we would want more. Specifically, the second requirement insists that we should be able to alter the behavior of the system by correcting mistaken beliefs and goals. Beliefs and goals thus cannot just show up after the fact in the output of an explanation module; they need to be able to govern how the system actually works.

So overall, we want systems with common sense that can learn to do better. This learning is not like the sort of automated machine learning that derives from repeated trials or massive amounts of data (although that learning is clearly useful as well). What we have in mind is something more like a focused one-on-one interaction between a teacher and a student, ideally a wise teacher and an obliging student. The ability to correct a mistaken belief or goal still does not mandate the use of a natural language such as English; some other interaction mechanism between the teacher and student might do the trick. But natural language will be tough to beat.

It is worth observing that the vision we have sketched above is an elaboration of what John McCarthy first proposed for AI back in 1958, as seen in chapter 1. The system he described, which was called the "Advice Taker," was intended to have commonsense knowledge represented in a symbolic language, and would make decisions about how to act in accordance with that knowledge. It would then be possible to modify the behavior of the system by changing the symbolic representations as appropriate—by giving advice.

We saw in chapter 4 that this McCarthy vision did not really come to fruition in AI for various reasons, perhaps the strongest of which was the detour into expertise—or at least what expertise was thought to be—and the resulting foray into so-called expert systems. Nothing in the original McCarthy manifesto suggested that particular emphasis. It remains to be seen whether a more concentrated effort on common sense—and especially on commonsense reasoning, over and above commonsense knowledge—will end up being more successful.

Trusting without Understanding

To conclude this chapter, let us return to the question noted above: How important will it be to have future AI systems that are *intelligible*—that is, systems that decide what to do based on considerations that we humans can make sense of? Perhaps tying their decision-making to our own understanding of it is asking too much, thereby shackling future technological progress to our own modest mental abilities.

First note that when we say that the behavior of an AI system should be intelligible, we should not be insisting that it be intelligible to everyone. Consider how we deal with people. When a crime is committed and a suspect is called to account for their behavior at a trial, we allow that they may be an expert of some sort and possibly did what they did for reasons a jury might not fully comprehend (without additional schooling). "Why did the suspect push button twenty-three rather than button seventeen at that point? Well, it's a long story." In cases like these, we might defer to other disinterested experts. They would have to be able to make sense of the reasons for the behavior and give us confidence that if we were to learn about the area, we would understand it too.

Similar considerations ought to apply to AI systems. We want to be able to say that the system did what it did for reasons that we, as a community, can make sense of. But we have to accept that these reasons need not be strictly commonsensical; they can also involve expert knowledge and puzzle-mode considerations such as advanced mathematics that not everyone will fully grasp (although these will ultimately rest on a stratum of common sense).

But why stop there? Maybe we want to allow for future AI systems that are so remarkably advanced, they have reasons for what they do that no human can fully grasp.

Consider the recent chess-playing program AlphaZero developed at DeepMind Technologies. This program started with only a rudimentary knowledge of the rules of chess, but learned to play well by playing against itself millions of times, eventually becoming what may prove to be the best chess player in the world. Such is the power of AI systems based on deep learning. As a recent article in the *New York Times* by mathematician Steven Strogatz observes,

Most unnerving was that AlphaZero seemed to express insight. It played like no computer ever has, intuitively and beautifully, with a romantic, attacking style. ... Grandmasters had never seen anything like it. AlphaZero had the finesse of a virtuoso and the power of a machine. It was humankind's first glimpse of an awesome new kind of intelligence. ...

What is frustrating about machine learning, however, is that the algorithms can't articulate what they're thinking. We don't know why they work, so we don't know if they can be trusted. AlphaZero gives every appearance of having discovered some important principles about chess, but it can't share that understanding with us. Not yet, at least. As human beings, we want more than answers. We want insight. This is going to be a source of tension in our interactions with computers from now on.

Strogatz goes on to speculate that maybe someday this lack of understanding on our part would not bother us that much—if the resulting technology was beneficial enough.

Is this right?

It is worth keeping in mind that chess is a closed, artificial environment. It is a game defined by rules that can be stipulated in advance. The deep learning technology behind AlphaZero might be applicable in other domains (in parts of biology, medicine, engineering design, or wherever), but these too will be artificially defined environments. As we have emphasized throughout, a world where totally unexpected things can happen is quite different from one where we can circumscribe the range of inputs to expect. There is no evidence whatsoever that an ability to work autonomously in the outside world will somehow emerge magically from abilities in these regulated areas. However impressive AlphaOne, DeltaTwo, or GammaNine will turn out to be, we should not be misled into thinking that they will deal well with the wide range of things that can happen in real life.

But let us put that issue aside and speculate further. Suppose, just for the sake of argument, that we could somehow build an AI system that operates autonomously in the real world and works extremely well as far as anyone can tell, but for reasons that we do not at all understand. Should we want such a technology?

The analogy with people is helpful. There are clearly wonderful things that people do for reasons we never expect to understand. Think of your favorite artists. Why did Pablo Picasso use that specific color there? Why did William Blake choose those very words? Why did Sergei Rachmaninoff settle on that particular musical phrase? Even the artists themselves likely do not know. We would be horribly impoverished as a society if we were to insist that people limit themselves to actions whose rationales could be clearly understood. And chess is an art. AlphaZero plays beautifully, we are told. Do we want to deprive ourselves of this because its play was produced for reasons we do not understand?

Yet life is not art. There are choices that people make that we clearly do insist on understanding. Imagine a defense attorney in a court case saying, "Your honor, my client is an artist. We do not deny that they acted as the prosecution said. But their act was a work of art and can only be assessed in artistic terms." Not the strongest sell. Even though we never really like to restrain imagination and creativity, we recognize that when it comes to actions in the world, and especially actions that can affect other people, there need to be limits.

So our position here is as follows: when it comes to operating in an artificial environment, on a chessboard or canvas, in a book or simulated world inside a computer, the sky's the limit. We should welcome and appreciate AI systems that display as much creativity and originality as they can muster, no holds barred, just as we would accept it from humans. No explanation necessary.

When it comes to actions in the real world, however, there are two cases. If the AI system is not acting autonomously—that is, if there are people supervising the system and supplying all the common sense—then we should treat what it does as if the people themselves were doing it. This is how we treat toasters and thermostats, for example. As a technology, a nonautonomous AI system (such as a face-recognition system, say) should be judged somewhat like an advanced appliance. In the end, a government using AI technology to spy on its citizens is not so different from a speeding driver using radar detection to avoid the highway patrol. In both cases, it is the *people* involved who are responsible and need to be held to account.

But consider an autonomous AI system making decisions for itself in the real world. Obviously, we should never accept what we would not be willing to accept from people. So we can start by asking ourselves, How much trust would we give to other people? How willing should we be to accept a rationale like this: "My behavior is too complex for you or anyone to understand, but I assure you that you're going to be happy with the final outcome"?

One way to think about this is as follows:

Suppose you are being asked to take some action that can clearly affect other people, perhaps negatively. You do not fully understand the rationale for the action, but you are told by some person that the final outcome will be proper and good. Furthermore, the person telling you this is somebody who, over a period of time, you have come to believe in and trust about a lot of things.

Should you just do it?

This is not an easy question, and we should not pretend it has an easy answer. In one sense, we are being asked for a leap of faith. In the movie *Miracle on 34th Street* (about a department store Santa Claus), there is the line, "Faith is believing in something when common sense tells you not to," and people without the capacity for faith are seen to be lacking something vital. But in another sense, we are being asked for what amounts to unquestioning obedience, and this can lead to disaster. Maybe it's not faith at all; maybe it's a cult.

So what is our opinion on this question, as AI researchers? Is it right to trust an AI system with a rock-solid track record that makes decisions we cannot quite follow?

In our view, *no*. A track record, even a flawless one, is just not enough given the long tail of strange things that can happen in the world. If we don't really understand how a system works, we have no way of knowing what it would do in exceptional circumstances that no one has yet thought about. A catastrophic blunder might be right around the corner.

This might seem a bit far-fetched. Is there any evidence at all that AI systems would ever blunder in this way? As it turns out, there is. This has come up in what are called *adversarial test cases*. It has been shown by researcher Christian Szegedy and others that deep learning systems that classify images such as AlexNet (mentioned in chapter 3) can be duped. It is possible to take an image that it classifies correctly, modify it in a way that is completely imperceptible to people, and have the result be classified incorrectly. The AlexNet system ended up categorizing a tweaked picture of a school bus as an ostrich. (There's no point in displaying the original and tweaked images here; they look like two identical images of a school bus!)

So what's the point? We already know these AI systems will not be *perfect*. There will be examples that the system gets wrong, just as there are ones that people get wrong. And these artificially constructed test cases do not even show up in naturally occurring images, or at least in any kind of statistically meaningful way. The performance of AlexNet is quite impressive by any statistical measure. So why should we care?

We should care because these examples show us that we do not really understand what the system has learned from all of its training. It decided that the school bus was an ostrich, but on what grounds? Statistics over test cases are totally beside the point. We are quite willing to accept that the system will sometimes classify images incorrectly, but we want to believe that it is nonetheless behaving *sensibly*, that images that look absolutely identical to us will be classified in the same way, correctly or incorrectly. Yet the AlexNet system simply does not have this property. So it's not that we care about those concocted test cases; it's that they show that the criterion the system is using to make decisions does not really make any sense to us.

Now imagine that instead of classifying images, the AI system is making mission-critical, life-and-death decisions. We want to trust the system. We want to be able to say, "The system will be fine. It ran into situations exactly like this before and it always did the right thing." But we can't. Even with a *perfect* track record, there may be something rare that has never come up before—something minute, imperceptible to us, that causes the system to completely misinterpret what it is dealing with. And recall from chapter 3 that extremely rare events are actually quite common.

In certain situations and for specific cases, individuals can and should let go and trust other individuals, including AI systems. But this should never be *policy*. It would be negligent for society as a whole to do this. Although this may well end up holding back our technological progress someday—in some speculative future anyway—it is the cost of acting responsibly.

In sum, if we are to pursue autonomous AI systems—again, a big if—it is our responsibility to ensure that the choices they make will be for reasons we can clearly understand, and largely in commonsense terms. Or to put it differently, it is our responsibility to ensure that systems that do not satisfy the two fundamental requirements above never get to operate autonomously in the world. A system without common sense should never be allowed to make decisions where common sense is needed. However a final decision is being made, whether by a human or future AI system, common sense should always be in the loop.

Epilogue

I may not have gone where I intended to go, but I think I have ended up where I needed to be.

—Douglas Adams, *The Long Dark Tea-Time of the Soul*

The road to common sense followed in this book is clearly at odds with the modern practice of AI, at least as it exists at the time of this writing. The bulk of the work in AI these days is about deep learning, for AI systems that somehow manage to do a lot without knowing a lot about what they are doing. As we have stated, for a wide range of tasks, this approach works surprisingly well, and for some tasks, exceedingly well. We see applications of deep learning in virtually all areas of modern technology where computers can be deployed.

This book was not about a better way of using AI to get things done—a better way of playing Go, translating English text, or diagnosing blood infections. It was about what it would take to get an AI system to behave in a reasonable way *outside* tasks like these. It was about what happens when you stop doing something and start thinking that maybe you should be doing something else. If you never have to stop what you're doing, then the fact that you might not know a lot about it is much less of a concern; nobody is going to notice. But if you do have to start considering whether continuing with your ongoing task is appropriate in your current situation, then you need an understanding of your task that goes beyond merely being able to carry it out.

What we have argued in this book is that what you really need in cases like this is an ability to step back from the actions available to you and consider how they fit into a larger picture. In a nutshell, you need to be able to see yourself as located in a world where there are different kinds of things with different kinds of properties that can be changed by different kinds of events, among which are those that result from the actions at your disposal. This is what we have called a *commonsense understanding of the world*. It is the view that we explored in considerable detail in the middle part of this book.

So the more general understanding that is required in these cases is broader than an ability to carry out any specific task or tasks. The moment a system designer gets to say something like "here is what I need my system to be able to do," a narrowing takes place. The task to be performed by the system can be demanding, and require considerable skill and expertise. It might be landing a lunar module, walking over rough terrain, or recommending a movie. But with the task in hand, an engineer can start to consider the range of inputs that need to be dealt with and maybe even how to train a system on sample inputs of the right sort. Anything deemed to be outside these parameters becomes the responsibility of someone else. The human operating the system will have to decide how loud to play the music at the party; the human will have to decide what to do when the traffic light is stuck on red.

There is nothing wrong with this design philosophy. It is what has been behind engineering practice since the Industrial Revolution. We expect things like washing machines, home stereos, and golf carts to do their jobs well, of course, but nothing else. It's not up to the washing machine to notice that somebody is hiding a birthday cake inside it. Why should we expect AI systems to be any different?

This is not an unreasonable position. We learn to adapt to the limitations and quirks of all sorts of technology. Maybe we need to accept that it is not worth the cost and effort to develop AI technology that is going to be truly intelligent the way humans are. Maybe intelligent machines are best thought of as some sort of fanciful gee-whiz dream for the future, on a par with hyperdrive rockets, gyro cars, and transporters like in *Star Trek*. Maybe we should just put this dream aside and continue to work on getting machines to work well on specific tasks we care about.

But our focus in this book has been quite different. We wanted to step back from these tasks and ask questions more like this: What would it take to build a washing machine controller that was able to figure out for itself that it would not be a good idea to run its cycle with a birthday cake hidden inside? We accept that these birthday cake considerations are really not part of the job to be done by the washing machine, yet they are certainly part of what a human with common sense would want to consider.

The idea we explored in this book is that what it takes to exhibit this kind of common sense is quite different from what it takes to perform particular tasks, even ones that seem to demand intelligence in people such as playing decent chess. Common sense, we claimed, is the ability to make good use of a broad spectrum of commonsense knowledge. Among other things, the washing machine controller would need to know about why people care about birthday cakes as distinct from clothes and what would happen to the cake if the machine were to start running, and then somehow use this knowledge to hold off on starting its washing cycle.

We do hope the reader will agree that making sense of common sense, thinking about what it would mean for a machine to make use of commonsense knowledge in this way, is rewarding in its own terms. And the picture presented in this book—computations over symbolic structures standing for this commonsense knowledge—is really the only game in town for this. We called it the *KR hypothesis*, although from a purely engineering point of view, there is no other proposal on the table for how a machine could decide what to do in a way that was not tied to the task at hand, but on a more comprehensive account of the world it finds itself in.

In the end, common sense is not about complex tasks at all. As McCarthy first said over sixty years ago, it's about being able to draw simple, immediate conclusions from what you know and what you've been told, and putting them to good use in whatever you're setting out to do.

If there is a future for machines with common sense, this is still it.

Appendix

This appendix collects a number of the more technical details having to do with representation and reasoning mentioned in chapters 7–8.

Finding Connections in a World Model

In chapter 7, a procedure **FIND-PATH** for finding a path between two symbols is described.

FIND-PATH[x;y]:

(The x and y here are symbols in a world model. Find all the shortest paths from x to y in the model. A path here is a sequence x (r_1, y_1) (r_2, y_2) ... (r_n, y_n) where (r_i, y_i) is as in the description of **GET-ADJACENT** below.)

1. Let P be the set that contains one path—the one with just x on it.
2. Repeatedly let P be the value of **EXTEND[P]**, until either P is the empty set or P contains a path whose last item is y.
3. Return those elements of P whose last item is y (if any).

EXTEND[P]:

(The P here is a set of paths. Return paths that are one step longer than those in P.)

Return all paths made up of p followed by (r, v) such that

1. p is an element of P.
2. (r, v) is an element of **GET-ADJACENT[z]**, where z is the last item of p.
3. v does not appear anywhere in the set P.

GET-ADJACENT[x]:

(The x here is a symbol. Find the neighbors of x in the world model.)

Return all pairs *(r, y)* such that the list "*x* has *y* as an *r*" is in the world model, together with all pairs *(r', y)* such that "*y* has *x* as an *r*" is in the world model.

(The *r'* here means that the connection involves the inverse of the role *r* in question.)

Inheritance in a Conceptual Model

In chapter 7, a procedure **GET-PARTS** for performing inheritance with cancellation is introduced. While it is possible to define this operation over the sentences in a conceptual model as is, it is easier to do so if we assume that these sentences have been expanded, as sketched at the end of the section on defaults in chapter 7 and as seen in figure 7.5. So for this operation, we assume that the conceptual model actually contains sentences of the form "*c* has *e* as a SUPERCONCEPT" and "*c* has *x* as a PART," where *c* and *e* are symbols for concepts, and *x* is a symbol for a role, restriction, or annotation.

GET-PARTS[c]:

(Find all parts inherited by the concept *c* in a conceptual model. A part here is a symbol representing a role, restriction, or annotation.)

1. Calculate all the items *p* such that there is a chain of "is a" links (that is, sentences of the form "*x* has *y* as a SUPERCONCEPT") from concept *c* to some concept *e*, and there is a sentence of the form "*e* has *p* as a PART" in the conceptual model. Call this set *P*.

2. Repeatedly do this:
   Find two elements *x* and *y* of *P*, where *y* cancels *x*, and where there is no *z* in *P* such that *z* cancels *y*. Then remove *x* from *P*.

   (Note: "*y* cancels *x*" means that "*y* is a CANCEL-ANNOTATION" and "*y* has *x* as a SUBJECT" are present in the expanded version of the conceptual model.)

3. When no further elements of *P* can be removed, the remaining parts in *P* are considered to be inherited by *c*. So return *P*.

Special Symbols for Numbers and Sequences

In the representation language $\mathcal{L}$ of chapter 8, it is convenient to include the usual arithmetic symbols with their normal interpretation. For example,

"$t_1 + t_2$" is a special term in $\mathcal{L}$ that can be read as "the sum of t_1 and t_2," and "$t_1 < t_2$" is a special atomic formula of $\mathcal{L}$ that can be read as "t_1 is less than t_2." For sequences, we include the special symbols [,], and |. For instance, "$[t_1, t_2, t_3]$" is a special term of $\mathcal{L}$ read as "the sequence consisting of just t_1, t_2, and t_3," while "$t_1 \mid t_2$" is a special term read as "the sequence made of all the elements of t_1 followed by the single element t_2."

Answering Questions

In chapter 8, two reasoning procedures are presented: **TEST** and **FIND-ALL**.

TEST[p]:

(Determine if a formula p with no free variables is true in the current world model.)

Return TRUE if any of the following conditions hold (and FALSE otherwise):

1. p is of the form "t is t," where t is some constant.

2. p is of the form "t is a c" or it is of the form "t_1 has t_2 as an r," and p is present as is in the current world model.

3. p is of the form "it is not the case that q," where **TEST**[q] = FALSE.

4. p is of the form "q_1 and q_2," where **TEST**[q_1] = **TEST**[q_2] = TRUE.

5. p is of the form "q_1 or q_2," where **TEST**[q_1] = TRUE or **TEST**[q_2] = TRUE.

6. p is of the form "there is a v where q," where **FIND-ALL**[v;q] is not the empty set.

FIND-ALL[$v_1, \ldots, v_n$;p]:

(Find all constants for which formula p, whose free variables are among $v_1, \ldots, v_n$, is true.)

Return the set of all combinations of constants $t_1, \ldots, t_n$ that appear in the world model such that

$$\textbf{TEST}[\textbf{SUBST}[v_1;t_1;\textbf{SUBST}[v_2;t_2; \ldots \textbf{SUBST}[v_n;t_n;p] \ldots]]] = \text{TRUE}.$$

SUBST[v;t;e]:

(Replace free variable v by term t in formula e.)

1. If e is of the form "p_1 and p_2," then return "q_1 and q_2," where q_1 = **SUBST**[v;t;p_1] and q_2 = **SUBST**[v;t;p_2].

2. If e is of the form "p_1 or p_2," then return "q_1 or q_2," where q_1 = **SUBST**[v;t;p_1] and q_2 = **SUBST**[v;t;p_2].

3. If e is of the form "it is not the case that p," then return the formula "it is not the case that q," where $q = $ **SUBST** $[v;t;p]$.

4. If e is of the form "there is a u where p," then if u is v then return e unchanged, and otherwise return "there is a u where q," where $q = $ **SUBST** $[v;t;p]$.

5. If e is any other formula made up of the sequence of symbols "$s_1 s_2 \dots s_n$," then return the sequence "$w_1 w_2 \dots w_n$," where w_i is t when s_i is the variable v, and w_i is s_i otherwise.

Handling Derived Properties

In chapter 8, derived clauses are introduced. The **TEST**$[p]$ procedure presented above should also return TRUE when there is a suitable derivation clause for p. Here is the idea:

Suppose there is a derivation clause "e when q" where e uses variables v_1, $v_2, \dots, v_n$. Suppose that p is a formula that is just like e, except that it uses terms $t_1, t_2, \dots, t_n$ instead:

$$p = \textbf{SUBST}[v_1;t_1;\textbf{SUBST}[v_2;t_2; \dots \textbf{SUBST}[v_n;t_n;e] \dots \ ]].$$

Then **TEST**$[p]$ should return TRUE if **TEST**$[q']$ = TRUE, where

$$q' = \textbf{SUBST}[v_1;t_1;\textbf{SUBST}[v_2;t_2; \dots \textbf{SUBST}[v_n;t_n;q] \dots \ ]].$$

In other words, **TEST**$[p]$ returns true whenever there is a derivation clause "e when q," where the e matches the p for some substitution of the variables, and the corresponding q is true. Note that clauses with top-level disjunctions in them like "e when q_1 or q_2" will then work the same for **TEST** as a collection of smaller clauses such as "e when q_1" and "e when q_2."

Dog Breeds as a Derived Property

The dog breed property discussed in chapter 6 can be handled as a derived property of dogs by using a large disjunction over all the cases:

```
Dog:d has Breed:b as a breed
     when
Dog:d is a pugDog and Breed:b is "Pug" or
Dog:d is a bichonFriseDog and Breed:b is "Bichon Frise" or
Dog:d is a jackRussellDog and Breed:b is "Jack Russell Terrier"
or ...
```

The disjunction would continue over all 339 breeds of dog. (We would probably want to represent the dog breeds not as strings but instead as things that have such strings as their English names. No matter.) So for example, if we had something like

    Dog#227 is a jackRussellDog.

in a world model, we could use **FIND-ALL** over the formula

    Dog#227 has Breed:u as a breed.

and get the string "Jack Russell Terrier" as the answer using this clause.

   In a more complex application, we can imagine starting with Dog#228 is a dog in a world model, learning that Dog#228 has "Pug" as a breed is true, and wanting to extend the model to incorporate this new information, as considered in chapter 7. We could use the clause for breed above, simplify the formula as necessary noting, for instance, that the equality "Pug" is "Pug" is always true, but that the equality "Pug" is "Bichon Frise" is always false, and reduce this to learning that the formula Dog#228 is a pug-Dog must be true, and then go from there to the typical properties like the bulging eyes and curly tail.

Reasoning about the Changes Resulting from Actions

Suppose that the world model contains representations for three door events, Event#816, Event#817, and Event#818:

    Event#816 is a doorOpeningEvent.
    Event#816 has Door#58 as an object.

    Event#817 is a doorClosingEvent.
    Event#817 has Door#58 as an object.

    Event#818 is a doorClosingEvent.
    Event#818 has Door#59 as an object.

We can see the reasoning behind the commonsense law of inertia unfolding in all of its glory in the following **FIND-ALL** operations over formulas with a single free variable State:u:

FIND-ALL[Door#58 has State:u as a doorState after []] = "open"

> After no events, Door#58 is open (since we are assuming it was open to start).

FIND-ALL[Door#58 has State:u as a doorState after
        [Event#817]] = "closed"
After the closing of Door#58, the door is closed.

FIND-ALL[Door#58 has State:u as a doorState after
        [Event#818]] = "open"
After the closing of Door#59, Door#58 remains open.

FIND-ALL[Door#58 has State:u as a doorState after
        [Event#817,Event#816]] = "open"
After the closing of Door#58 followed by its opening, the door is again open.

FIND-ALL[Door#58 has State:u as a doorState after
        [Event#817,Event#816,Event#817]] = "closed"
After the closing of Door#58, its opening, and its closing, Door#58 is closed.

FIND-ALL[Door#58 has State:u as a doorState after
        [Event#817,Event#816,Event#818]] = "open"
After the closing of Door#58, its opening, and a closing of Door#59, Door#58 is open.

Performing a Sequence of Actions

Recalling the convention on simulating change in chapter 8, we can use "after" with any derived property by distributing the "after" inside the embedded formula of the derivation clause. This includes the possible property as well. With this idea, we can have a derived property possibleSequence that says that a sequence of events can be made to occur by an agent, characterized by the following two clauses:

Seq:s is a possibleSequence for Agent:x when Seq:s is [].

Seq:s|Event:e is a possibleSequence for Agent:x
     when
Seq:s is a possibleSequence for Agent:x and
Event:e is possible for Agent:x after Seq:s.

This says that the empty sequence of actions can always be performed, and that a nonempty sequence $t_1 \mid t_2$ can be performed if (recursively) the sequence t_1 can be performed, and the final action t_2 is possible for the agent after the sequence t_1 has been performed.

Reasoning about What Actions Can Be Executed

Suppose that in the current state, Door#58 is open and Person#17 (John) is not near that door, but that there is a moving event, Event#357, John can perform in the current state, and it would put him near the door. Then we get the following:

TEST[Person#17 is near Door#58] = FALSE
> John is currently not near the door.

TEST[Person#17 is near Door#58 after [Event#357]] = TRUE
> John is near the door after moving.

TEST[Event#817 is possible for Person#17] = FALSE
> John cannot currently close the door.

TEST[Event#357 is possible for Person#17] = TRUE
> John can currently move near the door.

TEST[Event#817 is possible for Person#17 after [Event#357]] = TRUE
> John can close the door after moving near it.

TEST[[Event#357,Event#817] is a possibleSequence for Person#17] = TRUE
> John can do the sequence of moving near the door and closing it.

Abbreviations Used in Vivid Formulas

In the bonus chapter, the following formula abbreviations are used:

- The t_1, t_2, ... , t_n are distinct
  is used to stand for the formula
  It is not the case that ... or t_i is t_j or... ,
  where the disjuncts range over all pairs of indexes such that $i < j \le n$.
- The pairs $t_1\ t'_1$, $t_2\ t'_2$, ... , $t_n\ t'_n$ are distinct
  is used to stand for the formula
  It is not the case that ... or t_i is t_j and t'_i is t'_j or... ,
  where the disjuncts range over all pairs of indexes such that $i < j \le n$.
- There is at most n c (with the "is" and c possibly pluralized)
  is used to stand for the formula

It is not the case that

there is a v_1, ... , a v_n, and a v where

the v_1, ... , v_n, v are distinct,

v_1 is a c, ... , v_n is a c, and v is a c,

where the variables v_i and the v are all chosen to be distinct.

- There is at most n r (with the "is" and r possibly pluralized)

is used to stand for the formula

It is not the case that

there is a v_1, a u_1, ... , a v_n, a u_n, a v, and a u where

the pairs v_1, u_1, ... , v_n, u_n, v, u are distinct,

v_1 has u_1 as an r, ... , v_n has u_n as an r, and v has u as an r,

where the variables v_i, u_j, v, and u are all chosen to be distinct.

Bonus Chapter: The Logic of Common Sense

Logic, like whiskey, loses its beneficial effect when taken in too large quantities.

—Lord Dunsany, quoted in *The World of Mathematics,*
edited by James R. Newman

In chapters 7–8, we saw how knowledge could be represented in a world model (with help from a conceptual model and derivation clauses), and then how to compute from such a model which formulas of the language $\mathcal{L}$ should be considered to be true. In this bonus chapter, aimed at those who might want to dive a little deeper into the issues involved, we reconsider these reasoning operations from the standpoint of *logic*, where there are some significant lessons to learn.

The reasoning operations considered in the book are clearly related to what is seen in classical (deductive) logic. In logic, we start with certain premises or postulates, and the rules of logic tell us what other sentences should also be considered to be true as logical consequences. The only real difference is that in chapters 7–8, the reasoning starts with a world model, not a set of premises given initially to be true. Often in logic the premises are taken to be *axiomatic*—true with absolute mathematical certainty—so that the consequences will be guaranteed to be true as well—mathematical theorems. But logic is really about what follows from some premises being true, however certain they may be. An emphasis on certitude is not inherent in logic, and clearly not what is needed for common sense.

But in terms of the workings of common sense, how important is it to start with a world model as the representation of knowledge? Since we now have the formulas of $\mathcal{L}$ at our disposal, could we not simply use them to represent what is known and dispense with world models entirely? Other researchers, like Doug Lenat with Cyc, have argued that the representations for common sense must begin with rich and expressive logics, or even what are called higher-order logics. Why would we not do that?

In this bonus chapter, we are going to look at these questions more closely and show that while it might be possible to use formulas of $\mathcal{L}$ instead of world models as our representation of knowledge, there are some good reasons not to do so—reasons to take our logic in much smaller quantities. In particular, we will see that the sort of computation needed to draw conclusions from formulas of $\mathcal{L}$ *as premises* is too demanding in general to serve as the basis for common sense. In fact, we go further: we demonstrate that world models can be thought of as special formulas of $\mathcal{L}$ that are restricted enough to admit a more modest form of logical reasoning much better suited to the everyday mundane needs of common sense.

World Models as Vivid Formulas

Let us return to the world model with seven items used in the examples of chapter 7:

```
Person#17 is a person.
Person#17 has "John" as a firstName.
Person#17 has Event#23 as a birth.
TimePt#24 is a pointInTime.
TimePt#24 has 1979 as an enclosingYear.
Event#23 is a birthEvent.
Event#23 has TimePt#24 as a time.
```

What does this representation tell us about the world? Following the advice of Bertrand Russell (discussed in chapter 6), we should think of a world model like this as telling us what things exist and what properties they have: there is a person, birth event, and time point with certain properties. The choice of a name like Person#17 is not important. So the information carried by the world model is similar to what is said by a formula that replaces the constants above by variables:

```
There is a Person:x, a TimePt:y, and an Event:z where
  Person:x is a person,
```

```
Person:x has "John" as a firstName,
Person:x has Event:z as a birth,
TimePt:y is a pointInTime,
TimePt:y has 1979 as an enclosingYear,
Event:z is a birthEvent, and
Event:z has TimePt:y as a time.
```

But there is more to it than this. For instance, the formula

```
There is a Thing:u where Thing:u has "Harry" as a firstName.
```

is considered to be false according to the world model (and the TEST operation), but nothing in the formula above (that is, the one with Person:x, TimePt:y, and Event:z) suggests this.

In using a world model, we recognize that we are not modeling an entire world: there are too many things in the world and too many properties among them, most of which we will know nothing about. A world model captures only a fragment of the world in some state.

Once we accept that a world model deals with a fragment like this, however, we also accept that it presents all the things that exist and all the properties that hold in that fragment. This is what is sometimes called a "closed-world" interpretation of the representation. It allows us to treat a world model as an *analogue* of the fragment of the world it represents. There is a one-to-one correspondence between the things in the fragment and the symbols for them (containing a #) in the model. There is also a one-to-one correspondence between the basic properties of things in the fragment and the corresponding symbol structures in the model. The world model has a part-by-part correspondence with the world fragment in the same way a model airplane has a part-by-part correspondence with a real airplane.

There is a lot more to be said about this, yet suffice it to note that we draw conclusions from what a model has, but also from what it does not have. We conclude that an airplane has a jet engine below each wing based on the analogous pieces on the model. But we also conclude that the airplane does not have a jet engine on the tail fin from the *absence* of a corresponding piece on the model.

World models will be the same. So for example, we can find out how many individuals in the world have a certain property by counting how many symbols have a corresponding property in the world model. We can find out if a certain individual is related in some way to another in the world by checking if the symbol standing for the first individual is connected in the right way to the symbol standing for the second in the world model. This is exactly how we expect to be able to use analogical models.

With this closed-world understanding, there is a specific type of formula in $\mathcal{L}$ that captures all the information represented by a world model. It is called a *vivid* formula and has the following general form:

There is *variables* where *distinct*, *middle*, *at most*.

Here are the details: the *variables* part of the formula is a list of variables corresponding to each named individual in the world model (other than strings, numbers, and sequences); the *distinct* part is an abbreviation saying that these individuals are all different from each other (see the appendix for the exact details); *middle* is a sequence of atomic formulas that is identical to the world model except that the variables are used instead of the constants (as was done above); and finally, *at most* is a sequence of abbreviations (again described in the appendix) starting with the words "there is at most," and ranging over every concept and role used in the world model as well as taking into account the number of atomic formulas in the *middle* part that mention that concept or role.

For the world model with the seven items above, the vivid formula is shown in figure B.1. This vivid formula says that there are three distinct things in the world having the seven properties exactly as listed, no more, no less. (Strictly speaking, a vivid formula needs to say one additional thing: it needs to rule out the possibility of things without any properties among the named concepts and roles. We ignore that complication here.)

The vivid formula highlights just how restricted a world model actually is in terms of what it can represent. It does not allow for the possibility of there being things or properties they might have other than those it lists explicitly.

But how then to represent knowledge about a world where (say) John has a birth year that is not known? Or a world where we want to leave open the possibility of there being other people?

As first noted in chapter 6, this requires a different mode of representation. We have to change gears, and represent not things and their properties directly, as we have been doing with world models, but rather *information* about things and their properties. This can be done most easily using formulas of $\mathcal{L}$ that are not vivid.

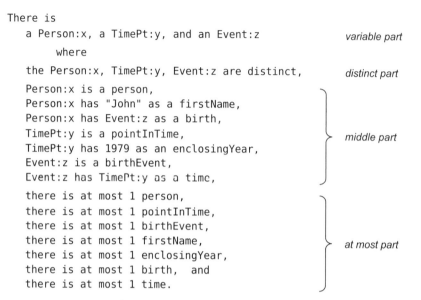

```
There is
    a Person:x, a TimePt:y, and an Event:z              variable part
        where
    the Person:x, TimePt:y, Event:z are distinct,       distinct part
    Person:x is a person,
    Person:x has "John" as a firstName,
    Person:x has Event:z as a birth,
    TimePt:y is a pointInTime,                          middle part
    TimePt:y has 1979 as an enclosingYear,
    Event:z is a birthEvent,
    Event:z has TimePt:y as a time,

    there is at most 1 person,
    there is at most 1 pointInTime,
    there is at most 1 birthEvent,
    there is at most 1 firstName,                       at most part
    there is at most 1 enclosingYear,
    there is at most 1 birth,   and
    there is at most 1 time.
```

Figure B.1
A vivid formula for the world model

Nonvivid Knowledge Representation

To see how this works, let us reconsider the high school prom example presented in chapter 6. For the first variant (figure 6.2), it is not too hard to construct a world model directly from the given information: all the relevant individuals and their properties are listed. It would look something like this:

```
Boy#51 is a boy. Boy#52 is a boy. Boy#53 is a boy.
Girl#54 is a girl. Girl#55 is a girl. Girl#56 is a girl.
Boy#51 has "Bob" as a name. Boy#52 has "Bill" as a name.
Boy#53 has "Brad" as a name. Girl#54 has "Gabby" as a name.
Girl#55 has "Gail" as a name. Girl#56 has "Gina" as a name.

Boy#51 has Girl#56 as a promDate.
Boy#52 has Girl#55 as a promDate.
Boy#53 has Girl#54 as a promDate.
```

This model has the three boys and three girls with their given names, with Bill (Boy#52) having Gail (Girl#55) as a prom date, and so on. (For

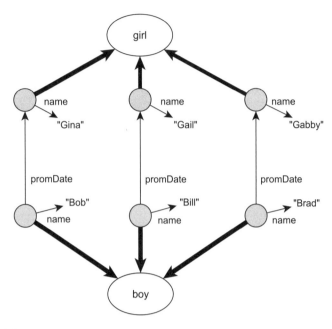

Figure B.2
A world model for the prom date example

simplicity, promDate is taken to be a property of the boys in question. A
more symmetrical representation is possible.) This world model is shown in
graphical form in figure B.2.

Following the recipe above, a somewhat-wordy vivid formula that captures this information is shown in figure B.3. In sum, there are exactly
three boys, three girls, six name properties, and three prom date properties,
exactly as listed in the world model.

Turning our attention now to the second variant of the prom in figure
B.3 (the logic puzzle), what is immediately clear is that we cannot construct
a world model for this variant. We would have to link the symbol for Bob to
his date for the prom, but all we are told is that it is someone other than Gail.
Where would the link go? While we cannot represent the given information
directly in a world model, we can still represent that information using a
nonvivid formula of $\mathcal{L}$. This formula is obtained by replacing the three items

```
Boy:u has Girl:z as a promDate
Boy:v has Girl:y as a promDate
Boy:w has Girl:x as a promDate
```

```
There is
    a Boy:u, a Boy:v, a Boy:w,
        a Girl:x, a Girl:y, a Girl:z              }  variable part
            where
    the Boy:u, Boy:v, Boy:w,
        Girl:x, Girl:y, Girl:z are distinct,      }  distinct part
    Boy:u is a boy,  Boy:v is a boy,
    Boy:w is a boy,  Girl:x is a girl,
    Girl:y is a girl,  Girl:z is a girl,
    Boy:u has "Bob" as a name,
    Boy:v has "Bill" as a name,
    Boy:w has "Brad" as a name,
    Girl:x has "Gabby" as a name,                 }  middle part
    Girl:y has "Gail" as a name,
    Girl:z has "Gina" as a name,
    Boy:u has Girl:z as a promDate,
    Boy:v has Girl:y as a promDate,
    Boy:w has Girl:x as a promDate,
    there are at most 3 boys,
    there are at most 3 girls,
    there are at most 6 names,  and               }  at most part
    there are at most 3 promDates.
```

Figure B.3
A vivid formula for the prom date example

in the vivid formula of figure B.3 by the following nine items:

```
There is a Person:p where Boy:u has Person:p as a promDate
There is a Person:p where Boy:v has Person:p as a promDate
There is a Person:p where Boy:w has Person:p as a promDate
There is a Person:p where Person:p has Girl:x as a promDate
There is a Person:p where Person:p has Girl:y as a promDate
There is a Person:p where Person:p has Girl:z as a promDate
It is not the case that Boy:u has Girl:y as a promDate
It is not the case that Boy:w has Girl:y as a promDate
Boy:w has Girl:x as a promDate or
    Boy:v has Girl:x as a promDate
```

The resulting formula no longer says who is going to the prom with whom. Instead it says that each of the three boys is going with someone and each of the three girls is going with someone, and then provides the three given

clues: Bob is not going with Gail, Gail is not going with Brad, and Gabby is
going with Brad or Bill.

What can we say about these two prom formulas—the vivid one and the
larger, nonvivid one? In terms of logic, the two formulas are *equivalent*: one
is true exactly when the other is. If we start with the vivid formula where
we are given that Bob is going with Gina and so on, we can see that the
nonvivid one will be true—for instance, that Bob is not going with Gail,
and that Gabby is going with Brad or Bill. Conversely, if we begin with the
nonvivid one where we are given that Bob is not going with Gail and all
the other clues, *and assuming that we now solve the puzzle*, we can see that
the vivid one will be true—for example, that Bob is going with Gina, Gail is
going with Bill, and Brad is going with Gabby.

And yet the two formulas are clearly not *identical*. As already noted, figuring out who Bob is taking to the prom in the first case is dead easy, but
figuring out who Bob is taking to the prom in the second case requires solving the puzzle.

To summarize, for every world model, there will be a formula of $\mathcal{L}$ car-
rying the same explicit information, but the converse does not hold. A
formula of $\mathcal{L}$ can omit details that would need to be spelled out in a world
model. In fact, we can easily construct other nonvivid formulas that leave
out even more than the nonvivid formula above.

For example, start with the vivid formula of figure B.3, and remove the
distinct and *at most* parts. Think of world models where the resulting formula would be true. It would say that Bob is going with Gina as before,
but now leave open other possibilities. The individual named "Bob" might
well be the same as the one named "Brad," for instance, and so might also
be going to the prom with Gabby. Furthermore, Bob may be taking other
girls beyond the three named ones (and some boys too, for that matter). In
this case, it is not a matter of solving a puzzle to determine if Bob is taking
someone other than Gina; the information is not there to be found.

So returning to the question at the beginning, could a formula of $\mathcal{L}$ take
the place of a world model as a representation of knowledge? We can now
see that the answer is *yes*. Under the closed-world interpretation, for every
world model, there is a vivid formula of $\mathcal{L}$ (with appropriate "distinct" and
"at most" subformulas) that says exactly the same thing. There are formulas
of $\mathcal{L}$, however, that go beyond what can be represented in world models.
The expressive power of a language like $\mathcal{L}$ lies in what it can leave open

and unresolved. By using world models as our representation of knowledge (together with conceptual models and derivation clauses, of course), we are plainly restricting ourselves in the kind of knowledge that can be represented.

Why are we doing this? Why are we limiting the kinds of knowledge that can be represented and reasoned with to what amounts to these vivid formulas? We will get to that in the final section. But let us first look more closely at the difference between the vivid and nonvivid cases in an even simpler example.

On the Boundary between Vivid and Nonvivid

In looking at the prom example from chapter 6, it was clear that the second version was some sort of logic puzzle. It had information like

> *Bob is going to the prom with someone other than Gail.*
>
> *Gabby is going to the prom with Brad or Bill.*

which had to be represented using logical operators such as "not," "or," and "there is." Yet it is possible to construct puzzles that do not require operators like these. Here is one:

> *Jack, Anne, and George are together in a room. Jack is looking at Anne, and Anne is looking at George. Jack is married, and George is divorced.*
>
> *Is a married person looking at a person who is not married?*

The first thing to observe is that the answer to the question is not immediately obvious. In fact, psychologists have tested people on this problem, and most subjects think that there is not enough information in the statement of the problem to answer the question one way or the other. How can you answer without knowing Anne's marital status?

As it turns out, the question can in fact be answered from the given information. To see this, consider Anne's marital status: if Anne is married, then she is a married person looking at an unmarried one (George); if Anne is not married, then Jack is a married person looking at an unmarried one (her). We are not told if Anne is married, but it doesn't matter; either way, a married person is looking at a person who is not married. So this is a puzzle not unlike the prom one, and the question can be answered by solving the puzzle. (Note that there is not enough information here to determine if an *unmarried* person is looking at a person who is not married.)

If our analysis from the previous section is correct, it should not be possible to use a world model (or vivid formula) to represent the given information. But consider this one:

```
Person#31 is a person.   Person#31 has "Jack" as a name.
Person#32 is a person.   Person#32 has "Anne" as a name.
Person#33 is a person.   Person#33 has "George" as a name.
Person#31 has Person#32 as an itemInView.
Person#32 has Person#33 as an itemInView.
Person#31 has "married" as a maritalStatus.
Person#33 has "divorced" as a maritalStatus.
```

This seems to represent the given information. Does a world model like this not do the job?

No, it does not. The problem is that according to the closed-world interpretation of world models, just as the formula

```
Person#33 has "married" as a maritalStatus.
```

would be considered to be false according to this model (as appropriate: George is divorced), the formula

```
Person#32 has "married" as a maritalStatus.
```

would also be considered to be false because there is no statement about Anne's marital status in the model. Indeed, the **TEST** operation would return the answer FALSE in both cases. In other words, as far as this model is concerned, neither Anne nor George have the property of being married, whereas in the puzzle itself, only the marital status of George is mentioned and Anne's is left open. To conclude that Anne is not married is a step too far. So the world model above (or corresponding vivid formula) does not correctly represent the given information. (It is possible to represent the given information faithfully using a nonvivid formula, much as we did in the previous section. We would use a "there is" within the formula to say that Anne does have a marital status, without spelling out what it is.)

What all of this suggests is that what makes these puzzles hard to solve is not the presence of operators such as "not" or "or" in the statement of the problem but rather the fact that some relevant details are left out—details we would need to know to represent the given information in a world model, and would need to puzzle through in order to solve the problem.

Note that if Anne's marital status had been provided as part of the statement of the problem, the effort would change completely. Consider this variant:

Jack, Anne, and George are together in a room. Jack is looking at Anne, and Anne is looking at George. Jack is married, Anne is single, and George is divorced.

Is a married person looking at a person who is not married?

The answer is now obvious. Not coincidentally, we can now also determine who the married and unmarried persons in the question are: Jack and Anne, respectively. The same would be true if Anne's marital status had been given as married, widowed, or divorced. In each case, it would be easy to see that a married person was looking at an unmarried one. From our point of view, what makes the variants that include Anne's marital status easy to reason with is that the relevant information can be captured exactly in a world model.

The Lesson for Common Sense

The observation that it is easier for people to reason with information that is specific enough to be represented in a world model is at the heart of what we are proposing in this book as a mechanism for common sense.

To see this, consider the prom example once again and the following formula that says that Bob is going to the prom with Gina:

```
There is a Person:x and a Person:y where
  Person:x has "Bob" as a name,
  Person:y has "Gina" as a name, and
  Person:x has Person:y as a promDate.
```

Both variants of the prom example have this formula as a logical consequence. That is, given either the vivid or nonvivid formula, it is possible to determine that the formula above is true using just the rules of logic: they both logically entail that Bob is going to the prom with Gina.

But there is a difference between the two cases, and it is a *computational* one. In the vivid case, the truth of the formula can be easily determined using the **TEST** procedure on the appropriate world model: find the pair of constants such that the three atomic formulas in the formula above appear in the model. It would not be hard to change **TEST** to work directly on the vivid formula instead of on the world model to obtain this answer.

But in the nonvivid case, this concrete strategy would not work. To determine that the above formula is true in that case requires taking what is given in the nonvivid formula and then doing what is necessary to solve the puzzle. In general, determining whether one formula is a logical consequence of another without the vivid restriction requires considerable logical machinery—just the sort seen in logic textbooks (and beyond the scope of this book). This computation is suitable for puzzle-mode reasoning perhaps, but well beyond what we can expect for ordinary common sense.

The key point here is this: we need commonsense reasoning to be easy enough that it can be computed routinely in a completely automated way, without much effort or careful monitoring, even over enormous knowledge bases. What we are suggesting is that there is a generic form of reasoning based on classical logic that has this property. This logic, however, must be limited to premises of a restricted form: vivid formulas. If we were to give up on the closed-world interpretation of world models, the required logical reasoning would become too demanding to serve for this purpose. (This is for reasoning about *truth*: what is true, what will be true, or how to make something true. Reasoning that is more associational, like how is x connected to y, or more analogical, like how is a P similar to a Q, would need its own analysis.)

This then is the crucial computational justification for using world models (augmented with conceptual models and derivation clauses) as the basis for commonsense reasoning. This is what explains how common sense can rest on a foundation of logical reasoning without having to be embroiled in the intricacies of logic. In the end, expertise in the use of logic is not a prerequisite for common sense.

It also helps make sense of a curious phenomenon. In a commonsense context outside of puzzles, humans seem to be compelled to fill in details left out of the information they are given. For example, when we are told that a dog chased a cat round and round a tree, we find it hard to think about it without imagining the animals moving in a clockwise or counterclockwise direction. If we are told that a young girl stood beside former president Ronald Reagan for a photograph, we find it hard to think about it without putting the girl on Reagan's left or right. This is related to what psychologists call *reconstructive memory*, which we touched on earlier. The idea is that when we try to remember something we experienced or were told about in the past, we end up recalling all sorts of details that might make sense, but were not part of what we were given at the time. In principle, logical formulas could have been used to represent the given information leaving those extra details unspecified (as we did with Gabby's date above), but we seem to be pushed toward using a mental representation that wants to be more specific. It might be argued that this is actually explainable in terms of visual imagery: we are not just thinking about an incident involving a dog and cat but are imagining a visual scene somehow in our mind's eye too, and the scene can't help but show a clockwise or counterclockwise direction for the chase. But as we saw in chapter 4, a visual image by itself is not the sort of representation well suited for commonsense reasoning. Maybe a better way of putting it is to say that real or imagined visual scenes give rise (or are connected in some way) to world models, which are analogues of the world not unlike images, which lend themselves to a readily computable form of reasoning.

There is a final but subtle connection between logic and common sense that is worth pointing out. First note that when we talk about a formula being believed, we mean that it is considered to be true according to a world model (as computed by the **TEST** operation). So we really have *two* distinct notions here: the information that can be represented directly in a world model, which as we argued, is restricted in logical form; and the formulas that can be believed—a much larger set—and thus get to use logical operators much more freely. The thing to remember is this: when we say that a logically complex formula is believed, there has to be a simple world model behind the scenes that supports that belief. So consider, for example, the formula that says that Bob is taking someone other than Gail to the prom. If that formula is believed at all, it is because in the underlying world model, Bob's date is specified and happens to be someone other than Gail.

This way of understanding belief leads to the following, somewhat-surprising conclusion:

If a formula P is believed and P logically entails Q,

then the formula Q will also be believed.

This is what is known as belief being "closed" under logical entailment. Yet it is important to stress that we cannot conclude from this fact that the agent must be some sort of logical wizard, able to carry out any amount of logical reasoning, to go from P to anything it entails. (This is what philosopher Jaakko Hintikka calls *logical omniscience*.) In fact, we have said nothing about the agent being able to work from a formula P in this way; it must start its work from a world model. The right conclusion to draw here is that if the agent can get to P from its world model (or vivid formula), it will also be able to get to Q from that same model. From the outside, we may be able to see that there is a logical connection from P to Q, but we are not insisting that a commonsense agent be able to see it.

Some Complications and Limitations

In this bonus chapter, we explored the idea that while drawing conclusions from a world model was a feasible form of commonsense reasoning, drawing conclusions from formulas more generally need not be. There are many subtleties we glossed over, however, both in terms of the representation and the reasoning, and we conclude by looking at some of them.

Let us consider reasoning first. Even though the **TEST** and **FIND-ALL** operations from before are indeed relatively easy compared to unrestricted logical reasoning, there are cases where what they have to do might still be too demanding for commonsense applications.

Imagine, for example, using **TEST** to determine if a "there is" formula is true where five variables are involved. In this case, **TEST** needs to see if it can find a combination of five constants in the world model to make the formula true. Let us suppose that the model mentions 1,000 constants. Then **TEST** might still have to look at as many as 10^{15} different combinations to see if any of them work. Even if it could consider a billion combinations every second, it would still take more than ten days to go through them all!

There are mitigating factors here, though. One is that it will seldom be necessary to find a combination of five interconnected things like this. Pairs of things, yes, and sometimes triples, but rarely beyond. The other is that **TEST** can do much better than to search exhaustively through all combinations. It can compute the answers to **FIND-ALL** for those five variables incrementally from the bottom up. For example, if the formula is a conjunction and contains

```
Person:x has Person:y as a friend
```

as one of its conjuncts, an answer only has to include values for `Person:x` and `Person:y` that are friend related in the world model, not all 10^6 combinations. If there are other conjuncts in the formula that just use these two variables, then that number can be further reduced. If for the next variable `Person:z`, there is a conjunct

> `Person:z has Person:y as a brother`

then an answer only has to include values of `Person:z` that are brother related in the world model to some `Person:y` in the answer so far, not all 10^9 triples. And so on. This is the basis of what is called *conjunctive query evaluation* for databases and has been found to be quite effective in practice even for extremely large databases.

Another complication with **TEST** concerns recursion. While it is nice to be able to say that we can have **TEST** look for chains of `parent` relationships in a model (as seen in chapter 8), this is in fact a powerful operation. Are we guaranteed that **TEST** will always stop expanding recursive definitions and come to a final answer? No. There are recursively defined properties that would keep **TEST** (or any computational engine) running forever. The mitigating factor here is that for commonsense purposes, recursion would only be used in limited ways, such as for transitive closures (like going from `parent` to `ancestor`), for which special-purpose machinery is available.

A related complication concerns numbers. We can easily modify **TEST** so that it will recognize a formula without variables like 2*3 < 5+4 as true by doing the necessary arithmetic. But we should not expect **TEST** to be able to evaluate arithmetic formulas with *variables* as part of commonsense reasoning. Is there an even number other than two that is not the sum of two prime numbers? Not even the experts know. One mitigating factor here is that when it comes to variables, the **TEST** and **FIND-ALL** operations are restricted to look for constants that appear in the model. So for example, **FIND-ALL** for the formula 6 < `Number:x` will only return the (finitely many) numerical constants greater than six that actually appear in the model and not attempt to return the infinite number of numbers that are greater than six.

The same issue applies to sequences, as discussed in the context of planning in chapter 8. An operation like **FIND-ALL** cannot be used to locate sequences of actions that achieve some goal, unless there are constants in the model representing them. What we would expect to see in a world model are representations of actions that have been found to be useful in the past. (This is one of the key elements of common sense discussed in chapter 2.) When the action is not primitive, it will be associated in the model with a sequence of primitive actions. The **FIND-ALL** operation should then be able to locate those remembered sequences of actions for planning purposes. As we saw in chapter 9, this much more limited notion of planning is more appropriate for commonsense purposes. The operation of assembling a totally new sequence of actions from first principles is a computationally demanding task best left for puzzle-mode reasoning.

Let us now turn to representation. What we have proposed is that basic knowledge would be represented in world models (chapter 7), and the beliefs expressed as formulas would be derived from them (chapter 8). This leaves out what to do with what we called in chapter 6 *incomplete knowledge*, where relevant details are missing about the specific things and properties involved. In this bonus chapter, we saw how dealing with this kind of knowledge can require solving logical puzzles, beyond what we can expect of common sense.

But there are other forms of incomplete knowledge. Consider, for example, reading a mystery novel where a murder was committed by one of three suspects. We can imagine starting with a world model with three constants representing the three individuals and various facts about them represented as in chapter 7. Once we discover that one of them is the murderer, however, this scheme breaks down. In one sense, the mystery novel does indeed become a puzzle. We accept that there may be clues to deal with and conclusions we will not get to until we find out who the murderer is, just like in the prom example above.

Still, it is clear that we also need to be able to reason about the murderer before solving the puzzle. For instance, it is common sense that the murderer was born somewhere, has a mother, needs to breathe, and so on, like any other person. We will not get far in our understanding of the novel if conclusions such as these have to wait until we know who the murderer is. If we find out early in the novel that the murderer had granola for breakfast, say, we should be able to conclude that the murderer ate something that morning without having to first figure out who the murderer is.

So how do we represent this kind of incomplete knowledge in a world model? The most obvious answer is that we should use a fourth constant in the model standing for the murderer. We can then represent information about the murderer as a person and draw conclusions from it, just as we would for each of the three suspects.

There are problems with this, though. First and foremost, we can no longer assume that every formula of $\mathcal{L}$ will be considered to be true or false. For example, if the first suspect is represented as `Person#92` and the murderer is represented as `UnknownPerson#17`, then the formula

    Person#92 is UnknownPerson#17.

cannot be taken to be false just because the two constants are different, as has been our convention so far. We have three people in this fictional world, but four constants. So the **TEST** operation clearly has to change. (A close reading of chapter 7 will show that we already have this problem. We represented the location of John's birth as `SpacePt#25`, but we do not really know whether this point is different from other points in the city of Boston we might have already considered.)

To get a glimpse of some of the complications involved, note that the formula

    There is a Person:x where Person:x is a person and
      it is not the case that Person:x is UnknownPerson#17.

should be considered to be true, even though we cannot name a constant among the four to substitute for `Person:x` to make the embedded formula true. So the **TEST** operation would need to behave quite differently not only on equality formulas but on the other formulas as well.

Now consider a different form of incomplete knowledge. Suppose there are some dogs in the backyard and we are told that they all belong to Jim. If we know there are four dogs involved, we can construct a model with representations of those four dogs, noting that each one of them is owned by Jim. No problem. But if we have no idea how many dogs there are, how can we represent the fact that they are all owned by Jim? It seems like we ought to be able to handle a fact like this without having to deal with the representation of each individual dog. A related issue came up in chapter 6 when we considered this statement:

All the paint cans in John's basement are covered in dust.

Again, it seems we should be able to represent this information without having to identify each individual paint can and represent its properties. This is even more obvious with something like

All the stars in the Milky Way galaxy are bigger than Neptune.

where one hundred billion individuals are involved.

This is once again a form of incomplete knowledge, with some logical puzzles lurking nearby. Here is one, adapted from an example by psychologist Philip Johnson-Laird:

> *Suppose there are some dogs in the backyard, and we have the following two facts:*
>
> *1. All the dogs in the backyard are owned by Jim.*
>
> *2. No small dogs are in the backyard.*
>
> *Then which of the following three statements must also be true?*
>
> *3. Some small dogs are not owned by Jim.*
>
> *4. Some dogs owned by Jim are not small.*
>
> *5. None of the dogs owned by Jim are small.*

This is a puzzle, and the correct answer here is (4). As before, we should not expect to be able to get to this conclusion from (1) and (2) alone, as a matter of mere common sense.

Yet the question we asked in chapter 6 remains: What exactly should be done with a basic fact like (1) by itself? Johnson-Laird proposes a representation that is similar to our world models, but with many additional features. Among other things, the Johnson-Laird models include symbols representing hypothetical objects which may or may not exist. So for example, we would have a certain number of symbols representing dogs in the backyard, all of which are marked as owned by Jim, and some representations of other objects owned by Jim that are not dogs in the backyard. The representation, in other words, postulates the existence of a number of individual things, and then uses the resulting model (or models) to derive general conclusions involving "all," "some," and "none" from them. (This is related to how a generic question about birds being flying animals was handled at the end of chapter 8.) This is an attractive proposal from the point of view of reasoning, although it needs further study as a general representational mechanism. How, for instance, do we avoid drawing spurious conclusions from these models about what actually does or does not exist?

Another possibility for dealing with incomplete knowledge in common-sense terms is to allow arbitrary general formulas to be part of the knowledge base after all (including negations, disjunctions, quantifications, modalities, or whatever), but to draw only certain superficial conclusions from them—too superficial to allow hard puzzles to be solved, but superficial enough to be readily computable. When the knowledge base happens to be vivid, the superficial reasoning might well align with the **TEST** operation. With a formula like (1) in the knowledge base, however, we might be able to draw certain obvious conclusions, such as the fact that all the *brown* dogs in the backyard are owned by Jim, but be unable to combine it with other facts like (2) to draw conclusions like (4), at least not without additional mental effort. The proposal again needs further study.

Incidentally, a big part of the research in the AI subarea of *knowledge representation and reasoning* involves looking for other "islands of tractability" in the sea of logical and probabilistic reasoning, with an eye toward common sense. In other words, what are forms of automated reasoning beyond those described in this book that make sense from the point of view of logic and probability, but that can be carried out in an automated way efficiently enough even over enormous symbolic representations of knowledge? This dovetails with a broader effort in the part of theoretical computer science called *computational complexity* to understand what it is that makes computational tasks easy or hard.

Acknowledgments

This book reflects our own views on what matters in AI and draws heavily on the topics we ended up exploring during our research careers. It's not just a coincidence that our names show up so often in the bibliography. One of us (RJB) worked mostly in industry, and the other (HJL), mostly in academia, but we were both fortunate to have worked with and learned from some of the smartest people in AI. After forty years, there are too many people to thank by name, but we do want to acknowledge our esteemed colleagues, students, postdoctoral fellows, and employees, without whom we would certainly have had a lot less to say.

Let's talk specifics. As we mention in the notes, we were inspired to take on this project after seeing the recent book by Gary Marcus and Ernest Davis as well as the one by Melanie Mitchell. Those three authors were willing to look at an early draft of our book and provided us with many helpful comments. We are also grateful for comments from Gerhard Lakemeyer, Gregg Vesonder, and three anonymous reviewers. We believe that the book is much better because of their advice. We had the final cut, of course, so any remaining errors and oversights in the book are our problem, not theirs. We especially thank Bruce Brachman for the terrific illustrations appearing as figures 8.4 and 9.1.

We also wish to acknowledge the good folks at MIT Press. Alex Hoopes and Elizabeth Swayze were invariably kind and encouraging, and helped us with excellent suggestions all the way through the process. Virginia Crossman, our editor, was a great partner and was critical to getting us across the finish line. We have no idea what other authors contend with at other publishing houses, but MIT Press has always been a joy to work with.

Last but not least, we wish to thank our families; they were there for us during the writing and myriad Zoom meetings where we hammered out all the details. So to Gwen and Pat: thank you for your love, support, and patience during all of that noisy hammering.

April 2021

Notes

This book draws to a great extent on what we have learned about AI over our long research careers. In this section of the book, we give pointers by author to a number of publications inside and outside AI that influenced our thinking. (We will refer to ourselves as RJB and HJL.) Details on these publications can be found in the bibliography. These notes are organized according to the chapters of the book, and can serve as starting points for a more comprehensive study of the issues raised.

While this book leans heavily on a broad spectrum of AI research going back to the 1950s, it was more directly inspired by three recent books: *Rebooting AI* by Gary Marcus and Ernest Davis, *Artificial Intelligence: A Guide for Thinking Humans* by Melanie Mitchell, and an earlier book by HJL titled *Common Sense, the Turing Test, and the Quest for Real AI*. What these three have in common was their focus on how the goals of current AI research fall short of the original vision of the field. All of them identified *common sense* as one of the main ingredients not being addressed in current AI work, despite so many achievements on other fronts. None of the three books, however, tried to analyze this idea of common sense in any depth. What is this common sense? How does it work? What would it take to build AI systems that had it? These, it seemed to us, were essential questions that needed to be investigated, and motivated us to try our hand at filling in some of the missing details. There are already some AI books on common sense, such as *Representations of Commonsense Knowledge* by Davis in 1990, *Formal Theories of the Commonsense World* by Jerry Hobbs and Robert Moore, *Formalizing Common Sense* by John McCarthy and Vladimir Lifschitz, and *Commonsense Reasoning* by Erik Mueller, but they tend to concentrate almost entirely on the formalization of the knowledge considered to lie behind common sense.

Two other recent books by colleagues of ours also influenced our approach. *The Book of Why* by Judea Pearl (with Dana Mackenzie) on causality made us believe it was possible to have a book on AI for general readers that included small technical examples. And the 2019 book *The Promise of Artificial Intelligence* by our good friend Brian Cantwell Smith made us think hard about the philosophical issues behind our and other approaches to AI.

Finally, we should mention that the book was also spurred by the large number of recent pieces written by people not directly involved in AI work. It is hard to read the technical or business sections of magazines and newspapers these days without finding commentary on the current state of the art in AI. Some of these will show up in the various sections below. For an early report on common sense, see the 1982 article "How Can Computers Get Common Sense?" by the science writer Gina Kolata. Two general critiques of AI worth noting are the book *Artifictional Intelligence* by sociologist Harry Collins, and the 2020 article "An Understanding of AI's Limitations Is Starting to Sink In" in the *Economist* by the science and technology correspondent Tim Cross.

Chapter 1: The Road to Common Sense

This introductory chapter motivates our approach and provides an overview of the rest of the book. The groundbreaking 1958 paper by John McCarthy that started all the thinking in AI on common sense was called, appropriately, "Programs with Common Sense." Much better known is a version that included a later article, "Situations, Actions, and Causal Laws," which appeared in Marvin Minsky's *Semantic Information Processing*, and was reprinted in RJB and HJL's *Readings* book. For more on these papers, see chapter 4 and the notes on chapter 8. The quote from Gary Marcus and Ernest Davis is taken from page 94 of their *Rebooting AI* book, written sixty years later.

As noted in the text, there have always been heated debates within and outside the field as to where AI should be going, and what will end up mattering the most. To get some idea of current opinions, see *Architects of Intelligence*, the 2018 book of interviews with AI researchers conducted by futurist Martin Ford. There is a curious mix of insight and overstatement in Ford's book, but certainly nothing resembling a consensus. Our opinion is that questions about how AI research should be conducted are best settled on the playing field, not by argumentation. Whatever works, works.

In this book, we will not be debating which direction to pursue in AI but instead exploring one particular road to common sense, if only to better understand what the journey entails. We first look at common sense in humans (chapter 2), the history of AI systems including deep learning (chapter 3), and where the idea of using symbols comes from along with the scientific hypothesis behind it (chapter 4). We then examine this hypothesis in some detail (chapters 5–8) before we try to make a connection with actual commonsense behavior (chapter 9). Then we consider two remaining questions: How we might put these ideas into practice (chapter 10), and why we might want to (chapter 11).

In our opinion, none of this settles the debate about how AI research should or should not be conducted. But our hope is that it will illuminate the issues having to do with common sense in a helpful way.

Chapter 2: Common Sense in Humans

Common sense has long been a subject of popular comment, but has been relatively resistant to detailed explication. Sometimes the term is just used as a stand-in for good sense or logical thinking. In the quotes at the start of this chapter, we illustrate several interesting perspectives on what it is about, and many others can be found online. Surprisingly, though, it is hard to find more than vague descriptions of what common sense in humans might be. There is a lot of speculation about when it is used and what is common (or uncommon) about it, but virtually nothing about what it actually *is*.

It is hard to find a scientific study of the phenomenon of common sense as it occurs in humans. Perhaps this is because it is difficult to draw a firm line separating common sense from other, more specialized modes of thinking. The Systems 1 and 2 distinction presented in Daniel Kahneman's *Thinking, Fast and Slow* is a useful way of understanding human psychology, but appears to be a different cut. Interestingly, Kahneman's book, which surveys his work with Amos Tversky on cognitive biases (including the Linda experiment discussed here), does not even have "common sense" as an item in its index.

As mentioned in the chapter, perhaps the most substantial line of work in psychology that deals directly with common sense is connected to what is termed *practical intelligence*. Robert Sternberg and colleagues have a series of publications related to the subject, including a comprehensive book called *Practical Intelligence in Everyday Life*, and there is a more recent survey, titled "Practical Intelligence," by Sternberg's collaborator Jennifer Hedlund. (The quotation in the text is the first line of the preface in the Sternberg book.) Sternberg's broader theory of adaptive intelligence is covered in his 2021 book, *Adaptive Intelligence*. Much of the discussion of practical intelligence in the literature is about measurement, largely in response to dissatisfaction with g, the single "general intelligence" factor supposedly measured by IQ tests. There is also a question regarding whether or not common sense can be taught; there are guidebooks and websites purporting to explain how to improve practical intelligence. While we leave all that aside here, insights from these debates may eventually prove valuable to AI.

Kenneth Hammond's work on the cognitive continuum is featured in a series of publications dating back to 1980. His 1987 article, "Direct Comparison of the Efficacy of Intuitive and Analytical Cognition in Expert Judgment," written with colleagues, is a good example. Hammond suggests that intuitive modes of cognition are pictorial, while analytical modes tend to be more verbal. Note that there is evidence that the more analytical capabilities are handled by a different part of the human brain (the prefrontal cortex) than those that control the routine autopilot activity (the amygdala and cerebellum). The temporal lobes, as the seat of memory, are probably important to human common sense, but the neuroscience will have to wait for another book.

On a different note, mirroring psychology's view of common sense emphasizing action, philosophers sometimes distinguish between reasoning that is concerned with what is true about the world and what they term *practical reasoning*, concerned with the actions that should be taken. Philosopher Elijah Millgram's edited volume *Varieties of Practical Reasoning* provides multiple perspectives on the subject. For more on the topic of rationality, see the 2021 book entitled *Rationality* by Steven Pinker.

A useful account of common sense from the perspective of sociology is due to Duncan Watts in his insightful *Everything Is Obvious*. We agree with much of his characterization, such as his emphasis on quick, simple, experience-based explanations and the practical nature of common sense.

But we differ from Watts on a couple of key points. First, as our definition of the term makes clear, for something to exhibit common sense, it must be able to make effective use of its experiential knowledge to achieve its goals. Watts focuses on the knowledge alone—important of course, but in our view, the *reasoning* aspect is equally crucial. Second, Watts speculates that the practicality of common sense means that there is no need to understand why something is commonsensical: "One does not need to know why [something is true] in order to benefit from the knowledge, and arguably one is better off not worrying about it too much" (page 9). We believe that it is critical to have at least an intuitive understanding of why a piece of common sense works, and as we observe in chapter 11, be able to unpack it in terms of the underlying knowledge it leans on.

Sir Frederic Bartlett's work on reconstructive memory in psychology is covered in his classic book on the subject, *Remembering: A Study in Experimental and Social Psychology*. We mention this again in chapter 7, and provide a reference there about eyewitness memory.

In the last section of the chapter, we mention several things that diverge from common sense. We say, for instance, that experts acquire specialized knowledge that often requires complex analytic modes of thinking. But it appears that experts also tend to develop a more intuitive understanding of their specialized worlds and what amounts to a kind of common sense shared by their narrow community of colleagues. In his book *The Power of Intuition*, psychologist Gary Klein talks in a compelling way about intuitive decision-making by experts and the frequency with which experts make critical decisions using intuition rather than rational, orderly analysis. We mention puzzle-mode thinking too; for a preliminary analysis of this idea, see HJL's 1988 paper, "Logic and the Complexity of Reasoning." Finally, regarding pattern recognition, the example presented in the chapter involves seeing a pattern over a linear sequence of letters. An interesting related task involving two-dimensional visual structures was proposed by computer scientist Mikhail Bongard and is discussed at some length in Melanie Mitchell's book *Artificial Intelligence*.

Chapter 3: Expertise in AI Systems

This chapter refers to a wide variety of different AI systems and projects. Pamela McCorduck and Nils Nilsson have both written informative overviews of the history of AI: respectively, *Machines Who Think* and *The Quest for Artificial Intelligence*. Articles with retrospectives on the field as a whole appear in special issues of the *AI Magazine* in 2005 and 2006 (edited by David Leake), the latter commemorating the fiftieth anniversary of the field. A 2020 issue of this magazine (edited by Ashok Goel) surveys the significant contribution made by researchers funded by DARPA in the United States.

Important speculation on what it would take for a machine to be considered intelligent was offered by Alan Turing as far back as the late 1940s. Turing's contemplation of a way to determine if a machine could think (via his imitation game, mentioned in the text), with all of its pros and cons, was a crucial early driver of thinking about AI. HJL's *Common Sense* book, and the Gary Marcus, Francesca Rossi, and Manuela Veloso 2016 special issue of *AI Magazine* provide insight into the Turing test. Less known perhaps is that Turing also contemplated how computers might be applied to strategic games in his 1953 article, "Digital Computers Applied to Games," building on the work of Claude Shannon in his "Programming a Computer Program for Playing Chess."

Many consider the field of AI to have begun at the famous Dartmouth Summer Research Project, an eight-week workshop in New Hampshire in 1956 based on "A Proposal for the Dartmouth Summer Research Project on Artificial Intelligence, August 31, 1955" by John McCarthy, Marvin Minsky, Nathaniel Rochester, and Shannon. The proposal to the Rockefeller Foundation for the meeting talked presciently about many topics that have continued to be of central interest to the field today, including reasoning using abstractions and concepts, learning (including neural nets), creativity, problem-solving, and game playing. Allen Newell, Herb Simon, and Cliff Shaw had actually been working on an AI program, called the Logic Theorist, since the year before the Dartmouth conference. In early 1956, Simon is reputed to have told one of his classes that "over the Christmas holiday, Al Newell and I invented a thinking machine" (quoted in an article by Byron Spice in the online *Pittsburgh Post-Gazette*, January 2, 2006).

Games and game-related search have always played an important role in the history of AI. Newell and Simon offered their ideas on search in their Turing Award lecture, published in 1976 as "Computer Science as Empirical Inquiry." Regarding checkers, a nice perspective on Arthur Samuel's contribution, subtitled "Pioneer in Machine Learning," was published on his death by John McCarthy and Ed Feigenbaum. Jonathan Schaeffer's eventual triumph over checkers is documented in his coauthored article "Checkers Is Solved" in *Science* in 2007. The success of Deep Blue in chess is much better known. (See, for example, Monty Newborn's book *Deep Blue*.) The backgammon and poker successes are described in the article "Backgammon Computer Program Beats World Champion" by Hans Berliner and "Superhuman AI for Heads-up No-Limit Poker" by Noam Brown and Tuomas Sandholm.

In regard to NLP, Terry Winograd's MIT thesis (published as "Understanding Natural Language" in *Cognitive Psychology* in 1972) was a milestone in the early history of NLP, although a number of other important efforts were already underway, such as "Transition Network Grammars for Natural Language Analysis" by William Woods. (Robert Simmons surveyed a number of question-answering systems in 1965 in his article "Answering English Questions by Computer.") Daniel Jurafsky and James Martin wrote a more recent textbook on NLP, *Speech and Language Processing*, with ongoing updates. On speech recognition and speech understanding, Mark Liberman and Charles Wayne provide a thorough review in "Human Language Technology." The recent attention to Winograd schemas arose out of a 2012 paper by HJL, Ernest Davis, and Leora Morgenstern, "The Winograd Schema Challenge," and were further discussed in HJL's *Common Sense* book. (For a lesson to learn from them, see the notes below on chapter 11.)

An early harbinger of the emergence of rule-based systems is *Semantic Information Processing*, edited by Minsky; it features the doctoral theses of several pioneers in the use of symbolic knowledge to support AI. Expert systems are described in comprehensive detail in the book *Building Expert Systems* by Frederick Hayes-Roth, Donald Waterman, and Douglas Lenat as well as *Introduction to Expert Systems* by Peter Jackson. The MYCIN system is presented in Edward Shortliffe's book *Computer-Based Medical Consultations*. MYCIN's competency in therapy recommendation for infectious meningitis was examined in a formal evaluation reported in "An Evaluation of MYCIN's Advice" by Victor Yu and colleagues in 1984. In a blinded, two-phase evaluation, its recommendations were rated as acceptable more often than those of seven physicians and a medical student. Details on Prospector were published by its inventors, Richard Duda, John Gaschnig, and Peter Hart, in "Model Design in the Prospector Consultant System for Mineral Exploration," and on XCON by its inventor, John McDermott, in "R1: A

Rule-Based Configurer of Computer Systems" (under its original name, R1) as well as in the later review "The Engineering of XCON" by Judith Bachant and Elliot Soloway. The quote from Melanie Mitchell about the brittleness of expert systems is from pages 39–40 of her book *Artificial Intelligence*.

Regarding integrated systems, AI, in the form of Shakey the robot, was first presented to the general public in a lengthy 1970 *Life Magazine* article by Brad Darrach. Shakey was given a provocative description in the article's title, "Meet Shaky [*sic*], the First Electronic Person," which also claimed that Shakey had "a mind of its own." The museum-guide robot was presented some thirty years later by Wolfram Burgard and colleagues in "Experiences with an Interactive Museum Tour-Guide Robot." The car that won the 2005 DARPA Grand Challenge for driving without human intervention is documented in detail by Sebastian Thrun and his team in "Stanley: The Robot That Won the DARPA Grand Challenge." The AI system aboard *Deep Space 1* is discussed by Nicola Muscettola and colleagues in "Remote Agent." The RoboCup competitions are described in the 1999 article "RoboCup" by Minoru Asada and company, and more recently by Asada and Oskar von Stryk in "Scientific and Technological Challenges in RoboCup." The Soar architecture is presented in John Laird's 2019 book, *The Soar Cognitive Architecture*. Other robotic and nonrobotic integrated AI systems are surveyed in the recent *AI Magazine* article "Integrated AI Systems" by RJB, David Gunning, and Murray Burke. For a review of robotics research that concentrates on the more cognitive aspects, see the article "Cognitive Robotics" by HJL and Gerhard Lakemeyer.

Speaking of robots, news reports or documentaries about the state of the art in AI invariably show robots that look human or move in a humanlike way. For the most part, these humanoid robots have little to do with AI. The emphasis is much more on the way they look than on what they can do. They might even be teleoperated by humans hiding on the sidelines—a tradition going back to the chess-playing automatons of the 1770s (a well-known one of which was called the Mechanical Turk).

Turning now to data-driven learning, what started out as a small effort in neural network modeling has grown to become the dominant force in AI today. A good place to learn about deep learning is the authoritative article "Deep Learning" in *Nature* by the recent Turing Award winners Yann LeCun, Yoshua Bengio, and Geoffrey Hinton. A more extensive survey with over three hundred references (including to some of the earlier work mentioned here), "A State-of-the-Art Survey on Deep Learning Theory and Architectures," was written by Md Zahangir Alom and colleagues. Many of the applications at Microsoft, IBM, Google, and other places are also discussed in this paper. The quote from Jeff Dean about the impact of deep learning on speech work is reported on page 180 of Mitchell's *Artificial Intelligence*. Christopher Shallue and Andrew Vanderburg discuss the use of deep learning in astronomy in "Identifying Exoplanets with Deep Learning." The *New York Times* ran an op-ed piece by Farhad Manjoo about GPT-3, "How Do You Know a Human Wrote This?," appearing on July 29, 2020. The Greek example of the GPT-2 transformer output was taken from Marcus's provocative "The Next Decade in AI" preprint. (Our birthday cake example was generated using the same program.) The methods based on deep learning for playing the game of Go are described in David Silver's multiauthor article "Mastering the Game of Go with Deep Neural Networks and Tree Search" in *Nature*. The quote from François Chollet on the limitations of deep learning is from his 2019 preprint "On the Measure of Intelligence," although other researchers have expressed similar misgivings. The "very next novel" whose first line is quoted here is *Geneva Farewell* by John Levesque. Information on the British National Corpus can be found online at http://www.natcorp .ox.ac.uk/. The observation concerning the large presence of rare words in this corpus is due to Ernest Davis, and the implication for common sense of long-tail distributions like this is discussed in chapter 7 of HJL's *Common Sense* book.

Chapter 4: Knowledge and Its Representation

This chapter is about some of the underpinnings of the study of common sense regarding knowledge, representation, and reasoning, and their connection to logic.

The topic of knowledge has been a mainstay of philosophical study since the time of the ancient Greeks. Two collections of papers in this area are *Knowledge and Belief* by A. Phillips Griffiths and *Knowing* by Michael Roth and Leon Galis. A groundbreaking mathematical analysis of knowledge was introduced in the book *Knowledge and Belief* by philosopher Jaakko Hintikka—work that has found further application in computer science, as seen in the book *Reasoning about Knowledge* by Ronald Fagin and colleagues. A study of knowledge that emphasizes its symbolic representation in knowledge bases can be found in the book *The Logic of Knowledge Bases* by HJL and Gerhard Lakemeyer.

Logic itself is a massive subject, incorporating a number of disparate ideas, difficult to even summarize. For our purposes, we can restrict our attention to deductive logic in the classical Western tradition, as in the Alex Malpass and Marianna Antonutti Marfori collection *The History of Philosophical and Formal Logic*. As noted in the text, the modern form of symbolic logic is due to Gottlob Frege, with a specific notation due to mathematician Giuseppe Peano, in the early 1900s. The key development was that of a formal system that included not only sentence-level operators like "and," "or," and "not" (the so-called Boolean operators, from the earlier logician George Boole) but also for the first time, predicates with arguments, variables, and quantifiers, all of which we will be making use of and further discussing in chapter 8.

The importance of symbols like words to the process of thinking in humans, especially through reading and writing, is addressed in the book *The Mind on Paper* by David Olson. An early originator in the work on representations such as words and numerals is Gottfried Leibniz, one of the most fascinating thinkers of all time. The Leibniz quote is from his 1677 *Preface to the General Science*, reprinted in the collection *The Cambridge Companion to Leibniz* by Nicholas Jolley. It has a clear reference to what we would now call *symbol processing*, but the actual characterization of that idea (as distinct from arithmetic) only came almost three hundred years later in the work of John McCarthy, Allen Newell, and others. (See McCarthy's 1960 paper, "Recursive Functions of Symbolic Expressions and Their Computation by Machine, Part I," for example.) Even the work of logician Kurt Gödel in the 1930s involving the processing of formulas of a logical language was cast in terms of arithmetic by first mapping these formulas onto numbers (in what has come to be called Gödelization).

The McCarthy quote on common sense was taken from his 1958 paper, "Programs with Common Sense," noted at the start of chapter 1. The knowledge representation hypothesis is quoted from Brian Cantwell Smith's PhD thesis "Reflection and Semantics in a Procedural Language." Credit for the idea is usually given to McCarthy, but other AI researchers were clearly on the same track. For Allen Newell and Herb Simon, the emphasis was more on the symbolic aspects, and their version is called the *physical symbol system hypothesis*, which they characterized this way in their 1976 paper

"Computer Science as Empirical Inquiry": "A physical symbol system has the necessary and sufficient means for general intelligent action."

McCarthy's ideas on the epistemological and heuristic adequacy of knowledge-based systems are discussed in his 1977 "Epistemological Problems of Artificial Intelligence" article.

The chapter mentions several key leaders who followed McCarthy's path in using logical formulas to represent commonsense knowledge. See, for example, the 1990 book *Representations of Commonsense Knowledge* by Ernest Davis, the 2017 book *Reasoning about Uncertainty* by Joseph Halpern, the 1985 book *Formal Theories of the Commonsense World* by Jerry Hobbs and Robert Moore, and the 2001 book *Knowledge in Action* by Raymond Reiter. On the need to consider extensions to logic to incorporate notions like defaults and typicality, see the collection *Readings in Nonmonotonic Reasoning* by Matthew Ginsberg. The Minsky quote about the inadequacy of logical reasoning is on page 262 of his 1985 paper, "A Framework for Representing Knowledge." (This paper is discussed at greater length in chapter 6, as is the work of Roger Schank and students.)

While probably the longest continuously running project in AI, Cyc has also been one of the most controversial—less because of its ambitious mission than because of the extreme lack of information flow about it. There have been peer-reviewed publications on Cyc, such as "Searching for Common Sense" by Cynthia Matuszek and colleagues and "An Interactive Dialogue System for Knowledge Acquisition in Cyc" by Michael Witbrock and colleagues, but they are rare given a thirty-five-year research project of this magnitude. Perhaps the most comprehensive account is the book *Building Large Knowledge-Based Systems* by Douglas Lenat and Ramanathan Guha, but this was deemed a "midterm report" and does not reflect the work after 1989. Many of the claims about Cyc appear only in popular magazines, such as the mentioned piece by Lenat from the July 2019 online issue of *Forbes* entitled "What AI Can Learn From Romeo & Juliet." (The quote by Lenat on "heuristic reasoning modules" is taken from that article.) Almost all information about the project has been carefully controlled by project and company leaders. For example, the quote on the actual size of Cyc is from the Cyc website and has not to our knowledge been independently confirmed. Ernest Davis and Gary Marcus comment on this somewhat unfortunate situation in their *Communications of the ACM* article "Commonsense Reasoning and Commonsense Knowledge in Artificial Intelligence" as follows:

The field might well benefit if CYC were systematically described and evaluated. If CYC has solved some significant fraction of commonsense reasoning, then it is critical to know that, both as a useful tool, and as a starting point for further research. If CYC has run into difficulties, it would be useful to learn from the mistakes that were made. If CYC is entirely useless, then researchers can at least stop worrying about whether they are reinventing the wheel.

The NELL project is described in a 2018 article "Never-Ending Learning" by Tom Mitchell and his team. The GOFAI term is from John Haugeland's book *Artificial Intelligence: The Very Idea*.

Reinforcing the criticality of the subject of our book, thought leaders in the deep learning community such as Yann LeCun, Yoshua Bengio, and Geoffrey Hinton have mentioned how important they think common sense will be for AI systems. Perhaps not surprisingly, they are confident that deep learning in some form will eventually account for it. (See, for example, interviews with them in the book *Architects of Intelligence* by Martin Ford.) The mentioned COMET system, which explores a more hybrid approach, is described in the preprint "COMET" by Antoine Bosselut and colleagues. See also the preprint "The Next Decade in AI" by Marcus on the need for hybrid systems like this, and the recent *Communications of the ACM* article "Seeking Artificial Common Sense" by Don Monroe on this topic and the lack of anything like common sense in deployed AI systems to date.

Chapter 5: A Commonsense Understanding of the World

In its broadest terms, this chapter is about what the knowledge of a commonsense agent needs to assume about the world. (This is not quite the same thing as trying to spell out what the world is *really* like, common sense aside.) As noted, there are different ways of looking at this, with different aspects being emphasized. In developmental psychology, researchers often concentrate on the more physical aspects of the world, with physical causality at the center, for example, and space playing as prominent a role as time. For this psychological perspective, see Gary Marcus's *The Birth of the Mind*, Steven Pinker's *The Language Instinct*, and Elizabeth Spelke and Katherine Kinzler's "Core Knowledge."

In AI, the breakdown of the sorts of things that a system will know about is sometimes called an *ontology*; Steffen Staab and Rudi Studer have produced the hefty *Handbook on Ontologies* on the subject. (Note that the term has a more metaphysical connotation in philosophy.) It is imagined that AI systems in different areas could work with quite different ontologies (for example, in archaeology versus endocrinology versus sociology versus mythology). Brian Cantwell Smith's quote on ontology at the end of the chapter is from page 142 of *The Promise of Artificial Intelligence*.

Along the lines of what was advocated in this chapter, the knowledge of an AI system is sometimes first classified into broad, general categories in what is called an upper or top-level ontology. (See the article "Understanding Top-Level Ontological Distinctions" by Aldo Gangemi and colleagues as well as "Towards a Standard Upper Ontology" by Ian Niles and Adam Pease.) The idea is to imagine a taxonomic classification of the entire subject matter, and look at what should be near the top of this taxonomy, above things like "living thing" or "physical object."

A "theory of everything" is the term physicists use to describe a unified mathematical account of the entire universe. (Of course, their notion of "everything" is for the physical world, and does not include things like online surveys or the songs on the Beatles' *Abbey Road*.) For many researchers, common sense is first and foremost concerned with what we have called medial macro-objects (with an emphasis on location, shape, enclosure, and the like). See the 2020 article "Artificial Intelligence and the Common Sense of Animals" by Murray Shanahan and colleagues, for example. The term "naive physics" (sometimes called "folk physics") was popularized by Patrick Hayes in his "Naive Physics Manifesto," which was followed by a sequel, "The Second Naive Physics Manifesto." The term "qualitative physics" is sometimes used to underscore the nonnumerical reasoning about physical objects and properties so typical of common sense. Much of the work on qualitative physics owes its origins to ideas from Johan de Kleer, subsequently elaborated by Ken Forbus, among others. (See the collection *Readings in Qualitative Reasoning about Physical Systems* by Daniel Weld and de Kleer.) Of special interest in regard to qualitative physics is reasoning about space and time themselves, as in the articles "The Challenge of Qualitative Spatial Reasoning" by Anthony Cohn and "Maintaining Knowledge about Temporal Intervals" by James Allen. The commonsense law of inertia is explored in detail by Shanahan in his 1997 book, *Solving the Frame Problem*, and chapter 5 of Erik Mueller's *Commonsense Reasoning*. It is related to what is called the frame problem, taken up in the notes on chapter 8. The displacement property of language, and how it makes human language use so different from other forms of animal communication, is discussed in Derek Bickerton's book *Adam's Tongue*.

Regarding quantities and limits, the goal of reasoning about quantities in a qualitative way—that is, without the use of real numbers or large integers (where, for instance, variables might take on only one of three possible values: positive, negative, or zero)—is at the root of the work in qualitative physics noted above and the order of magnitude reasoning examined in the next chapter. The example about kings and knights getting to squares on a chessboard is taken from David McAllester's "Observations on Cognitive Judgments."

Naive psychology (by analogy with naive physics) is explored in the articles "From Folk Psychology to Naive Psychology" by Andy Clark and "A Brief Naive Psychology Manifesto" by Stuart Watt. The idea of modeling an agent as something governed by beliefs, desires, and intentions is presented in the 2005 paper "Toward a Large-Scale Formal Theory of Commonsense Psychology for Metacognition" by Jerry Hobbs and Andrew Gordon, and an earlier one by Anand Rao and Michael Georgeff, titled "Modeling Rational Agents within a BDI-Architecture." A more comprehensive account of "how people think people think" appears in *A Formal Theory of Commonsense Psychology* by Gordon and Hobbs. Intentions themselves are sometimes seen as derivative properties, or combinations of certain beliefs and goals, as seen in the 1990 article "Intention Is Choice with Commitment" by Philip Cohen and HJL. Another property seen as deriving from beliefs is that of know-how or *epistemic ability*, considered in the *Studia Logica* article "Ability and Knowing How in the Situation Calculus" by Yves Lespérance and company. The idea that children need to be of a certain age before they realize that people may be acting on *false* beliefs is discussed by Alison Gopnik and Janet Astington in "Children's Understanding of Representational Change." Speech acts are covered in John Searle's *Expression and Meaning*, and as an application for AI in the 1979 article "Elements of a Plan-Based Theory of Speech Acts" by Cohen and C. Raymond Perrault. The idea of joint intentions among a team of agents is discussed by Cohen and HJL in "Teamwork," and Searle in his "Collective Intentions and Actions." For a broader perspective on multiagent groups—that is, on what might be called "naive sociology"—see Michael Wooldridge's book *An Introduction to Multiagent Systems*.

The study of causality in AI is mainly associated with the work of Judea Pearl in his two books—*Causality* and *The Book of Why* (with Dana

Mackenzie)—and in collaboration with Joseph Halpern. (See Halpern's *Actual Causality*.) The emphasis there is on deriving appropriate conclusions from a given set of basic causal facts (often represented in graphical form) and distinguishing causality from mere statistical correlation.

Chapter 6: Commonsense Knowledge

In the analysis of the previous chapter, the world is taken to be made of things with properties that change over time. This chapter is concerned with what we might know about these things and their properties, and in particular, what ideas or concepts we might form about them.

The notion that a concept can be fully characterized by a definition of some sort is a common misconception that needs to be abandoned. While it is certainly true that a birthday party is no more and no less than a party whose purpose is to celebrate the birthday of someone, the *idea* of a birthday party goes further: there's the cake, candles, and song (in the Western tradition, at least). Philosophers like Willard Van Orman Quine (in *From a Logical Point of View*) and Ludwig Wittgenstein (in his *Philosophical Investigations*) have argued against understanding concepts in terms of categorical definitions, and much of the chapter examined what had to be considered beyond necessary and sufficient conditions when thinking about things such as birthday parties.

Much of the exploration here was inspired by the work of Marvin Minsky. From the beginning of the field, Minsky's concern with humanlike reasoning differentiated his work from his colleague John McCarthy's, as he stated on page 323 of his *Society of Mind*: "McCarthy was more concerned with establishing logical and mathematical foundations for reasoning, while I was more involved with theories of how we actually reason using pattern recognition and analogy." Minsky's writing suggested alternative ideas for building knowledge-based AI systems—one of the most influential of which was his notion of frame systems. The extended quote here is from his MIT AI Laboratory Memo 306 from June 1974 ("A Framework for Representing Knowledge"), available online as well as reprinted in RJB and HJL's *Readings in Knowledge Representation* book. For an interesting and more comprehensive account of Minsky's overall view, see his *Society of Mind* book. The example concerning elephants and trees was taken from RJB's "I Lied about the Trees."

The general notion of remembering situations in a stereotyped way and then, having been reminded of prior experience, adapting remembered structures to the current situation is an important one, and has undergirded a significant, if somewhat undervalued, thread in AI. This memory-based notion of reasoning also infuses the research of Roger Schank and his students. This is covered in Schank's "Language and Memory" article and *Dynamic Memory* book as well as his book *Scripts, Plans, Goals, and Understanding* with Robert Abelson. In what could serve as a summation of this line of thinking, Jaime Carbonell and Steven Minton proposed an *experiential reasoning hypothesis* (which could just as well have been written by Minsky) in their "Metaphor and Commonsense Reasoning" piece: "Reasoning in mundane, experience-rich recurrent situations is qualitatively different from formal, deductive reasoning evident in more abstract, experimentally contrived, or otherwise nonrecurrent situations (such as some mathematical or puzzle-solving domains)." Janet Kolodner and others extended memory-based reasoning to problem-solving situations related to medical diagnosis, design, conflict resolution, planning, and other areas, through what they called *case-based reasoning*. See her 1993 book, *Case-Based Reasoning*.

As should now be evident, much about concepts and categories relates to human language and thinking, and important relevant ideas come from psychology and philosophy. The idea of prototypes, for example, is mainly seen in the psychological literature. See the review article "Concepts and Concept Formation" by Douglas Medin and Edward Smith, and the volume *Cognition and Categorization* edited by Eleanor Rosch and Barbara Lloyd. The distinction between knowing that and knowing who is discussed by Jaakko Hintikka in his *Knowledge and Belief*. Bertrand Russell's idea regarding names, noun phrases, and individuals can be found in his "On Denoting" article and will have an impact on how we use symbols for individuals in the next two chapters.

The Brian Cantwell Smith quote in the final subsection is from page 63 of his *The Promise of Artificial Intelligence* book. Rod Brooks's statement about the world and its models is paraphrased from page 139 of his "Intelligence without Representation." The idea that it should always be possible to further refine or annotate concepts is sometimes known as elaboration tolerance—a notion discussed by McCarthy in his 1998 paper, "Elaboration Tolerance." On the idea of graded concepts and properties holding only to a degree, see George Klir and Bo Yuan's collection of papers by Lotfi

Zadeh, titled *Fuzzy Sets, Fuzzy Logic, and Fuzzy Systems*. For more on the use of indexical knowledge in AI, see the 1995 article "Indexical Knowledge and Robot Action" by Yves Lespérance and HJL in *Artificial Intelligence*. The children's dictionary mentioned earlier in the chapter is John Trevaskis and Robin Hyman's *Boys' and Girls' First Dictionary*. Thinking about how concepts are understood by children will also be relevant in chapter 10.

Chapter 7: Representation and Reasoning, Part I

This chapter and the next are concerned with symbolic representations of commonsense knowledge along with the reasoning operations defined over them. This subarea of AI is usually called *knowledge representation and reasoning*. An early collection of research articles in this area is the *Readings in Knowledge Representation* book by RJB and HJL. A more recent (and advanced) collection of review articles is the *Handbook of Knowledge Representation* edited by Frank van Harmelen and colleagues. Most of the issues seen in this chapter and the next are covered in more depth in the textbook *Knowledge Representation and Reasoning* by RJB and HJL.

The world and conceptual models introduced in this chapter focus on individual things as well as their links to other things. This connection-oriented style of representation became quite popular in the 1970s under the general umbrella of *semantic* (or *conceptual* or *associative*) *networks*. Nicholas Findler's edited book *Associative Networks* has a collection of related articles, and RJB's "On the Epistemological Status of Semantic Networks" contribution surveys that field as of the late 1970s. Some credit philosopher Charles Sanders Peirce with the original idea of using networks in this way early in the twentieth century; see the book *The Existential Graphs of Charles S. Peirce* by Don Roberts for that observation. Among the more influential work of the 1960s that led directly to extensive exploration in AI was that of Ross Quillian, as seen in his "Semantic Memory" article. As Quillian noted, because of their connectivity, semantic networks lend themselves to path-based processing, such as passing markers along links in the network to detect connections between items. This was later exploited to good effect in the systems discussed in the book *NETL* by Scott Fahlman and the article "Path-Based and Node-Based Inference in Semantic Networks" by Stuart Shapiro.

A fundamental feature of semantic networks as presented here is the taxonomic organization of concepts and attendant inheritance of properties.

But what looks like a simple idea in terms of nodes and links actually hides a number of subtle conceptual traps. In his influential "What's in a Link," William Woods examined a number of intuitive but wrongheaded assumptions made about links in such networks. RJB followed with related observations and additional challenges for network representations in his "What's in a Concept" and "What 'IS-A' Is and Isn't."

To get a sense of some of the issues involved, consider the symbol SpacePt#25 used in the world model of this chapter. Does this symbol represent some specific location in Boston that happens to be where Event#23 (John's birth) took place, or does it actually represent the location where Event#23 took place, which happens to be somewhere in Boston? In the terminology of Woods, the location link from Event#23 to SpacePt#25 is *assertional* in the former case and *structural* in the latter. The difference shows up if we were to discover that we were mistaken, and that John was actually born in Pittsburgh. In the former case, we would want to change the location link from Event#23 to go to a different symbol—say, SpacePt#37—standing for somewhere in Pittsburgh; in the latter case, we would want to leave the location link as is, but change the enclosingCity link from SpacePt#25 to go to the symbol standing for Pittsburgh. (To be clear, we have not spelled out in this chapter which interpretation to use, or if there are others, or where this might make a difference in what is believed. This will only be taken up in the bonus chapter, where we try to be more precise about the total information carried by the nodes and links of a world model.)

Out of these analyses and considerations emerged the widely known KL-ONE knowledge representation system, documented by RJB and James Schmolze in "An Overview of the KL-ONE Knowledge Representation System," which ultimately set the stage for an extensive body of work on what came to be known as *description logics*. Franz Baader and colleagues offer a comprehensive view in their *Description Logic Handbook*. The distinction in this chapter between a world model and a conceptual model derives from a similar one made in description logics between what are called the *ABox* and *TBox* (*A* for *assertion*, and *T* for *terminology*). The idea of a Minsky frame from chapter 6 is closely related to the symbolic expressions in description logics. Interpretations of frame structures are discussed in Charles Fillmore's "Frame Semantics" and Patrick Hayes's "The Logic of Frames." This work is also related to earlier thinking on what were called *case frames* in linguistics—an area in which Fillmore is a prominent contributor. (See his 1968 paper "The Case for Case.") This was an important foundation for the notion of a role, as used here and in the KL-ONE system. It should be noted that KL-ONE went well beyond the representation presented here in having a rich language of so-called *structural descriptions* for capturing relationships among the roles of a concept (as discussed in the RJB and Schmolze paper).

One of the more sophisticated representation frameworks in this lineage was KRL, nicely documented in the 1977 article "An Overview of KRL, a Knowledge Representation Language" by Daniel Bobrow and Terry Winograd. The KRL language had a number of interesting constructs, including a style of annotation similar to the one considered here. KRL also explored some of the metalevel representation and reasoning touched on in this chapter.

Prototypes and exemplars were discussed in chapter 6. As mentioned, the idea of reconstructive memory goes back to Sir Frederic Bartlett's book *Remembering* (and see also the bonus chapter). Important work on eyewitness memory is documented in the book *Eyewitness Testimony* by Elizabeth Loftus.

Finally, as hinted toward the end of the chapter, what is known about the world is subject to constant amending and changing, as default assumptions are discovered to be untenable. Matthew Ginsberg's *Readings in Nonmonotonic Reasoning* highlights the thorny issues that arise in reasoning about exceptional cases under assumptions of typicality. Simple updates with no ramifications are fairly easy to handle, but changes to underlying beliefs on which many inferences have rested can be complicated. A substantive area of research around belief revision explores this space. Of particular note are the book *Belief Revision* edited by Peter Gärdenfors and the article "A Knowledge Level Analysis of Belief Revision" by Bernhard Nebel. Support for belief change in AI systems has often been implemented through what are called truth maintenance systems, covered by Johan de Kleer in "An Assumption-Based TMS" and Jon Doyle in "A Truth Maintenance System"—both as contributions to *Artificial Intelligence*.

Chapter 8: Representation and Reasoning, Part II

While the previous chapter was mainly concerned with the kinds of *representations* that might be needed for commonsense knowledge (that is, world models and conceptual models), this chapter is mainly about *reasoning*: computing what should be believed about the world given these models. The premise is that a "species of calculus" is needed (to use Leibniz's phrase from chapter 4) that not only results in appropriate beliefs but rather, as stated in the bonus chapter, that can be "computed routinely in a completely automated way, without much effort or careful monitoring, even over enormous knowledge bases."

The first step is to come up with a symbolic language to represent the propositions to be believed. The language $\mathcal{L}$ introduced here is a dialect of the first-order predicate calculus noted in chapter 4, but with unary and binary predicates only, and where constants are handled in a special way, similar to the treatment of standard names in HJL and Gerhard Lakemeyer's *The Logic of Knowledge Bases*. (Introductions to the predicate calculus can be found in the books *A Mathematical Introduction to Logic* by Herbert Enderton and *Introduction to Mathematical Logic* by Elliott Mendelson.) Actually, because of its use of the word "after" to talk about events and change, $\mathcal{L}$ is more like a dialect of the *situation calculus*, the language introduced by John McCarthy in his "Situations, Actions, and Causal Laws." The situation calculus was later adapted and formalized by Raymond Reiter and colleagues, as documented in Reiter's 2001 book, *Knowledge in Action*, and the 2008 article "Situation Calculus" by Fangzhen Lin. Further extensions to $\mathcal{L}$ may be necessary to deal with notions such as time and modality, as per McCarthy and Patrick Hayes's "Some Philosophical Problems from the Standpoint of Artificial Intelligence" paper.

The next step was to understand a world model as representing only the *basic* properties of the world and use special clauses involving formulas of $\mathcal{L}$ for properties to be derived from them. These clauses make the overall representation system look more like Datalog, and once numbers and sequences are taken into account, like Prolog, most often seen as a programming language. Datalog is documented in the book *Foundations of Databases* by Serge Abiteboul and colleagues. The history of Prolog is covered in the article "The Birth of Prolog" by Alain Colmerauer and Philippe Roussel, and its programming aspects in William Clocksin and Christopher Mellish's *Programming in Prolog* as well as HJL's *Thinking as Computation*.

When it comes to reasoning about change in logical terms, perhaps the foremost issue that arises is what is called the *frame problem*. (See McCarthy and Hayes's "Some Philosophical Problems" as well as Murray Shanahan's

Solving the Frame Problem.) In a nutshell, the problem is how to draw conclusions about what is unaffected by events, given premises that deal only with what is affected. The way of reasoning about change proposed in this chapter is based on the solution to the frame problem first presented by Reiter in his 1991 article "The Frame Problem in the Situation Calculus" and elaborated in *Knowledge in Action.* Roughly speaking, this involves a logical quantification over events—that is, being able to say that the *only* events affecting a certain property are certain ones to be named explicitly. For Reiter, these statements become logical axioms (called *successor state axioms*) to be reasoned with; in our case, they become derivation clauses of a certain form.

(Note that this way of handling change does not talk about what events will take place without further intervention—that is, the ongoing exogenous processes. This requires a representation for such processes as complex events as seen, for example, in the language Golog in the context of the situation calculus. See Reiter's book for details.)

Turning to planning, the first characterization of it as a form of logical reasoning is due to McCarthy in his "Situations, Actions, and Causal Laws." Since then, automated planning has had a long history in AI, with a number of specialized representation and reasoning schemes, among which was the influential STRIPS representation, introduced by Richard Fikes and Nils Nilsson in "STRIPS: A New Approach to the Application of Theorem Proving to Problem Solving." Some of these specialized planning schemes are covered in the textbook *Automated Planning* by Malik Ghallab, Dana Nau and Paolo Traverso.

As noted, in addition to reasoning about the effects of actions, it is necessary to reason about their prerequisites, which show up for Reiter as so-called *precondition axioms,* and which we characterized as yet another derived property. This raises what McCarthy called in his "Epistemological Problems of Artificial Intelligence" the *qualification problem*: roughly, how to categorize prerequisites of actions without having to list all the various, perhaps quite-remote stumbling blocks that could arise in principle. This is a special case of the problem discussed in chapter 6 of wanting to make blunt, unqualified statements, but also wanting to be able to elaborate and annotate them over time.

Finally, the way proposed in the text for answering generic questions such as "Would a pomegranate fit inside a laundry basket?" by instantiating the concepts involved and then asking questions about the hypothesized individuals is related to the way Philip Johnson-Laird postulates answering questions using mental models, discussed in the bonus chapter.

Chapter 9: Common Sense in Action

This chapter is, in a way, a culmination of the previous four chapters. It attempts to show how symbolic representations of commonsense knowledge and the computational operations over them can play a determining role in the decisions an agent will need to make when dealing in a commonsensical way with something unanticipated.

The picture presented in the chapter was that of an agent encountering a problem while following a plan of some sort. The agent had to step away from the execution of the plan and decide what to do, taking into account the structure of the plan, what had been discovered about the current situation, and general commonsense knowledge of the world.

In this book, plans were taken to be simple actions or perhaps sequences of them. But this is clearly too limited. A plan to board an airplane to fly somewhere might involve going to the appropriate gate at the airport, but that gate would normally not be named in the plan. Instead, the plan would specify a sensing or *knowledge-producing* action to be executed at the airport to find out which gate to use. (HJL and Gerhard Lakemeyer talk about such actions in their "Cognitive Robotics" article.) This might trigger an addition to the world model to incorporate the new information. A plan of this sort, which can involve branches and loops, is sometimes called a *generalized* plan in AI. See "A Review of Generalized Planning" by Sergio Jiménez and colleagues.

The idea of deciding what to do in a way that takes both cost and benefit into account is a mainstay of *decision theory*; see Martin Peterson's *An Introduction to Decision Theory* book for an introduction. Some of this work is philosophical or economic in nature, but some of it is within AI and deals with the issue in computational terms; an example is "Decision Theory in Expert Systems and Artificial Intelligence" by Eric Horvitz and his collaborators. Especially relevant here is the work on decision-theoretic planning, such as in the article "Decision-Theoretic Planning" by Craig Boutilier and colleagues as well as "Planning and Acting in Partially Observable Stochastic Domains" by Leslie Pack Kaelbling and colleagues. Note that while this

AI work emphasizes the quality of plans and uncertainty about the domain, it does tend to downplay the role of general commonsense knowledge in the planning process.

The bulk of the reasoning in this chapter involves using common-sense knowledge to modify a plan when something unexpected happens. This process is sometimes called *plan repair*. (See, for example, the papers "Explaining and Repairing Plans That Fail" by Kristian Hammond and "A Validation-Structure-Based Theory of Plan Modification and Reuse" by Subbarao Kambhampati and James Hendler). Interestingly, there is a sense in which plan repair is actually more difficult as a computational task than planning itself since in the worst case at least, it can still require planning from scratch, as observed in the article "Plan Reuse versus Plan Generation" by Bernhard Nebel and Jana Koehler.

The chapter concludes by claiming that it was not appropriate to think of common sense as the main driving force within the cognitive architecture of an agent with common sense. But what should this architecture look like, then? It's far from clear. For a recent review of what other researchers have had to say on this, see the 2020 survey "40 Years of Cognitive Architectures" by Iuliia Kotseruba and John Tsotsos.

Chapter 10: Steps toward Implementation

This chapter was about the practical difficulties in building computer systems with common sense. The problem was broken down into building reasoners and building knowledge bases. For commonsense reasoners, the idea of using neural nets to learn how to perform symbolic operations (such as those involved in commonsense reasoning) is discussed in the Łukasz Kaiser and Ilya Sutskever article "Neural GPUs Learn Algorithms." Most of the chapter, however, was about building knowledge bases.

In the expert system era, building a knowledge base typically involved interviewing experts and getting them to provide the sort of IF/THEN rules required. What made this task challenging is that experts are not usually in the habit of articulating how they make their decisions. Introspection appears to be a poor guide for where things like hunches come from. This became known as the *knowledge acquisition bottleneck*—a major challenge in the expert system development process. For more on knowledge acquisition, see the book *Knowledge Acquisition* by James Brulé and Alexander

Blount as well as the edited volume *Knowledge Acquisition for Expert Systems* by Alison Kidd.

The issues are somewhat different when it comes to commonsense knowledge, where everyone is seemingly an expert. The Cyc project, discussed in chapter 4, is the preeminent example of an attempt to build a broad commonsense knowledge base by hand. In terms of automated efforts, two notable instances are ConceptNet (documented in the paper "Representing General Relational Knowledge in ConceptNet 5" by Robert Speer and Catherine Havasi) and NELL (mentioned in chapter 4). The critique of ConceptNet and NELL by Gary Marcus and Ernest Davis is in their *Rebooting AI*, pages 151–153. The story by Ted Chiang with the quote about common sense appears in his book *Exhalation*. The symbol grounding problem is discussed by Stevan Harnad in "The Symbol Grounding Problem."

One suggestion for automatically capturing the meaning of words from a collection of texts is the following: given texts T_1, T_2, ... , T_N, where N is assumed to be large, represent the meaning of a word by a vector of N binary numbers, where component i is 1 if the word appears in text T_i. (Fancier vectors are possible.) The expectation is that words with related meanings will have similar vectors and "you shall know a word by the company it keeps" (from John Firth's 1957 article, "A Synopsis of Linguistic Theory, 1930–1955," page 11). This so-called distributed representation of words appears to be quite useful for aggregating words based on their meanings and other similarity-based operations. (See, for example, the paper "Linguistic Regularities in Continuous Space Word Representations" by Tomáš Mikolov, Wen-tau Yih, and Geoffrey Zweig.) But it does not lend itself to the operations that go beyond word meanings needed for commonsense reasoning.

The idea of constructing a knowledge base layer by layer is sometimes called *bootstrap learning*, outlined in the article "Bootstrap Learning of Foundational Representations" by Benjamin Kuipers and colleagues. The wonderful book by Judy Herr from which much of the material on ECE was drawn is her *Creative Resources for the Early Childhood Classroom*. The book *Goodnight Moon* that is quoted in the text is a toddler's classic by Margaret Wise Brown and Clement Hurd.

The Basic English project was an attempt to get a small but expressively adequate core of English that would be easier for people to learn, created by Charles Ogden, and presented in his book *Basic English*. This project is well documented online, and there are many examples of texts written in Basic English, including *The Bible in Basic English* by Samuel Hooke and *The General Basic English Dictionary* of over twenty thousand words by Ogden. For other ideas on using limited forms of English or other natural languages for knowledge representation or other purposes, see Tobias Kuhn's "A Survey and Classification of Controlled Natural Languages" in *Computational Linguistics* and the references therein.

The KidzSearch website is https://wiki.kidzsearch.com/wiki. Note that this site is unfortunately quite volatile. The quote on gophers used in the text is currently buried in a flurry of other links, and the website itself is now marred by ads and other distractions.

Chapter 11: Building Trust

This chapter considers common sense as it might apply to autonomous AI technology of the future. Much has been written of late on the limitations and risks in AI technology, but almost invariably the articles concentrate on what might be called "nonautonomous AI."

To take one example, an article in the December 2019 *New York Times* by Natasha Singer and Cade Metz reported that various forms of AI facial-recognition technology misidentified African American and Asian faces ten to a hundred times more frequently than Caucasian faces. These sorts of errors can be extremely harmful in the context of law enforcement. We have every reason to demand technology that does not reinforce biases that might be present in the training data used. Systems of this kind are not operating autonomously, though. In the end, it is the law enforcement personnel (humans, in other words) who must take full responsibility for the limitations of these AI tools, and make the final call on how or if they should be used in their current state.

The topic of this chapter, however, was somewhat different. It was about AI systems in some conceivable future that might be asked to make the final call for themselves. These are autonomous AI systems, sometimes known as *artificial general intelligence*. (See the volume *Artificial General Intelligence* edited by Ben Goertzel and Cassio Pennachin.)

In terms of the specific references in this chapter, the notion of superintelligence (and the so-called singularity it gives rise to) is discussed in *Our Final Invention* by James Barrat, *The Singularity Is Near* by Ray Kurzweil, and

The Technological Singularity by Murray Shanahan. The "move fast and break things" saying is (or was until 2014) the motto of Facebook. (See the short article "Move Fast and Break Things" by Moshe Vardi.) The quote by Roger McNamee, an early Facebook supporter, comes from his *Zucked*. For more on the state of verification of mission-critical software, see the article "Model Checking"—based on a Turing Award lecture—by Edmund Clarke, E. Allen Emerson, and Joseph Sifakis. The Donald Rumsfeld notion of "unknown unknowns" is from a US Defense Department briefing on February 12, 2002. On trolley problems in general, see the article "The Trolley Problem" by Judith Thomson, and for criticism, see "Away from Trolley Problems and toward Risk Management" by Noah Goodall. Daniel Dennett's intentional stance is presented in his 1989 book, *The Intentional Stance*. The critique of the AI approach to common sense as being overly concerned with language and its use was made most recently in "Artificial Intelligence and the Common Sense of Animals" by Shanahan and colleagues.

Asimov's three laws of robotics appeared in his 1950 book, *I, Robot*. Within the plot, the laws are quoted from a robotics handbook to be published in 2058 and are the following:

1. A robot may not injure a human being or, through inaction, allow a human being to come to harm.
2. A robot must obey the orders given it by human beings except where such orders would conflict with the First Law.
3. A robot must protect its own existence as long as such protection does not conflict with the First or Second Laws.

(Arguably, additional laws are needed to deal with humanity as a whole.) When it comes to machines running amok, the Nick Bostrom example involving paper clips appears in his 2014 book, *Superintelligence*. Philip K. Dick's story "Autofac" appears in his *Selected Stories*. For a survey on explanation as it applies to machine learning systems (sometimes called explainable AI), see the article "Explanation and Justification in Machine Learning" by Or Biran and Courtenay Cotton. The quote from Steven Strogatz about AlphaZero was taken from an article he wrote in the *New York Times*, December 25, 2018. The adversarial examples for AlexNet mentioned at the end of the chapter were first presented by Christian Szegedy and colleagues in 2014 in "Intriguing Properties of Neural Networks," and further discussed in Melanie Mitchell's *Artificial Intelligence*.

Incidentally, these adversarial examples raise an important methodological issue. Success in AI research is usually measured in terms of statistical performance on suites of test cases. For instance, a recent effort on Winograd schemas reported by Keisuke Sakaguchi and colleagues in "Wino-Grande" got the answers correct 90 percent of the time on a comprehensive series of test cases—an impressive achievement! So does this mean that the problem is essentially solved, give or take some fine tuning? The answer depends on how well we can extrapolate from those test cases. Can we predict that the system will behave sensibly in the large? In the end, this is the question that matters. Recalling the experience with AlexNet, do we understand the system well enough to be confident that it would still get about 90 percent of the answers correct were someone to tweak those inputs in some irrelevant way? Without an understanding of how the system works and how it goes about making its decisions, we should not trust it to be doing the right thing, no matter its rate of success on particular test cases.

Finally, there is the recent book *Human Compatible* by well-known AI researcher Stuart Russell that also deals with designing autonomous AI technology in a responsible way. Russell's position, roughly speaking, is that we must build AI systems with goals (or preferences or reward functions) that push them toward finding out and acting on the goals that *humans* have, or what he calls "maximizing the realization of human preferences." This seems quite right to us, but perhaps does not go far enough. We can imagine an AI system, for example, whose model of the world is totally wrongheaded, but that acts in what it mistakenly takes to be a helpful and constructive way, exactly as advocated by Russell. If the system is not required to be *knowledge based*, we may not be able to make sense of the particular choices it makes, just like those of AlphaZero or AlexNet, even if we believe it to be acting in good faith. In other words, we should want AI systems that do what we want, as Russell says, but we also need them to be able to *show their work* so that we can understand where they get it wrong and advise them what to do about it.

Bonus Chapter: The Logic of Common Sense

The bonus chapter was about the somewhat complex relationship between commonsense reasoning and logical reasoning as it is normally understood (as in the 1982 Willard Van Orman Quine book *Methods of Logic*, say). The two notions overlap to a large extent, but there are cases where common sense admits conclusions not sanctioned by classical logic (as in the use of defaults), and others where logic sanctions conclusions that are not really part of common sense (as in the answers to logical puzzles).

For those interested in research in this area, the place to start is with an understanding of classical logic and logical reasoning, such as that presented in the books *Introduction to Mathematical Logic* by Elliott Mendelson and *A Mathematical Introduction to Logic* by Herbert Enderton. The connection to knowledge and the issue of logical omniscience are discussed in Jaakko Hintikka's *Knowledge and Belief*.

Many of the topics examined in this chapter came up in our own research and were first presented in HJL's 1986 "Making Believers Out of Computers." The idea of viewing world models as logical formulas of a limited *vivid* form was introduced there, although the exact formulation was somewhat different. The idea derived from work by Raymond Reiter in 1981 ("On Closed World Data Bases") on interpreting databases in logical terms. Other authors went on to show how more general forms of information might be reducible to this form. See, for example, the article "Vivid Knowledge and Tractable Reasoning" by David Etherington and colleagues, and the book *Vivid Logic* by Gerd Wagner. A critique of this approach can be found in the 1991 technical report *Lucid Representations* by Ernest Davis. The connection between vivid representations and visual images was discussed in the HJL paper above, based on ideas in the article "Mental Representations" by Elliott Sober. The example puzzle involving Jack, Anne, and George was also first presented in the HJL paper, adapted from a related illustration in the 1982 article "The Role of Logic in Knowledge Representation and Commonsense Reasoning" by Robert Moore, and then picked up later by psychologist Keith Stanovich in his article "Rational and Irrational Thought," with slightly different lessons to learn. The idea of evaluating a conjunctive query from the bottom up is a mainstay of relational databases, as seen in the textbook *Foundations of Databases* by Serge Abiteboul and colleagues.

The idea that the expressiveness of a more general representation language like $\mathcal{L}$ involves what it can leave *unsaid* appears in the article "Knowledge Representation and Reasoning" by HJL. The strong connection between expressiveness and the demands it then places on the associated reasoning is outlined in the 1987 article "Expressiveness and Tractability in Knowledge Representation and Reasoning" by HJL and RJB, and explored in chapter 16 of the 2004 textbook, *Knowledge Representation and Reasoning*, by RJB and HJL.

A number of efforts have been made to look at the connection between expressiveness and tractability. The work is somewhat technical in nature, but the basic idea is to investigate what sorts of extensions to representations like world models would still allow certain questions to be answered efficiently. See the 1998 article "A Completeness Result for Reasoning with Incomplete First-Order Knowledge Bases" by HJL as well as the 2011 article "Efficient Reasoning in Proper Knowledge Bases with Unknown Individuals" by Giuseppe De Giacomo, Yves Lespérance, and HJL, for example.

One especially tricky case involves the use of *disjunctions* in a world model. Going back to chapter 7, this would allow us to represent the birthplace of Sue as Phoenix or Tucson in a world model, for instance. Interestingly, nobody knows whether this move must inherently be more difficult for reasoning. The question is equivalent to the famous *P=NP* question, first posed by Stephen Cook in his groundbreaking 1971 article, "The Complexity of Theorem-Proving Procedures." Despite the best efforts of thousands of computer scientists and mathematicians since then, nobody knows the answer. Because of its connection to many other computational problems, this question is considered to be *the* most important open problem in computer science. (See the article "The Status of the P versus NP Problem" by Lance Fortnow.) To further complicate matters, there are computer programs called *SAT solvers* that do appear to work quite well in practice even on enormous inputs, although they stumble occasionally. (See the "Satisfiability Solvers" article by Carla Gomes and company.)

The work by psychologist Philip Johnson-Laird on mental models begins with his 1983 book, *Mental Models*. The example puzzle in the text involving dogs is adapted from one on page 67 (with bankers recast as dogs in the backyard, athletes as Jim's dogs, and councillors as small dogs). More recent thoughts on mental models can be found in the article "Mental Models and Human Reasoning" by Johnson-Laird in 2010, and "Facts and Possibilities" by Sangeet Khemlani and colleagues in 2018. For historical grounding, Johnson-Laird cites inspiration from the work of Charles Sanders Peirce, gathered in the 1931 volume *Collected Papers of Charles Sanders Peirce*. Johnson-Laird also credits philosopher Kenneth Craik for proposing in the 1943 *The Nature of Explanation* "that thinking is the manipulation of internal representations of the world."

As suggested at the end of the chapter, another way to ensure that commonsense reasoning is not overly demanding is to allow unrestricted (nonvivid) formulas in the knowledge base, but to limit the sorts of reasoning that can be done with them. The resulting notion of belief would no longer be closed under logical entailment, and the problem is to find out what "species of calculus" should replace it. An early example of work on this is in the article "A Logic of Implicit and Explicit Belief" by HJL from 1984; a recent proposal along the same lines, but now allowing for quantifiers, can be found in the 2020 article "A First-Order Logic of Limited Belief Based on Possible Worlds" by Lakemeyer and HJL. As noted, much of the research in the area of knowledge representation and reasoning can be understood as looking for additional alternatives in this space of possibilities. See the article "Knowledge Representation and Reasoning" by HJL.

Bibliography

Abiteboul, Serge, Richard Hull, and Victor Vianu. *Foundations of Databases*. Reading, MA: Addison-Wesley, 1995.

Allen, James F. "Maintaining Knowledge about Temporal Intervals." *Communications of the ACM* 26, no. 11 (1983): 832–843.

Alom, Md Zahangir, Tarek M. Taha, Chris Yakopcic, Stefan Westberg, Paheding Sidike, Mst Shamima Nasrin, Mahmudul Hasan, et al. "A State-of-the-Art Survey on Deep Learning Theory and Architectures." *Electronics* 8, no. 3 (2019): 1–66.

Asada, Minoru, Hiroaki Kitano, Itsuki Noda, and Manuela Veloso. "RoboCup: Today and Tomorrow—What We Have Learned." *Artificial Intelligence* 110, no. 2 (1999): 193–214.

Asada, Minoru, and Oskar von Stryk. "Scientific and Technological Challenges in RoboCup." *Annual Review of Control, Robotics, and Autonomous Systems* 3 (2020): 441–471.

Asimov, Isaac. *I, Robot*. New York: Gnome Press, 1950.

Baader, Franz, Diego Calvanese, Deborah L. McGuinness, Daniele Nardi, and Peter F. Patel-Schneider, eds. *The Description Logic Handbook: Theory, Implementation and Applications*. Cambridge: Cambridge University Press, 2003.

Bachant, Judith, and Elliot Soloway. "The Engineering of XCON." *Communications of the ACM* 32, no. 3 (1989): 311–319.

Barrat, James. *Our Final Invention: Artificial Intelligence and the End of the Human Era*. New York: Thomas Dunne Books, 2013.

Bartlett, Sir Frederic C. *Remembering: A Study in Experimental and Social Psychology*. Cambridge: Cambridge University Press, 1932.

Berliner, Hans J. "Backgammon Computer Program Beats World Champion." *Artificial Intelligence* 14, no. 2 (1980): 205–220.

Bickerton, Derek. *Adam's Tongue: How Humans Made Language, How Language Made Humans.* New York: Hill and Wang, 2009.

Biran, Or, and Courtenay Cotton. "Explanation and Justification in Machine Learning: A Survey." In *Proceedings of the IJCAI-17 Workshop on Explainable AI (XAI)*, 8–13, Melbourne, August 2017.

Bobrow, Daniel G., and Terry Winograd. "An Overview of KRL, a Knowledge Representation Language." *Cognitive Science* 1, no. 1 (1977): 3–46.

Bosselut, Antoine, Hannah Rashkin, Maarten Sap, Chaitanya Malaviya, Asli Celikyilmaz, and Yejin Choi. "COMET: Commonsense Transformers for Automatic Knowledge Graph Construction." Submitted June 12, 2019. https://arxiv.org/abs/1906.05317.

Bostrom, Nick. *Superintelligence: Paths, Dangers, Strategies.* Oxford: Oxford University Press, 2014.

Boutilier, Craig, Thomas Dean, and Steve Hanks. "Decision-Theoretic Planning: Structural Assumptions and Computational Leverage." *Journal of Artificial Intelligence Research* 11 (1999): 1–94.

Brachman, Ronald J. "'I Lied about the Trees' (or, Defaults and Definitions in Knowledge Representation)." *AI Magazine* 6, no. 3 (1985): 80–92.

Brachman, Ronald J. "On the Epistemological Status of Semantic Networks." In *Associative Networks: Representation and Use of Knowledge by Computers*, edited by Nicholas V. Findler, 3–50. New York: Academic Press, 1979.

Brachman, Ronald J. "What 'IS-A' Is and Isn't: An Analysis of Taxonomic Links in Semantic Networks." *IEEE Computer Special Issue on Knowledge Representation* 16, no. 10 (1983): 67–73.

Brachman, Ronald J. "What's in a Concept: Structural Foundations for Semantic Networks." *International Journal of Man-Machine Studies* 9, no. 2 (1977): 127–152.

Brachman, Ronald J., David Gunning, and Murray Burke. "Integrated AI Systems." *AI Magazine* 41, no. 2 (2020): 66–82.

Brachman, Ronald J., and Hector J. Levesque. *Knowledge Representation and Reasoning.* Amsterdam: Morgan Kaufmann Publishers, Inc., 2004.

Brachman, Ronald J., and Hector J. Levesque, eds. *Readings in Knowledge Representation.* Los Altos, CA: Morgan Kaufmann Publishers, Inc., 1985.

Brachman, Ronald J., and James G. Schmolze. "An Overview of the KL-ONE Knowledge Representation System." In *Readings in Artificial Intelligence and Databases*, edited by John Mylopoulos and Michael L. Brodie, 207–230. San Mateo, CA: Morgan Kaufmann Publishers, Inc., 1989.

Brooks, Rodney A. "Intelligence without Representation." *Artificial Intelligence* 47, no. 1–3 (1991): 139–159.

Brown, Margaret Wise, and Clement Hurd. *Goodnight Moon.* New York: Scholastic Book Services, 1947.

Brown, Noam, and Tuomas Sandholm. "Superhuman AI for Heads-up No-Limit Poker: Libratus Beats Top Professionals." *Science* 359, no. 6374 (2018): 418–424.

Brulé, James F., and Alexander Blount. *Knowledge Acquisition.* New York: McGraw Hill, Inc., 1989.

Burgard, Wolfram, Armin B. Cremers, Dieter Fox, Dirk Hähnel, Gerhard Lakemeyer, Dirk Schulz, Walter Steiner, and Sebastian Thrun. "Experiences with an Interactive Museum Tour-Guide Robot." *Artificial Intelligence* 114, no. 1–2 (1999): 3–55.

Carbonell, Jaime G., and Steven Minton. "Metaphor and Commonsense Reasoning." In *Formal Theories of the Commonsense World*, edited by Jerry R. Hobbs and Robert C. Moore, 405–426. Norwood, NJ: Ablex Publishing Corporation, 1985.

Chiang, Ted. *Exhalation: Stories.* New York: Alfred A. Knopf, 2019.

Chollet, François. "On the Measure of Intelligence." Submitted November 25, 2019. https://arxiv.org/abs/1911.01547.

Clark, Andy. "From Folk Psychology to Naive Psychology." *Cognitive Science* 11, no. 2 (1987): 139–154.

Clarke, Edmund M., E. Allen Emerson, and Joseph Sifakis. "Model Checking: Algorithmic Verification and Debugging." *Communications of the ACM* 52, no. 11 (2009): 74–84.

Clocksin, William F., and Christopher S. Mellish. *Programming in Prolog: Using the ISO Standard.* Berlin: Springer-Verlag, 2012.

Cohen, Philip R., and Hector J. Levesque. "Intention Is Choice with Commitment." *Artificial Intelligence* 42, no. 2–3 (1990): 213–261.

Cohen, Philip R., and Hector J. Levesque. "Teamwork." *Noûs* 25, no. 4 (1991): 487–512.

Cohen, Philip R., and C. Raymond Perrault. "Elements of a Plan-Based Theory of Speech Acts." *Cognitive Science* 3, no. 3 (1979): 177–212.

Cohn, Anthony G. "The Challenge of Qualitative Spatial Reasoning." *ACM Computing Surveys* 27, no. 3 (1995): 323–325.

Collins, Harry. *Artifictional Intelligence: Against Humanity's Surrender to Computers.* Medford, MA: Polity Press, 2018.

Colmerauer, Alain, and Philippe Roussel. "The Birth of Prolog." In *History of Programming Languages—II*, edited by Thomas J. Bergin and Richard G. Gibson, 331–367. New York: ACM Press, 1996.

Cook, Stephen A. "The Complexity of Theorem-Proving Procedures." In *Proceedings of the Third Annual ACM Symposium on Theory of Computing (STOC'71)*, 151–158, Shaker Heights, OH, May 1971.

Craik, Kenneth J. W. *The Nature of Explanation*. Cambridge: Cambridge University Press, 1943.

Cross, Tim. "An Understanding of AI's Limitations Is Starting to Sink In." *Economist, Technical Quarterly*, June 2020.

Darrach, Brad. "Meet Shaky [*sic*], the First Electronic Person: The Fascinating and Fearsome Reality of a Machine with a Mind of Its Own." *Life*, November 20, 1970, 58B–68.

Davis, Ernest. *Lucid Representations*. Technical report 565. New York: Computer Science Department, Courant Institute of Mathematical Sciences, New York University, 1991.

Davis, Ernest. *Representations of Commonsense Knowledge*. San Mateo, CA: Morgan Kaufmann Publishers, Inc., 1990.

Davis, Ernest, and Gary Marcus. "Commonsense Reasoning and Commonsense Knowledge in Artificial Intelligence." *Communications of the ACM* 58, no. 9 (2015): 92–103.

De Giacomo, Giuseppe, Yves Lespérance, and Hector J. Levesque. "Efficient Reasoning in Proper Knowledge Bases with Unknown Individuals." In *Proceedings of the Twenty-Second International Joint Conference on Artificial Intelligence (IJCAI-11)*, 827–832, Barcelona, July 2011.

de Kleer, Johan. "An Assumption-Based TMS." *Artificial Intelligence* 28, no. 2 (1986): 127–162.

Dennett, Daniel C. *The Intentional Stance*. Cambridge, MA: MIT Press, 1989.

Dick, Philip K. "Autofac." In *Selected Stories of Philip K. Dick*, 199–222. Boston: Houghton Mifflin Harcourt, 2013.

Doyle, Jon. "A Truth Maintenance System." *Artificial Intelligence* 12, no. 3 (1979): 231–272.

Duda, Richard, John Gaschnig, and Peter Hart. "Model Design in the Prospector Consultant System for Mineral Exploration." In *Readings in Artificial Intelligence*, edited by Bonnie Lynn Webber and Nils J. Nilsson, 334–348. Los Altos, CA: Morgan Kaufmann Publishers, Inc., 1981.

Enderton, Herbert B. *A Mathematical Introduction to Logic.* San Diego: Academic Press, 2001.

Etherington, David W., Alex Borgida, Ronald J. Brachman, and Henry Kautz. "Vivid Knowledge and Tractable Reasoning: Preliminary Report." In *Proceedings of the Eleventh International Joint Conference on Artificial Intelligence (IJCAI-89)*, 1146–1152, Detroit, August 1989.

Fagin, Ronald, Joseph Y. Halpern, Yoram Moses, and Moshe Y. Vardi. *Reasoning about Knowledge.* Cambridge, MA: MIT Press, 2003.

Fahlman, Scott E. *NETL: A System for Representing Real-World Knowledge.* Cambridge, MA: MIT Press, 1979.

Fikes, Richard E., and Nils J. Nilsson. "STRIPS: A New Approach to the Application of Theorem Proving to Problem Solving." *Artificial Intelligence* 2, no. 3–4 (1971): 189–208.

Fillmore, Charles J. "The Case for Case." In *Universals in Linguistic Theory*, edited by Emmon W. Bach and Robert T. Harms, 1–88. New York: Holt, Rinehart and Winston, 1968.

Fillmore, Charles J. "Frame Semantics." In *Cognitive Linguistics: Basic Readings*, edited by Dirk Geeraerts, 34:373–400. New York: Mouton de Gruyter, 2006.

Findler, Nicholas V., ed. *Associative Networks: Representation and Use of Knowledge by Computers.* New York: Academic Press, 1979.

Firth, John. "A Synopsis of Linguistic Theory, 1930–1955." In *Studies in Linguistic Analysis*, edited by John Firth, 1–32. Oxford: Basil Blackwell, 1957.

Ford, Martin. *Architects of Intelligence: The Truth about AI from the People Building It.* Birmingham, UK: Packt Publishing Ltd., 2018.

Fortnow, Lance. "The Status of the P versus NP Problem." *Communications of the ACM* 52, no. 9 (2009): 78–86.

Gangemi, Aldo, Nicola Guarino, Claudio Masolo, and Alessandro Oltramari. "Understanding Top-Level Ontological Distinctions." In *Proceedings of the IJCAI-01 Workshop on Ontologies and Information Sharing*, 26–33, Seattle, August 2001.

Gärdenfors, Peter, ed. *Belief Revision.* Cambridge Tracts in Theoretical Computer Science 29. Cambridge: Cambridge University Press, 2003.

Ghallab, Malik, Dana Nau, and Paolo Traverso. *Automated Planning: Theory and Practice.* Amsterdam: Elsevier, 2004.

Ginsberg, Matthew L., ed. *Readings in Nonmonotonic Reasoning.* Los Altos, CA: Morgan Kaufman Publishers, Inc., 1987.

Goel, Ashok K., ed. Special issue, *AI Magazine* 41, no. 2 (Summer 2020).

Goertzel, Ben, and Cassio Pennachin, eds. *Artificial General Intelligence*. New York: Springer, 2007.

Gomes, Carla P., Henry Kautz, Ashish Sabharwal, and Bart Selman. "Satisfiability Solvers." In *Handbook of Knowledge Representation*, edited by Frank van Harmelen, Vladimir Lifschitz, and Bruce Porter, 89–134. Amsterdam: Elsevier, 2008.

Goodall, Noah J. "Away from Trolley Problems and toward Risk Management." *Applied Artificial Intelligence* 30, no. 8 (2016): 810–821.

Gopnik, Alison, and Janet W. Astington. "Children's Understanding of Representational Change and Its Relation to the Understanding of False Belief and the Appearance-Reality Distinction." *Child Development* 59, no. 1 (1988): 26–37.

Gordon, Andrew S., and Jerry R. Hobbs. *A Formal Theory of Commonsense Psychology: How People Think People Think*. Cambridge: Cambridge University Press, 2017.

Griffiths, A. Phillips, ed. *Knowledge and Belief*. London: Oxford University Press, 1967.

Halpern, Joseph Y. *Actual Causality*. Cambridge, MA: MIT Press, 2016.

Halpern, Joseph Y. *Reasoning about Uncertainty*. Cambridge, MA: MIT Press, 2017.

Hammond, Kenneth R., Robert M. Hamm, Janet Grassia, and Tamra Pearson. "Direct Comparison of the Efficacy of Intuitive and Analytical Cognition in Expert Judgment." *IEEE Transactions on Systems, Man, and Cybernetics* 17, no. 5 (1987): 753–770.

Hammond, Kristian J. "Explaining and Repairing Plans That Fail." *Artificial Intelligence* 45, no. 1–2 (1990): 173–228.

Harnad, Stevan. "The Symbol Grounding Problem." *Physica D: Nonlinear Phenomena* 42, no. 1–3 (1990): 335–346.

Haugeland, John. *Artificial Intelligence: The Very Idea*. Cambridge, MA: MIT Press, 1985.

Hayes, Patrick J. "The Logic of Frames." In *Readings in Artificial Intelligence*, edited by Bonnie Lynn Webber and Nils J. Nilsson, 451–458. Los Altos, CA: Morgan Kaufmann Publishers, Inc., 1981.

Hayes, Patrick J. "The Naive Physics Manifesto I: Ontology for Liquids." In *Formal Theories of the Commonsense World*, edited by Jerry R. Hobbs and Robert C. Moore, 71–107. Norwood, NJ: Ablex Publishing Corporation, 1985.

Hayes, Patrick J. "The Second Naive Physics Manifesto." In *Formal Theories of the Commonsense World*, edited by Jerry R. Hobbs and Robert C. Moore, 1–36. Norwood, NJ: Ablex Publishing Corporation, 1985.

Hayes-Roth, Frederick, Donald A. Waterman, and Douglas B. Lenat. *Building Expert Systems*. Reading, MA: Addison-Wesley, 1983.

Hedlund, Jennifer. "Practical Intelligence." In *The Cambridge Handbook of Intelligence, Second Edition*, edited by Robert J. Sternberg, 736–755. Cambridge: Cambridge University Press, 2020.

Herr, Judy. *Creative Resources for the Early Childhood Classroom*. Belmont, CA: Wadsworth Cengage Learning, 2009.

Hintikka, Jaakko. *Knowledge and Belief*. Ithaca, NY: Cornell University Press, 1962.

Hobbs, Jerry R., and Andrew S. Gordon. "Toward a Large-Scale Formal Theory of Commonsense Psychology for Metacognition." In *Proceedings of the AAAI Spring Symposium: Metacognition in Computation*, 49–54, Palo Alto, CA, March 2005.

Hobbs, Jerry R., and Robert C. Moore, eds. *Formal Theories of the Commonsense World*. Norwood, NJ: Ablex Publishing Corporation, 1985.

Hooke, Samuel H. *The Bible in Basic English*. Cambridge: Cambridge University Press, 1949.

Horvitz, Eric J., John S. Breese, and Max Henrion. "Decision Theory in Expert Systems and Artificial Intelligence." *International Journal of Approximate Reasoning* 2, no. 3 (1988): 247–302.

Jackson, Peter. *Introduction to Expert Systems*. Reading, MA: Addison-Wesley, 1990.

Jiménez, Sergio, Javier Segovia-Aguas, and Anders Jonsson. "A Review of Generalized Planning." *Knowledge Engineering Review* 34, no. e5 (2019): 1–28.

Johnson-Laird, Philip N. "Mental Models and Human Reasoning." *Proceedings of the National Academy of Sciences* 107, no. 43 (2010): 18243–18250.

Johnson-Laird, Philip N. *Mental Models: Towards a Cognitive Science of Language, Inference, and Consciousness*. Cambridge, MA: Harvard University Press, 1983.

Jolley, Nicholas, ed. *The Cambridge Companion to Leibniz*. Cambridge: Cambridge University Press, 1994.

Jurafsky, Daniel, and James H. Martin. *Speech and Language Processing: An Introduction to Speech Recognition, Computational Linguistics and Natural Language Processing*. Upper Saddle River, NJ: Prentice Hall, 2008.

Kaelbling, Leslie Pack, Michael L. Littman, and Anthony R. Cassandra. "Planning and Acting in Partially Observable Stochastic Domains." *Artificial Intelligence* 101, no. 1–2 (1998): 99–134.

Kahneman, Daniel. *Thinking, Fast and Slow*. New York: Farrar, Straus and Giroux, 2011.

Kaiser, Łukasz, and Ilya Sutskever. "Neural GPUs Learn Algorithms." In *Proceedings of the Fourth International Conference on Learning Representations (ICLR 2016)*, San Juan, Puerto Rico, May 2016.

Kambhampati, Subbarao, and James A. Hendler. "A Validation-Structure-Based Theory of Plan Modification and Reuse." *Artificial Intelligence* 55, no. 2–3 (1992): 193–258.

Khemlani, Sangeet S., Ruth M. J. Byrne, and Philip N. Johnson-Laird. "Facts and Possibilities: A Model-Based Theory of Sentential Reasoning." *Cognitive Science* 42, no. 6 (2018): 1887–1924.

Kidd, Alison L., ed. *Knowledge Acquisition for Expert Systems: A Practical Handbook.* New York: Plenum Press, 1987.

Klein, Gary. *The Power of Intuition: How to Use Your Gut Feelings to Make Better Decisions at Work.* New York: Doubleday, 2007.

Klir, George J., and Bo Yuan, eds. *Fuzzy Sets, Fuzzy Logic, and Fuzzy Systems: Selected Papers by Lotfi A. Zadeh.* Advances in Fuzzy Systems—Applications and Theory 6. River Edge, NJ: World Scientific Publishing Co. Pte. Ltd., 1996.

Kolata, Gina. "How Can Computers Get Common Sense?" *Science* 217, no. 4566 (1982): 1237–1238.

Kolodner, Janet. *Case-Based Reasoning.* San Mateo, CA: Morgan Kaufmann Publishers, Inc., 1993.

Kotseruba, Iuliia, and John K. Tsotsos. "40 Years of Cognitive Architectures: Core Cognitive Abilities and Practical Applications." *Artificial Intelligence Review* 53, no. 1 (2020): 17–94.

Kuhn, Tobias. "A Survey and Classification of Controlled Natural Languages." *Computational Linguistics* 40, no. 1 (2014): 121–170.

Kuipers, Benjamin J., Patrick Beeson, Joseph Modayil, and Jefferson Provost. "Bootstrap Learning of Foundational Representations." *Connection Science* 18, no. 2 (2006): 145–158.

Kurzweil, Ray. *The Singularity Is Near: When Humans Transcend Biology.* New York: Penguin Books, 2005.

Laird, John E. *The Soar Cognitive Architecture.* Cambridge, MA: MIT Press, 2019.

Lakemeyer, Gerhard, and Hector J. Levesque. "A First-Order Logic of Limited Belief Based on Possible Worlds." In *Proceedings of the Seventeenth International Conference on Principles of Knowledge Representation and Reasoning (KR2020)*, 624–635, Rhodes, Greece, September 2020.

Leake, David, ed. Special issue, *AI Magazine* 26, no. 2 (Winter 2005).

Leake, David, ed. Special issue, *AI Magazine* 27, no. 4 (Winter 2006).

LeCun, Yann, Yoshua Bengio, and Geoffrey Hinton. "Deep Learning." *Nature* 521, no. 7553 (2015): 436–444.

Lenat, Douglas B. "Not Good as Gold: Today's AI's Are Dangerously Lacking in AU (Artificial Understanding)." *Forbes*, February 18, 2019.

Lenat, Douglas B. "What AI Can Learn from Romeo & Juliet." *Forbes*, July 3, 2019.

Lenat, Douglas B., and Ramanathan V. Guha. *Building Large Knowledge-Based Systems: Representation and Inference in the Cyc Project*. Reading, MA: Addison-Wesley, 1989.

Lespérance, Yves, and Hector J. Levesque. "Indexical Knowledge and Robot Action— a Logical Account." *Artificial Intelligence* 73, no. 1–2 (1995): 69–115.

Lespérance, Yves, Hector J. Levesque, Fangzhen Lin, and Richard B. Scherl. "Ability and Knowing How in the Situation Calculus." *Studia Logica* 66, no. 1 (2000): 165–186.

Levesque, Hector J. *Common Sense, the Turing Test, and the Quest for Real AI*. Cambridge, MA: MIT Press, 2017.

Levesque, Hector J. "A Completeness Result for Reasoning with Incomplete First-Order Knowledge Bases." In *Proceedings of the Sixth International Conference on Principles of Knowledge Representation and Reasoning (KR'98)*, 14–23, Trento, June 1998.

Levesque, Hector J. "Knowledge Representation and Reasoning." *Annual Review of Computer Science* 1, no. 1 (1986): 255–287.

Levesque, Hector J. "Logic and the Complexity of Reasoning." *Journal of Philosophical Logic* 17, no. 4 (1988): 355–389.

Levesque, Hector J. "A Logic of Implicit and Explicit Belief." In *Proceedings of the Fourth National Conference on Artificial Intelligence (AAAI-84)*, 198–202, Austin, TX, August 1984.

Levesque, Hector J. "Making Believers Out of Computers." *Artificial Intelligence* 30, no. 1 (1986): 81–108.

Levesque, Hector J. *Thinking as Computation: A First Course*. Cambridge, MA: MIT Press, 2012.

Levesque, Hector J., and Ronald J. Brachman. "Expressiveness and Tractability in Knowledge Representation and Reasoning." *Computational Intelligence* 3, no. 1 (1987): 78–93.

Levesque, Hector J., Ernest Davis, and Leora Morgenstern. "The Winograd Schema Challenge." In *Proceedings of the Thirteenth International Conference on Principles of Knowledge Representation and Reasoning (KR2012)*, 552–561, Rome, June 2012.

Levesque, Hector J., and Gerhard Lakemeyer. "Cognitive Robotics." In *Handbook of Knowledge Representation*, edited by Frank van Harmelen, Vladimir Lifschitz, and Bruce Porter, 869–886. Amsterdam: Elsevier, 2008.

Levesque, Hector J., and Gerhard Lakemeyer. *The Logic of Knowledge Bases*. Cambridge, MA: MIT Press, 2001.

Levesque, John. *Geneva Farewell*. Oakville, ON: Mosaic Press, 2020.

Liberman, Mark, and Charles Wayne. "Human Language Technology." *AI Magazine* 41, no. 2 (2020): 22–35.

Lin, Fangzhen. "Situation Calculus." In *Handbook of Knowledge Representation*, edited by Frank van Harmelen, Vladimir Lifschitz, and Bruce Porter, 649–669. Amsterdam: Elsevier, 2008.

Loftus, Elizabeth F. *Eyewitness Testimony*. Cambridge, MA: Harvard University Press, 1996.

Malpass, Alex, and Marianna Antonutti Marfori, eds. *The History of Philosophical and Formal Logic: From Aristotle to Tarski*. London: Bloomsbury Publishing Plc., 2017.

Manjoo, Farhad. "How Do You Know a Human Wrote This?" *New York Times*, July 29, 2020.

Marcus, Gary. *The Birth of the Mind: How a Tiny Number of Genes Creates the Complexities of Human Thought*. New York: Basic Books, 2004.

Marcus, Gary. "The Next Decade in AI: Four Steps towards Robust Artificial Intelligence." Submitted February 19, 2020. https://arxiv.org/abs/2002.06177.

Marcus, Gary, and Ernest Davis. *Rebooting AI: Building Artificial Intelligence We Can Trust*. New York: Pantheon Books, 2019.

Marcus, Gary, Francesca Rossi, and Manuela Veloso, eds. "Beyond the Turing Test." Special issue, *AI Magazine* 37, no. 1 (Spring 2016).

Matuszek, Cynthia, Michael Witbrock, Robert C. Kahlert, John Cabral, Dave Schneider, Purvesh Shall, and Douglas B. Lenat. "Searching for Common Sense: Populating Cyc from the Web." In *Proceedings of the Twentieth National Conference on Artificial Intelligence (AAAI-05)*, 3:1430–1435, Pittsburgh, July 2005.

McAllester, David. "Observations on Cognitive Judgments." In *Proceedings of the Ninth National Conference on Artificial Intelligence (AAAI-91)*, 910–914, Anaheim, CA, July 1991.

McCarthy, John. "Elaboration Tolerance." In *Proceedings of the Fourth Symposium on Logical Formalizations of Common Sense Reasoning*, London, January 1998.

McCarthy, John. "Epistemological Problems of Artificial Intelligence." In *Proceedings of the Fifth International Joint Conference on Artificial Intelligence (IJCAI-77)*, 1038–1044, Cambridge, MA, August, 1977.

McCarthy, John. "Programs with Common Sense." In *Symposium on the Mechanization of Thought Processes*, 77–84. Teddington, UK: National Physical Laboratory, November 1958.

McCarthy, John. "Recursive Functions of Symbolic Expressions and Their Computation by Machine, Part I." *Communications of the ACM* 3, no. 4 (1960): 184–195.

McCarthy, John. "Situations, Actions, and Causal Laws." In *Semantic Information Processing*, edited by Marvin L. Minsky, 410–418. Cambridge, MA: MIT Press, 1968.

McCarthy, John, and Edward A. Feigenbaum. "In Memoriam: Arthur Samuel: Pioneer in Machine Learning." *AI Magazine* 11, no. 3 (1990): 10–11.

McCarthy, John, and Patrick J. Hayes. "Some Philosophical Problems from the Standpoint of Artificial Intelligence." In *Readings in Artificial Intelligence*, edited by Bonnie Lynn Webber and Nils J. Nilsson, 431–450. Los Altos, CA: Morgan Kaufmann Publishers, Inc., 1981.

McCarthy, John, and Vladimir Lifschitz. *Formalizing Common Sense: Papers by John McCarthy*. Norwood, NJ: Ablex Publishing Corporation, 1990.

McCarthy, John, Marvin L. Minsky, Nathaniel Rochester, and Claude E. Shannon. "A Proposal for the Dartmouth Summer Research Project on Artificial Intelligence, August 31, 1955." *AI Magazine* 27, no. 4 (2006): 12–14.

McCorduck, Pamela. *Machines Who Think: A Personal Inquiry into the History and Prospects of Artificial Intelligence*. Boca Raton, FL: CRC Press, 2018.

McDermott, John. "R1: A Rule-Based Configurer of Computer Systems." *Artificial Intelligence* 19, no. 1 (1982): 39–88.

McNamee, Roger. *Zucked: Waking up to the Facebook Catastrophe*. New York: Penguin Books, 2020.

Medin, Douglas L., and Edward E. Smith. "Concepts and Concept Formation." *Annual Review of Psychology* 35, no. 1 (1984): 113–138.

Mendelson, Elliott. *Introduction to Mathematical Logic*. Boca Raton, FL: CRC Press, 2009.

Mikolov, Tomáš, Wen-tau Yih, and Geoffrey Zweig. "Linguistic Regularities in Continuous Space Word Representations." In *Proceedings of the 2013 Conference of the North American Chapter of the Association for Computational Linguistics: Human Language Technologies (NAACL-HLT 2013)*, 746–751, Atlanta, June 2013.

Millgram, Elijah, ed. *Varieties of Practical Reasoning*. Cambridge, MA: MIT Press, 2001.

Minsky, Marvin L. "A Framework for Representing Knowledge." In *Readings in Knowledge Representation*, edited by Ronald J. Brachman and Hector J. Levesque, 245–262. Los Altos, CA: Morgan Kaufmann Publishers, Inc., 1985.

Minsky, Marvin L., ed. *Semantic Information Processing*. Cambridge, MA: MIT Press, 1968.

Minsky, Marvin L. *Society of Mind*. New York: Simon and Schuster, 1986.

Mitchell, Melanie. *Artificial Intelligence: A Guide for Thinking Humans*. New York: Farrar, Straus and Giroux, 2019.

Mitchell, Tom, William Cohen, Estevam Hruschka, Partha Talukdar, Bishan Yang, Justin Betteridge, Andrew Carlson, et al. "Never-Ending Learning." *Communications of the ACM* 61, no. 5 (2018): 103–115.

Monroe, Don. "Seeking Artificial Common Sense." *Communications of the ACM* 63, no. 11 (2020): 14–16.

Moore, Robert C. "The Role of Logic in Knowledge Representation and Commonsense Reasoning." In *Proceedings of the Second National Conference on Artificial Intelligence (AAAI-82)*, 428–433, Pittsburgh, August 1982.

Mueller, Erik T. *Commonsense Reasoning: An Event Calculus-Based Approach*. Amsterdam: Morgan Kaufmann Publishers, Inc., 2014.

Muscettola, Nicola, P. Pandurang Nayak, Barney Pell, and Brian C. Williams. "Remote Agent: To Boldly Go Where No AI System Has Gone Before." *Artificial Intelligence* 103, no. 1–2 (1998): 5–47.

Nebel, Bernhard. "A Knowledge Level Analysis of Belief Revision." In *Proceedings of the First International Conference on Principles of Knowledge Representation and Reasoning (KR'89)*, 301–311, Toronto, May 1989.

Nebel, Bernhard, and Jana Koehler. "Plan Reuse versus Plan Generation: A Theoretical and Empirical Analysis." *Artificial Intelligence* 76, no. 1–2 (1995): 427–454.

Newborn, Monty. *Deep Blue: An Artificial Intelligence Milestone*. New York: Springer-Verlag, 2003.

Newell, Allen, and Herbert A. Simon. "Computer Science as Empirical Inquiry: Symbols and Search." *Communications of the ACM* 19, no. 3 (1976): 113–126.

Niles, Ian, and Adam Pease. "Towards a Standard Upper Ontology." In *Proceedings of the International Conference on Formal Ontology in Information Systems—Volume 2001*, 2–9, Ogunquit, ME, October 2001.

Nilsson, Nils J. *The Quest for Artificial Intelligence: A History of Ideas and Achievements*. Cambridge: Cambridge University Press, 2009.

Ogden, Charles K. *Basic English*. London: Kegan Paul Trench Trubner, 1935.

Ogden, Charles K. *The General Basic English Dictionary*. New York: W. W. Norton and Co., 1942.

Olson, David R. *The Mind on Paper*. Cambridge: Cambridge University Press, 2016.

Pearl, Judea. *Causality: Models, Reasoning, and Inference*. Cambridge: Cambridge University Press, 2009.

Pearl, Judea, and Dana Mackenzie. *The Book of Why: The New Science of Cause and Effect*. New York: Basic Books, 2018.

Peirce, Charles Sanders, Charles Hartshorne, Paul Weiss, and Arthur W. Burks. *Collected Papers of Charles Sanders Peirce*. Vol. 1. Cambridge, MA: Harvard University Press, 1931.

Peterson, Martin. *An Introduction to Decision Theory*. Cambridge: Cambridge University Press, 2017.

Pinker, Steven. *The Language Instinct: How the Mind Creates Language*. London: Penguin Books, 2003.

Pinker, Steven. *Rationality: What It Is, Why It Seems Scarce, Why It Matters*. New York: Penguin Books, 2021.

Quillian, M. Ross. "Semantic Memory." In *Semantic Information Processing*, edited by Marvin L. Minsky, 227–270. Cambridge, MA: MIT Press, 1968.

Quine, Willard Van Orman. *From a Logical Point of View: Nine Logico-Philosophical Essays*. Cambridge, MA: Harvard University Press, 1953.

Quine, Willard Van Orman. *Methods of Logic*. Cambridge, MA: Harvard University Press, 1982.

Rao, Anand S., and Michael P. Georgeff. "Modeling Rational Agents within a BDI-Architecture." In *Proceedings of the Second International Conference on Principles of Knowledge Representation and Reasoning (KR'91)*, 473–484, Cambridge, MA, April 1991.

Reiter, Raymond. "The Frame Problem in the Situation Calculus: A Simple Solution (Sometimes) and a Completeness Result for Goal Regression." In *Artificial and Mathematical Theory of Computation: Papers in Honor of John McCarthy*, edited by Vladimir Lifschitz, 359–380. Boston: Academic Press, 1991.

Reiter, Raymond. *Knowledge in Action: Logical Foundations for Specifying and Implementing Dynamical Systems*. Cambridge, MA: MIT Press, 2001.

Reiter, Raymond. "On Closed World Data Bases." In *Readings in Artificial Intelligence*, edited by Bonnie Lynn Webber and Nils J. Nilsson, 119–140. Los Altos, CA: Morgan Kaufmann Publishers, Inc., 1981.

Roberts, Don D. *The Existential Graphs of Charles S. Peirce*. The Hague: Mouton, 1973.

Rosch, Eleanor, and Barbara B. Lloyd, eds. *Cognition and Categorization*. Hillsdale, NJ: Lawrence Erlbaum Associates, Publishers, 1978.

Roth, Michael D., and Leon Galis. *Knowing: Essays in the Analysis of Knowledge*. Lanham, MD: University Press of America, 1984.

Russell, Bertrand. "On Denoting." *Mind* 14, no. 56 (1905): 479–493.

Russell, Stuart. *Human Compatible: Artificial Intelligence and the Problem of Control*. New York: Penguin Books, 2019.

Sakaguchi, Keisuke, Ronan Le Bras, Chandra Bhagavatula, and Yejin Choi. "Wino-Grande: An Adversarial Winograd Schema Challenge at Scale." In *Proceedings of the Thirty-Fourth National Conference on Artificial Intelligence (AAAI-20)*, 34:8732–8740, New York, February 2020.

Schaeffer, Jonathan, Neil Burch, Yngvi Björnsson, Akihiro Kishimoto, Martin Müller, Robert Lake, Paul Lu, and Steve Sutphen. "Checkers Is Solved." *Science* 317, no. 5844 (2007): 1518–1522.

Schank, Roger C. *Dynamic Memory: A Theory of Reminding and Learning in Computers and People*. Cambridge: Cambridge University Press, 1982.

Schank, Roger C. "Language and Memory." *Cognitive Science* 4, no. 3 (1980): 243–284.

Schank, Roger C., and Robert P. Abelson. *Scripts, Plans, Goals, and Understanding: An Inquiry into Human Knowledge Structures*. Hillsdale, NJ: Lawrence Erlbaum Associates, Publishers, 1977.

Searle, John R. "Collective Intentions and Actions." In *Intentions in Communication*, edited by Philip R. Cohen, Jerry Morgan, and Martha E. Pollack, 401–415. Cambridge, MA: MIT Press, 1990.

Searle, John R. *Expression and Meaning: Studies in the Theory of Speech Acts*. Cambridge: Cambridge University Press, 1985.

Shallue, Christopher J., and Andrew Vanderburg. "Identifying Exoplanets with Deep Learning: A Five-Planet Resonant Chain around Kepler-80 and an Eighth Planet around Kepler-90." *Astronomical Journal* 155, no. 2 (2018): 94.

Shanahan, Murray. *Solving the Frame Problem: A Mathematical Investigation of the Common Sense Law of Inertia*. Cambridge, MA: MIT Press, 1997.

Shanahan, Murray. *The Technological Singularity*. Cambridge, MA: MIT Press, 2015.

Shanahan, Murray, Matthew Crosby, Benjamin Beyret, and Lucy Cheke. "Artificial Intelligence and the Common Sense of Animals." *Trends in Cognitive Sciences* 24, no. 11 (2020): 862–872.

Shannon, Claude E. "Programming a Computer for Playing Chess." *London, Edinburgh, and Dublin Philosophical Magazine and Journal of Science* ser. 7, vol. 41, no. 314 (1950): 256–275.

Shapiro, Stuart C. "Path-Based and Node-Based Inference in Semantic Networks." *American Journal of Computational Linguistics* (1978): 38–44.

Shortliffe, Edward H. *Computer-Based Medical Consultations: MYCIN.* New York: American Elsevier Publishing Co., Inc., 1976.

Silver, David, Julian Schrittwieser, Karen Simonyan, Ioannis Antonoglou, Aja Huang, Arthur Guez, Thomas Hubert, et al. "Mastering the Game of Go with Deep Neural Networks and Tree Search." *Nature* 529, no. 7587 (2016): 484–489.

Simmons, Robert F. "Answering English Questions by Computer: A Survey." *Communications of the ACM* 8, no. 1 (1965): 53–70.

Smith, Brian Cantwell. *The Promise of Artificial Intelligence: Reckoning and Judgment.* Cambridge, MA: MIT Press, 2019.

Smith, Brian Cantwell. "Reflection and Semantics in a Procedural Language." PhD thesis, MIT Laboratory for Computer Science, 1982.

Sober, Elliott. "Mental Representations." *Synthese* 33, no. 1 (1976): 101–148.

Speer, Robert, and Catherine Havasi. "Representing General Relational Knowledge in ConceptNet 5." In *Proceedings of the Eighth International Conference on Language Resources and Evaluation (LREC'12)*, 3679–3686, Istanbul, May 2012.

Spelke, Elizabeth S., and Katherine D. Kinzler. "Core Knowledge." *Developmental Science* 10, no. 1 (2007): 89–96.

Staab, Steffen, and Rudi Studer, eds. *Handbook on Ontologies.* Berlin: Springer-Verlag, 2009.

Stanovich, Keith E. "Rational and Irrational Thought: The Thinking That IQ Tests Miss." *Scientific American Mind* 20, no. 6 (2009): 34–39.

Sternberg, Robert J. *Adaptive Intelligence: Surviving and Thriving in a World of Uncertainty.* New York: Cambridge University Press, 2021.

Sternberg, Robert J., George B. Forsythe, Jennifer Hedlund, Joseph A. Horvath, Richard K. Wagner, Wendy M. Williams, Scott A. Snook, and Elena L. Grigorenko. *Practical Intelligence in Everyday Life.* New York: Cambridge University Press, 2000.

Szegedy, Christian, Wojciech Zaremba, Ilya Sutskever, Joan Bruna, Dumitru Erhan, Ian Goodfellow, and Rob Fergus. "Intriguing Properties of Neural Networks." In *Proceedings of the Second International Conference on Learning Representations ICLR 2014*, Banff, Canada, April 2014.

Thomson, Judith Jarvis. "The Trolley Problem." *Yale Law Journal* 94, no. 6 (1985): 1395–1415.

Thrun, Sebastian, Mike Montemerlo, Hendrik Dahlkamp, David Stavens, Andrei Aron, James Diebel, Philip Fong, et al. "Stanley: The Robot That Won the DARPA Grand Challenge." *Journal of Field Robotics* 23, no. 9 (2006): 661–692.

Trevaskis, John, and Robin Hyman. *Boys' and Girls' First Dictionary.* Toronto: Copp Clark Pitman, 1983.

Turing, Alan M. "Digital Computers Applied to Games." In *Faster than Thought: A Symposium on Digital Computing Machines,* edited by Bertram Bowden, 286–310. London: Sir Isaac Pitman and Sons, Ltd., 1953.

van Harmelen, Frank, Vladimir Lifschitz, and Bruce Porter, eds. *Handbook of Knowledge Representation.* Amsterdam: Elsevier, 2008.

Vardi, Moshe Y. "Move Fast and Break Things." *Communications of the ACM* 61, no. 9 (2018): 7.

Wagner, Gerd. *Vivid Logic: Knowledge-Based Reasoning with Two Kinds of Negation.* Lecture Notes in Artificial Intelligence 764. Berlin: Springer, 1994.

Watt, Stuart. "A Brief Naive Psychology Manifesto." *Informatica* 19, no. 4 (1995): 495–500.

Watts, Duncan J. *Everything Is Obvious* (*Once You Know the Answer): How Common Sense Fails Us.* New York: Crown Business, 2011.

Weld, Daniel S., and Johan de Kleer, eds. *Readings in Qualitative Reasoning about Physical Systems.* San Mateo, CA: Morgan Kaufmann Publishers, Inc., 1989.

Winograd, Terry. "Understanding Natural Language." *Cognitive Psychology* 3, no. 1 (1972): 1–191.

Witbrock, Michael, David Baxter, Jon Curtis, Dave Schneider, Robert C. Kahlert, Pierluigi Miraglia, Peter Wagner, et al. "An Interactive Dialogue System for Knowledge Acquisition in Cyc." In *Proceedings of the Eighteenth International Joint Conference on Artificial Intelligence (IJCAI-03),* 138–145, Acapulco, August 2003.

Wittgenstein, Ludwig. *Philosophical Investigations.* New York: Macmillan Company, 1953.

Woods, William A. "Transition Network Grammars for Natural Language Analysis." *Communications of the ACM* 13, no. 10 (1970): 591–606.

Woods, William A. "What's in a Link: Foundations for Semantic Networks." In *Representation and Understanding: Studies in Cognitive Science,* edited by Daniel G. Bobrow and Allan Collins, 35–82. New York: Academic Press, Inc., 1975.

Wooldridge, Michael. *An Introduction to Multiagent Systems*. Hoboken, NJ: John Wiley and Sons, 2009.

Yu, Victor L., Lawrence M. Fagan, Sharon Wraith Bennett, William J. Clancey, A. Carlisle Scott, John F. Hannigan, Robert L. Blum, et al. "An Evaluation of MYCIN's Advice." In *Rule-Based Expert Systems: The MYCIN Experiments of the Stanford Heuristic Programming Project*, edited by Bruce G. Buchanan and Edward H. Shortliffe, 589–596. Reading, MA: Addison-Wesley Publishing Co., 1984.

Index

About the Authors

Ron Brachman's career has been spent mostly in industry as a research scientist and research leader. In his seventeen years at AT&T Bell Labs/ AT&T Labs, he built a world-class AI and machine learning team, eventually becoming a vice president. He was later the head of Yahoo Labs and also served as Yahoo's chief scientist. He spent several years as the director of the Information Processing Technology Office at DARPA, during which time he created the program that eventually led to the development of Siri. Brachman currently works as the director of the Jacobs Technion-Cornell Institute at Cornell Tech in New York City, and is a professor of computer science at Cornell University. He is a fellow of the Association for Computing Machinery, Institute of Electrical and Electronics Engineers, and American Association for the Advancement of Science (AAAS).

Hector Levesque spent most of his career in the Department of Computer Science at the University of Toronto, where he is now a professor emeritus. He is the author or coauthor of a number of prizewinning AI research papers and several books, including an undergraduate textbook, *Thinking as Computation: A First Course* (2012), and a book for nonspecialists, *Common Sense, the Turing Test, and the Quest for Real AI* (2017). Levesque is a fellow of the Royal Society of Canada and AAAS.

Brachman and Levesque are prominent members of the two most prestigious AI research organizations, the Association for the Advancement of AI (AAAI), which has over four thousand members, and International Joint Conferences on AI (IJCAI), which has held biennial conferences on AI since 1969. Brachman has served as president of the AAAI and secretary-treasurer of the IJCAI. Levesque has served on the executive council of AAAI and as president of the board of trustees of the IJCAI. They are both founding fellows of the AAAI and have won best paper awards at the annual AAAI conferences. Levesque is the only researcher to have won both the IJCAI Computers and Thought award at the start of his academic career, and the IJCAI Research Excellence award at the end.

Together, Brachman and Levesque have collaborated on a wide variety of projects, and have been lead players since the 1970s in knowledge representation and reasoning, the subarea of AI that is central to the topic of this book. With Raymond Reiter, they launched the first major international conference in this area, which has continued now for thirty years, and together they wrote the popular graduate textbook *Knowledge Representation and Reasoning* (2004).